my one-night stand with cancer

my
one-night
stand
with

cancer

tania katan

alyson books
los angeles
Celebrating Twenty-Five Years

THIS IS, IN FACT, A TRUE STORY. THAT SAID, THE TIMELINE OF EVENTS, CERTAIN CONVERSATIONS, AND UNSAVORY SITUATIONS HAVE BEEN ALTERED TO SERVE THE MEMOIR.

MANUFACTURED IN THE UNITED STATES OF AMERICA.

THIS TRADE PAPERBACK ORIGINAL IS PUBLISHED BY ALYSON BOOKS,
P.O. BOX 4371, LOS ANGELES, CALIFORNIA 90078-4371.
DISTRIBUTION IN THE UNITED KINGDOM BY
    TURNAROUND PUBLISHER SERVICES LTD.,
UNIT 3, OLYMPIA TRADING ESTATE, COBURG ROAD, WOOD GREEN,
LONDON N22 6TZ ENGLAND.

FIRST EDITION: SEPTEMBER 2005

05 06 07 08 09 a 10 9 8 7 6 5 4 3 2 1

ISBN 1-55583-890-1
ISBN-13 978-1-55583-890-4

LIBRARY OF CONGRESS CATALOGING-IN-PUBLICATION DATA
    KATAN, TANIA, 1971–
        MY ONE-NIGHT STAND WITH CANCER / TANIA KATAN.—1ST ED.
        ISBN 1-55583-890-1; ISBN-13 978-1-55583-890-4
        1. KATAN, TANIA—HEALTH. 2. BREAST—CANCER—PATIENTS—UNITED
STATES—BIOGRAPHY. 3. LESBIANS—UNITED STATES—BIOGRAPHY. I. TITLE.
RC280.B8K355 2005
362.196'99449'0092—DC22   2005048066
    [B]

CREDITS
COVER PHOTOGRAPHY BY DIANA KOENIGSBERG/STONE/GETTY IMAGES.
COVER DESIGN BY MATT SAMS.

for Joëlle Katan, Elliott Richards,
and Angela Ellsworth

acknowledgments

A warm thank-you to the following people for their enormous support, silly demeanors, and extraordinary ideas:

The boys (and girl) at Peet's, John V. Buckley III, Elizabeth Cutler, Paul Domaleski, Liz Gail, Sue Hamilton, Julie Hampton, Mike Josephson, Tori King, Mildred Light, Scout McNamara, Daniele Nathanson, Lisa Petty, Jen Sincero, Jet Tennant, Barbi Wengerd, James White, and Mary Kay Zeeb

Without my mentors I might have ended up a professional golfer with a bad attitude, so a huge thank-you to the writers and performers who have given freely of their time, talents, and letters of recommendation:

Jim Fountain, Michael Grady, William Hoffman, Victoria Holloway, Jim Leonard, Marshall W. Mason, Susan Welch, and the women at the Creative Center in New York

Thank you to my family for allowing me the luxury to write about them without being mean to me at Thanksgiving:

Paul Katan, Joelle Katan, Tessa Katan, and Elliott Richards

I would also like to acknowledge the many coffeehouses whose rich coffee and cute barista girls inspired my numerous hours writing stories. Note: If any of the following businesses are interested in the corporate sponsorship of a writer, give me a call. Thanks to: Starbucks on Church and Market, Coffee Bean and Tea Leaf on Ocean Park, Le Grande Orange on 40th and Campbell, and Peet's Coffee on Market. I've bought plenty of coffee; now it's time for you to buy a book!

Thank you to Angela Brown for the opportunity to write a book and the guidance to make it clear, focused, and resonant.

And to Angela Ellsworth, the most amazing person I know: Thank you for choosing to be with me.

"Where are my breasts? *Where are my breasts?*"
—*Myra Breckinridge*

the early detection decathlon
(left breast—2002)

It started with a lump. It always starts with a lump. No, actually it started with a girlfriend who found the lump. Wait. It started before the lump, before the idea of having girlfriends even entered my mind; it started five years earlier when I was sixteen years old. See, my oncologist told me that by the time you find cancer it usually has been growing for at least five years.

The Breast Clinic. A clinical setting or...a lesbian mixer? As a lesbian and optimist, I choose the latter. I'm here to get a small lump checked out. I'm a little nervous. I didn't anticipate being nervous. It's not my first trip to the Breast Clinic, and when I'm nervous I tend to pretend I'm somebody else, somebody less nervous than me—like a politician, or a therapist, or a...rock star. Today, I'm a rock star. Maybe that's a bit of a stretch. Due to my five-foot-four stature and the small rectangular tortoiseshell glasses perched on my nose, always sliding down my face at the wrong time, I don't usually incite the question *Do you wanna rock with me?!*

I sign in while verbally asserting my new persona, "What up? Tania Katan in the house." It's working. I feel infinitely more calm. My glasses inch toward the tip of my nose, but my forefinger responds in the usual fashion by giving the hard plastic bridge a quick nudge back into place. I'm cool again. Maria, the hot young receptionist, looks at me like she wants to hump me, or maybe she has something stuck in her throat. According to the pastel yellow sticky note stuck on the front of Maria's computer, next to her screen, with my name written on it in blue swirly cursive writing, I'm a VIP at the Breast Clinic. My breast cancer–survivor status has kicked me up to Platinum Level. Maria, my groupie, hands me a clipboard's worth of paper and instructs me to, "Fill out all the forms and then I will take you back...*stage, Miss Katan.*"

She blushes and turns away.

Name: Tania Katan
Age: 30
Date of Birth: 9/28/71

(Other info, such as address and phone numbers, have been omitted due to the high volume of groupies trying to get a piece of me.)

Sexually active: extremely
Form of birth control: lesbian sex

Have you ever had a mammogram? yes
Have you ever had an ultrasound? yes
Have you ever had breast cancer? yes
If "yes," at what age? 21
Did you have surgery? yes, a modified radical mastectomy.
If "yes," did you have reconstructive surgery? No, I
opted for tattoo surgery performed by Stag, the Venice
Beach artist who dons a pop-top tattoo on top of his bald
head. Blue Shield didn't cover that.
List any prior surgeries (and at what age): Removal of a
9 cm fibroid tumor attached to my uterus. Age: 23
Why are you here today? I found a lump in my remain-
ing breast.

Five years can represent the amount of time it takes to finish college, or to pay off a high-interest car loan, or to
grow a cancerous tumor. I was twenty-one when they
found my cancer, which means that when I was sixteen
years old, driving around cones at the DMV in hopes of
getting my license, my cells were developing an obstacle
course of their own.
Maria leads me to my dressing room. The walls are a
mosaic of mirrors stained with red wine and cocaine. She
licks her glossy pink lips and asks me to take off everything from the waist up. She tosses me a flimsy, obviously
Mizrahi vest to put on. Wait, this whole rock star thing
isn't working. I'm not a rock star. Even in tight leather
pants and a chunky silver chain I'm still a nervous, lopsided lesbian. And right now, as I'm surrounded by the
smell of disinfected medical equipment, the reason I'm
here feels very real, like even a well-constructed persona

can't help me now. I wrap the paper vest around my cold and anxious upper body. I pull back the curtain. There is no audience waiting for me.

When I was sixteen years old I finished, and submitted for publication, my award-winning novel *Sixteen, Dateless, and Jewish*. As the title might suggest, it was about an awkward, chubby, Jewish girl who was trying to fit in to the social landscape of high school, a place where football bullies and blond cheerleaders are adored and celebrated. I could identify with my main character's struggles; after all, I did spend the first few years of high school trying to convince my classmates that Jews do, in fact, celebrate Thanksgiving. Equipped with a typewriter, a case of correction fluid, a desire to fit in, and an interest in making money, I set out to transcend my sorrowful sixteen-year-old life by writing a book based on it. All seventy-three typo-filled, Wite-Out–smudged pages of *fiction* were quickly written and ready to be sold. If I could sell *Sixteen, Dateless, and Jewish*, I thought, maybe I could afford to help my struggling mom out with the bills and still have enough money to buy Gummy Bears so my school lunch would look like everyone else's.

I never got my huge cash advance. In fact, my book didn't even receive the readership I'd expected, because it was never published. Perhaps it was because I wrote the query letter on Culture Club stationery. Simon & Schuster sent me what I would come to know as a "form letter," but at the time it seemed like a wonderful form of optimism: "Your book doesn't fit our needs at this time," and "We look forward to future submissions." Harper & Row essentially said the same thing—actually they said the exact same thing, which led me to believe my writing was genius. Sadly, however, my youthful entrée into the literary world was denied.

The first event in the Early Detection Decathlon is the Mammogram. The nurse conducting the mammogram seems sweet, sort of nondescript, like someone else's mom, not ugly or unattractive, but definitely not someone you'd think about having sex with unless you were on a reality show or forced to wait for days in a doctor's office. The nurse kindly asks me to disrobe.

"Great tattoo. Keith Haring, right?" she says in response to the tiny colorful men dancing where my right breast used to be. She's read my chart. You can always tell when they know your history because they compliment you. A lot. "Great glasses! Where'd you get them? Look at your earrings! Do you have anything else pierced?! You're just…FUN!"

When I was sixteen, my existence in high school was less than desirable, even *Less Than Zero*, which I read when I was sixteen and secretly wished that I, too, could be rich and fucked up beyond recognition, but my single mother's social-work income made cocaine hard to come by. Although I owned all of the requisite eighties regalia— brooches, thrift-store blazers, and bangs—I didn't have the most important accessory: friends. Maybe it was because I was new, or poor, or different in some profound and intrinsic way that kids couldn't put their fingers on and, quite frankly, didn't want to touch anyway. For some reason no one accepted my invitation to come over to the wrong side of the tracks and listen to Bronski Beat.

When I was sixteen I also discovered high school drama. My brother, Paul, was rehearsing a scene with this sexy girl named Christy who looked like Madonna circa 1988. The scene seemed to have a little bit of dialogue, with a lot of kissing.

"You get to do that for class, man?" I asked.

"Yeah, dumb fuck."

Right then and there I made up my mind to have drama with women forever. If my freckly, buck-toothed brother could get a chick by becoming a character, surely performing was for me. Finally there was a field that not only facilitated my creativity but also covertly encouraged my homosexuality. I was a sixteen-year-old drama fag and proud of it. In order to help me survive a high school life without friends, my sense of humor, which had been present well before high school, had suddenly kicked into high gear. I wrote stand-up comedy routines in hopes of showing my peers how totally cool and piss-your-pants funny I was. Unfortunately, sixteen-year-olds were not allowed into the Improv, which was holding a National Lampoon comedy competition, so I lied about my age in order to compete. None of my peers were there to see me beat out hundreds of adults, make it to the final round, and win grown-up prizes like wine, scented candles, and hotel stays. Because I was sixteen and didn't see much use for any of the prizes, I gave them to the people who'd come to the Improv to support me: my mom, my drama teacher, and my speech coach. I proved, once again, that I was a dork—a funny dork, but a dork nonetheless.

I'm positioned in front of the sci-fi machine as the nurse pulls on my A-size booby. Like someone who works with taffy, she stretches and folds until it lies just right on the cool flat surface. She runs behind the magic curtain and gently yells, "Hold it! Hold it!" as she flips a switch that activates the Booby-Smusher-Downer, which in turn sends a signal to the Intense Atomic Ray, which then radiates through my booby. We are successful. We have imaging. It's time for the next event at the Early Detection Decathlon: the Ultrasound.

I lie on a table that's barely large enough to accommodate one of my butt cheeks, let alone two. I love Ben and Jerry's. Dr. Comack comes into the room; he's very kind, sort of young, and maybe queer, like Richard Chamberlain in *The Thorn Birds*.

The nurse quickly places a round, rubber disc on the ultra-sound wand. She's rolling it down when I realize what it is—a condom! Where am I? And when the nurse squeezes a mountain of lube on the condom-clad wand, I know exactly where I am: on the set of a hot new lesbo porno called *The Magic Wand*. I'm the star awaiting my first scene. The nurse is, in fact, the fluff girl and the doctor is the lascivious director. The nurse is just about to show me a "magic trick" when the slap of the cold, slimy wand winding around my breast snaps me back to the Breast Clinic. The three of us stare at the screen like it's Must-See TV.

"OK, see that? It appears to be…" Dr. Comack leans into the screen. "A…junky cyst."

A what? "What's a junky cyst?" I ask as my breast begins to creep out of the paper vest, perhaps trying to get a glimpse of the monitor herself.

"It's a benign cyst filled with fluid. Nothing to worry about," Dr. Comack says, no longer looking at the screen, mentally moving on to his next patient.

A junky cyst, huh? I kinda like the sound of that, like my cyst wears a beret, smokes colorful European cigarettes, and shoots up heroin for fun. My junky cyst is intriguing, cunning, and usually running from the law. We're looking for chicks, for kicks, for our next fix, me and my junky cyst.

When I was sixteen, my breasts started to come into their own. Up until that point, they had been fine, functional, friendly, but at sixteen something happened, like an ethereal spring had sprung and my boobies were looking *good*. My breasts had become "Perfect Boobs," given their title by random boys and men. They were full but not overflowing C cups. Round and perky, pert and funky, they were openly adored by many boys who tossed off quick, unsolicited quips like, "Nice tits," and "Seriously, you've got some hot hooters," and "I'd like to fuck those titties," and other flattering phrases. It's not like my boobs saw a lot of action that year, because they didn't, but they were definitely ready to.

The Early Detection Decathlon has become a Tittie Triathlon, and the final event of today's games is the Core Biopsy. Dr. Comack explains this procedure to me.

"I will start the procedure," he says, "by injecting your breast with one of the *caines*: novo, lido…Michael." He smirks and continues. "You're going to hear a loud noise, something akin to a gun being fired, as I shoot this tremendously large, hollowed-out steel cylinder—which we will refer to as a *needle*—through your breast. I will shoot your breast three times." He pantomimes shooting a gun with a lot of kickback. "A nice cross section of your mass, which means chunks of bloody and fibrous tissue, will be gathered. You won't feel a thing, assuming we gave you enough anesthetic." He laughs. "You may experience some discomfort, light bleeding, intense fever, excessive bleeding, light bruising, horrible bruising, for a day or two or six. Don't shower for two days. This will take about five seconds. Ready?"

"When will I know the results?"

"We'll give you a call Thursday or Friday. OK, are you ready?"

In all honesty, I'm not, but what other options do I have?

"Yeah, I'm ready."

In five years, cells divide, collide, converge, and decide the next line of text in your ongoing memoir. When I was sixteen, I was growing a cancer that I wouldn't discover until I was twenty-one. Actually, I wouldn't discover it—my girlfriend Dawn would.

lesbianism: a form of early detection (right breast—1992)

It's Thursday night, Trash Disco at my favorite bar in Phoenix, Arizona: Fosters. Alexander Billingford III, my best gay boyfriend, and I are twenty-one years old, queer, and single. The only thing that could be better is if we were both rich, but Alexander Billingford III was born into relative poverty with a touch of verbal abuse. That's why he says his name in its entirety every time someone asks him. ("It's Alexander Billingford III," like it exalts him to some kind of aristocratic status.) Me? I'm the offspring of a New York City cabbie and a French social worker. What's a trust fund?

Tonight is my night. I can feel it. During my past two years of active lesbian duty, my responsibilities have included drinking far too many cocktails and trying to get the attention of the cutest girl in the bar. The latter has been a bit more difficult for me. Maybe it's because my body goes completely stiff and my upper lip starts to quiver whenever a cute girl is within a three-mile radius? Or maybe it's because girls don't think I'd be very good at lesbianism? Whatever the reason, tonight all of this changes.

Alexander Billingford III and I hit the dance floor, and Alexander quickly launches into his famous dance move, the Bump and Grind. Clutching his big silver belt buckle with one hand while holding a cigarette and cocktail in the other, he swivels his hips as if he were a stripper working over a high-paying client. The movement from his hips works its way down to his knees, forcing them to bend while his torso stays perfectly erect. It looks like he's going to sit down or sexily pick up a pile of dollar bills without losing his victim's gaze. Instead he allows the bass line of the song to infiltrate his groin, making him grind his way up to a standing position. He repeats this move over and over again. He is amazing. When I try to dance, I end up spending half my time pulling up my extra-baggy jeans before they expose my predilection for not wearing panties.

The other half of my time is dedicated to hiding the sweat and discoloration under the arms of my white V-neck T-shirt—which is caused by a flailing arm move I patented at my cousin's bat mitzvah several years ago.

Alexander and I are drunk, half falling over, and looking good. We are kung fu fighting. *Everybody* is kung fu fighting until someone shouts, "Play that funky music, white boy!" The vodka collins I sucked down in 1.5 minutes has allowed me to believe I *can* dance. I am the *Dance* in *Dance Fever*, the *Soul* in *Soul Train*. A chick is checking me out. She's the cutest girl in the bar, and perhaps in surrounding bars. Oh, no, maybe she's checking out my lips. Shit. Almost every day of my life, there's a moment when some well-meaning passerby catches a glimpse of my lips and kindly alerts me to what I must be completely obliviously to: "Ah, excuse me, but you have some chocolate on your upper lip...OH, and your bottom one too." When in fact, the Arizona sun is to blame for permanently staining the perimeter of my mouth with organic, chocolate-brown lip liner. The cute girl doesn't seem to notice my lips, or she's playing it cool.

She has no hips. This is a good sign. Alexander always says you should date someone who looks totally different from you—that way you can help put a stop to what he sees as a major issue in the gay community: twinning. I have hips; this could work. Casually hanging from her waist are light-blue Girbaud jeans, which are loose enough to be boyish but tight enough to reveal that she has a really great butt. Her thick, dark hair is short in the back, with a floppy but coiffed top, much like Paul McCartney in the Beatles' early years. Until she casually leans back on the bar, her black leather jacket almost completely covers up a chambray shirt outfitted with numerous cartoon character appliqués. I find the juxtaposition of her chunky black Doc Martens and Mickey Mouse waving, "Hello, boys and girls!" from her shirt to be sexy in a way I don't understand. She is a brick…house. We make eye contact, as much as my eyes are capable of making.

I don't know what to do! As an enthusiastic baby dyke with limited sexual encounters, I'm not real smooth with the ladies. Alexander Billingford III is my sexual guru. His experience with men is vast—he dated men three times his age when he was in his teens. And with his spiky red hair, pale freckly skin, and gap between his two front teeth, it's obvious why men like Alexander: He's exotic.

"That girl over there is looking at me. What should I do?" I ask him. I fidget with my hair, making sure the bulk of it is flopped on the right side of my head, providing my nose, which feels stark and large in the neon light of the club, with a much needed "hair visor."

"Hang on, honey," he says while doing the Hustle and taking a long drag from his menthol Marlboro. He holds the smoke in his mouth like a wine connoisseur savors a gulp of pinot noir, with hints of mint, tobacco, and earth. When he purposefully blows a stream of smoke straight across the dance floor, like a human fog machine, I follow the smoke with my eyes to a clean-cut Hispanic boy who's staring seductively at Alexander.

"OK, what's it this time?" Alexander says to me, holding the gaze of the boy.

"That girl, over there, she's checking me out."

He turns to the source of my anxiety. "The one who's

fried, dyed, and laid to the side?" he says, referring to the girl whose damaged, bleach-blond hair suggests that if she hasn't had one too many cocktails, her hair has.

"No, the one next to her."

"Thank God! I saw that ratty bleach-blond tail peeking over her collar like it was coming to get us! You mean the one who looks like a boy?"

"Yes."

"She's cute. Of course she's checking you out, Katan—you are looking G-O-O-D."

"So what do I do?"

"I've got three words for you, Miss Katanalicious: alcohol replacement therapy. There, I said it. Here's what you do: First, you identify the emotion you're feeling—in your case, *fear*. Then, with a large but glamorous cocktail, you *replace* that fear with a warm surge of confidence. Watch." Alexander takes the first sip of his fourth drink while doing the Freak over to the clean-cut Hispanic boy, leaving me alone. I run to the bar, where I optimistically purchase a Sex on the Beach, suck it down, and approach the brick…house. I'm mighty, mighty. I'm gonna let it all hang out.

"Um, hi. My name is Tania. What's your name?" I'm a nerd…that slurs.

"Dawn," she says, pushing both of her hands deeper into her saggy jean pockets.

"Nice to meet you, Dawn," I say, really meaning it. Dawn continues to stare into my eyes but doesn't say anything. Dawn: concise, one syllable, to the point, doesn't really have a lot to say—but hey, who wants to talk? Alcohol replacement therapy is working. I grab a Creamy

Cowgirl and invite Dawn into my unofficial office: the bathroom. I feel a bit like Fonzie's younger sister as I lean against the slightly unhinged door. I'm not sure what I slur, but before I know it, in the fluorescent light of the bathroom stall, to the sound of urination and gossip, Dawn and I are kissing. We're not just kissing—we're exchanging visions in each other's mouths. A spontaneous dating contract is drawn up, reviewed, and signed with our collective saliva.

Before I was familiar with the joke "What do lesbians bring to a first date?" Dawn and I had moved in together, thus becoming the punch line. The first week of living together is really great. We don't have a whole lot to talk about, or a whole lot in common, or… But the sex is phenomenal! The best sex I've ever had. True, Dawn is only the second person I've had sex with, but she is so much better than the first. And Dawn is so cute. I'm lucky that she opted to be with me. I'm not that cute. I will never be that cute. She's like predetermined-by-genetics cute. Sometimes I'm kind of smart or very funny, but smart plus funny does not equal sex, and even if it does equal sex, it equals sex with someone who's also smart and funny, which is redundant. Not only is Dawn cute, but she's brooding too. Dawn is the lesbian equivalent to Ponyboy in *The Outsiders,* or Rusty James in *Rumble Fish,* or basically any character from any movie, play, or novel that is sexy and on the periphery of society. Her looks are so compelling to me that they almost pull focus away from some of her quirks, like communication. See, Dawn's prime method of communication is the fuck-you-slam-the-door-

I'm-leaving method. For example, I will say something that irritates her like, "Have a great day!" She will then say, "Fuck you!" slam the door, and leave.

Another of Dawn's quirks is her unique sense of language; she uses words that sound familiar in the framework of unfamiliar definitions. For example, "She was so skinny, you know, Tania, she was *emancipated*." So…she's free to be skinny? As our relationship continues it's obvious that my optimism plus her cynicism equals: our cataclysm. Eventually, Dawn's malapropistic ways, along with her short fuse, lose their luster and I'm stuck with a girl who by definition is not the one for me. And even though we've grown estranged, we're strangely still attracted to each other. Sex is our staple activity, and at twenty-one years old, that's OK by me. I can get my intellectual needs met at school, my emotional needs met through friends, and all that's left is sex.

So, Dawn's going down on me while simultaneously grabbing my breasts. She's a multitasker. She stops abruptly and places my hand on my right breast.

"Do you feel that? It feels weird," she says with an intensity she usually reserves for violent outbursts.

"Um…no, I don't feel anything." I arch back and gently nudge her head into its previous position.

"I'm serious, Tania. There's a lump. Do you feel that?" Her tone shifts from intensity to tender concern.

Why would she stop the only way in which we communicate to tell me this? I'm on the cusp of having an orgasm. A lump, in the scheme of things, is not a big deal.

"Fine, I feel the lump. Are you happy?"

She doesn't seem happy, but then again she never seems

happy. "It just feels a little strange, that's all," she says. And I say that our relationship feels a little strange, but I don't stop to evaluate it. We continue having sex.

will the real lump please stand up?
(left breast—2002)

It's 2 A.M. I'm lying next to the lump who found my lump, Sal, aware this will be the last time we sleep together. In the morning, I will break up with Sal. The reason I'm breaking up with her is simple: Sal is toxic. Am I thinking too loudly? How many times have I been thinking loudly in someone else's bed? I can't sleep. Why am I even here? These sheets are so stiff. Low thread count. That should have been the first red flag. Never date a girl with less than 300 threads. Tania, please, try to sleep. I can't sleep. OK, just try not to think.

Why did I leave San Francisco?
Why am I in Long Beach, California?
Why am I working at a crappy job?
What if my lump is…something?
How does one know when they've reached rock bottom?
How long is Long Beach?

Long Beach, or Idaho-by-the-Sea, is a mishmash of newly-weds, nearly deads, quirky queens, and outdated dykes, all set to the backdrop of stucco strip malls and the *Queen Mary*. I moved here from San Francisco six months ago to transition from being a poor-but-produced playwright to being a salaried-and-successful sitcom writer. I set up temporary residence at my father's more-than-humble Long Beach apartment. My writing partner, Daniele Nathanson, and I would meet twice a week trying to write the definitive *Will & Grace* spec script. We were determined to find an agent, land a job, and become amazingly wealthy before our respective cushions ran out. My cushion consisted of $4,000. My monthly bills consisted of $2,000. Although I was never good at math, I knew I had about three months to "make it." Two months into our Southern California tour, our cushions, our steam, and our connections all seemed to run out. Daniele took to writing "hour-longs" by herself, and I took to watching television, a form of research, if you will. I mean, the last time I really watched TV was when Gilda Radner was on *Saturday Night Live*, and if I was going to write for TV, I needed to fully understand TV. Who knew TV was so chock-full of crap? Why didn't anyone tell me this? I would have reconsidered the whole writing-for-TV thing. The only two channels with any artistic merit, and any obvious connection to each other, are the Food Network and the Spice Channel. For months I flipped back and forth between *Hot off the Grill* and *Hot on the Girl*. After several failed attempts at writing a *Will & Grace* spec script on my own—in which Will fell in love with a chef and Grace fell in love with a porn star—I decided it was time for me to go to therapy or start dating. The latter was cheaper…initially.

She's snoring. In the entire five months we've been together, I've never heard Sal snore. That pinched, tense look she usually carries between her eyes and on the sides of her nose seems smoothed out. She looks sweet right now. They always do that, you know, look sweet before you break up with them. Wow, I just realized this is the first time I've ever felt completely comfortable around Sal.

2:30 A.M. epiphany: When the only time you truly feel comfortable around your lover is when she's asleep, it's time to break up, right?

Six months ago I was living in San Francisco. My five-year relationship with Fran, the love of my life—or at least that portion of my life—had ended, and I was ready to start anew. San Francisco seemed like the right place for a single twenty-seven-year-old lesbian who had always felt out of place in Arizona. All the kids from high school who had ever been ridiculed for being ugly, silly, witty, nerdy, or edgy colonized San Francisco. Wearing glasses, supporting the arts, and being disheveled was hot. I had finally found my peeps. The most important thing I found in San Francisco, however, was that attractive women found *me* attractive. This was a startling and welcome addition to my tenuous lesbian self-image. Everywhere I went there seemed to be a cute queer girl who wanted to say hello: at a coffee house, in a grocery store, on the street, near a boat, next to a goat. It was like I was in the lesbian version of a Dr. Seuss book: *One girl, two girl, three girl, NEW girl!* In San Francisco my status temporarily shifted from Nerdy to Sexy. I loved San Francisco.

Long Beach was a different creature, a South-Going Zax, if you will. After being a single—and dating—babe in S.F. for the past three years, I was ready to scope out the Long Beach scene. I arrived in L.B. to find that all the cute lesbians were clearly on vacation, leaving their older, Trans Am–driving, cigarette-smoking, Alcoholics

Anonymous–attending, stereotypical counterparts to hold their places at the neighborhood bar named, quite cleverly, after the street it was on, Club Broadway. I would not be going to Broadway unless it was to see Patti LuPone. Just driving by Broadway brought back images from the bar scene in Arizona, complete with characters like Michelle, the faux Eurobabe with the homemade accent and raspberry-red lipstick who used her sex appeal to seduce naïve girls (me), dump them, seduce them again, dump them, seduce them one more time for good measure, then dump them for good. The bar scene also brought me random make-out sessions with stalkers, psychos, and sycophants. The Bar Scene was the dysfunctional undertow that crept below the cocktail-stained carpet, constantly trying to pull me into its clutches. I would not be seduced by Broadway's promises of two-for-one well drinks.

Ow! Bob just bit me. I know *hate* is a strong word, and God will probably punish me in some theatrical way for saying this, but here goes: I hate cats. No, I hate Sal's cat. I wish I could sleep. I wish I didn't have a lump. I wish I didn't have to break up with Sal. I wish she had asked me some questions, or just one question. It was the questions that started it. Two months into our five-month relationship, when I'd emerged from the blissed-out-sex phase of our connection, I realized that Sal never asked me questions, ever. She never asked about my childhood, my goals, my bout with cancer—nothing. When someone doesn't ask you questions it can only mean one thing: They don't want to know you. Eventually I confronted Sal about it. She told me she didn't ask questions because her parents taught her that asking questions was rude and intrusive. Since I'm a Jew, we had a problem.

A friend of mine suggested an alternative to the bar scene, to take a trip to a planet far, far away—PlanetOut: a place where lesbians of all shapes and sizes can love each other in two dimensions. The love of my life was just a "click here" away. A pop-up message informed me to: "Sign up now to receive great personal services for as low as $9.95 a month." It seemed a small price to pay for love, but I was a broke writer in search of a day job. Can a Jew "Jew" someone down? I grabbed my only remaining credit card—the rest were thriving in the nineties—and optimistically entered the numbers. My entrance into the lesbian dating world was...accepted.

Snapshots of my future girlfriend appeared with catchy headlines like, "Looking for HOT Bi-Sexual PUSSY?" and "Snuggle up with this fifty-something recovering drug addict," and "I've suffered a great deal of emotional trauma, but now I'm ready for fun!" I clicked "next" so fast and furiously that I almost bypassed the cute butch girl the spiky hair and cool glasses whose headline read: "Semantics." At the time I thought "Semantics" was a succinct way of saying, "I'm smart," but in fact it was a red flag warning, "You can expect a lifetime of arguments and clarification if you pick PlanetOut girl #55."

She was a lesbian into Middle Eastern food and foreign films and lived within a ten-mile radius. Perfect. I shot off an extremely clever e-mail—I'm certain—and waited for her response. After 2.5 days of checking my e-mail every 8.5 minutes, I heard the mellifluous cries of the Bar Scene

Siren beckoning me to, *Come back to earth, Tania… You can't meet a girl in cyberspace… Come to Broadway… $1 well drinks and all the cute girls in Long Beach will be here… Come, come, come, come m'lady… Sugar pie honey… I'll make your knees weak, you make me go crazy…*

Broadway. The cocktails are priced according to size and for $1 I get a Dixie-cup cosmopolitan. It's a tasty hors d'oeuvre before the main course of three Dixie-cup cosmopolitans, and by that time I'm too drunk to realize I just paid $4 for one regular-size drink, so I have another and head over to the pool table.

You become an instant superstar when you're running it, you lean on it when you're drunk, and you hide underneath it when your ex enters the bar: the pool table. Stability in an unstable environment. My father taught me how to play pool the summer I came out to him; I was nineteen, and he lived next to a gay bar. At the Crowbar, with sailors and naval officers as onlookers, my dad showed me how to chalk, break, stroke, massé, and jump my way into coming out on top. As we would leave the Crowbar, each of us glowing from that one shot that shouldn't have gone in but did, my father's arm around my shoulder, a baseball cap anchored onto my head, the older guys would give my dad a sort of thumbs-up nod.

"What's that about?" he'd ask.

"They think I'm your Boy, Daddy. You're, like, the king of NAMBLA around here. I'm hot property."

Once at the pool table, barely able to stand, I chalk my cue, shake my opponent's hand, and proceed to kick her astonished ass. My daddy taught me well. Six opponents

down, eight cosmos down—which is really like two regular-size drinks—I sit down and watch as the two cutest
girls in all of Long Beach stroll into the bar and sit near
me. One of them is a girly girl: lipstick, exposed-midriff
top, seductive smirk. The other is barely a girl: messy
auburn rock-star hair, black Buddy Holly glasses, a faded
HOT WHEELS T-shirt, and a hyphen for a mouth. I
approach them with the confidence of a fraternity guy at a
high school party.

"Hello, ladies." I slide into their booth, because if I don't
sit down I might fall over. The girly girl, my aesthetic
ideal, is the first to respond: "Great, now that you're here."
I let out an audible gulp.

The other girl, the boyish one, seems a bit tentative. "Fine,"
she says.

"I'm Tania," I tell them.

"I'm Sally, but I like being called Sal," the butch one says.

"I'm Carrie, but I like being called…all the time."

I'm immediately attracted to Carrie, whose honey-brown
hair seems to oscillate whenever she looks at me. "You girls
look too cool to be from Long Beach," I say. "Where are
you from?"

"San Francisco," Carrie says. I am in love with Carrie.

"Me too! What part?"

"Noe Valley."

"I love Noe Valley!" We have so much in common already.

"I'm actually from Long Beach," Sal says with an impish
grin.

"I know you *live* in Long Beach," I say, "but you weren't
born and raised here? I mean, no one's really *from* Long
Beach, right?"

"Yeah, actually, I am," she says, again offering a sneaky smile. I'm not sure whether Sal has a facial tic or if she's a touch "special."

For the next twenty minutes Carrie and I play out a scene from a lesbian romance movie: We discuss early-childhood trauma in slow motion, we laugh spontaneously while feigning falling off our chairs, we talk about past lovers and all of *their* issues. We are falling in love. Sal finally says something.

"You know you responded to my personal ad on PlanetOut, right?"

What?! This is the butch girl who's into foreign films and hummus?

"How come you didn't mention that when I first sat down?"

"Sorry. I thought it was kind of fun that I knew and you didn't." Sal smiles, finally coming to life.

I'm feeling a little exposed, but I'm intrigued by Sal. She's different from me, from Carrie. Here's a girl who appears to be completely removed from the conversation, when, in fact, she is hyperaware, totally engaged, a bit sneaky, but definitely present. I like that. There's something to this Sal, some substance. My focus shifts from Carrie and our easy banter to Sal and her intrinsic mystery.

Sal is still snoring; Bob, the flea-ridden cat, is still biting; and I am still unable to sleep. I'm doomed to repeat the story of how I got here over and over in my head until the alarm goes off, in about three hours, at which point I'll turn to her and say, "Good morning, I'm breaking up with you. Do you want some coffee?" Why does hindsight always beat foresight to the punch? If you listen, people will tell you exactly who they are and how they'll handle situations within the first few hours of your meeting them. The difficulty comes when we don't listen, when we see a red flag waving and choose to view it as a decorative banner rather than a giant foreboding gesture. Red Flag #1 was waved during month one of our five-month relationship, in the form of an e-mail.

E-mail to: Sal
Subject: Hey, Super Cutie!
Sal: Can't wait to have coffee with you Saturday. Do you mind if my friend Julia comes? I'd really like for you guys to meet, since I adore both of you. Hope you're having an amazing day!
xo tania

E-mail to: Tania
Subject: I'm going to count to 10...
I thought just YOU and I were going to coffee. What's up with inviting Julia? I'm going to count to ten cuz I'm really pissed. Call me. —Sal

I took note of the red flag, but I also noted that I was ready to be in a relationship—and there is nothing more powerful than being ready.

Sal e-mailed me the minute she got home from the bar:

E-mail to: Tania
Subject: I wouldn't give Carrie your e-mail address...
...because I wanted it all for myself! Sorry I didn't return

your PlanetOut message sooner, didn't realize you were so cute in real life. Can I take you out to dinner sometime?
Cheers, Sal

I e-mailed her back—the next day.

E-mail to: Sal
Subject: I'm a cheap date sexually…
…but when it comes to a culinary encounter, I can be very expensive! Dinner sounds great. How about Saturday? Let me know.
Take care, Tania

Saturday night arrives, and Sal shows up at my door carrying flowers. *She* brought *me* flowers. As a rather androgynous woman who's historically been attracted to girly girls, I have fallen into the role of the Boy (different from the Boy of my pool-playing days with Daddy at the Crowbar. Being gay is very complicated), which means paying for things, making reservations, and buying flowers. It takes a lot of energy to be the Boy. I don't know how real boys do it. Still, Sal's chivalry is not lost on me. I love it. Not since Dawn have I encountered a butch girl who wants to help with dating duties.
Sal nervously leads me to her enormous navy-blue sport utility vehicle. Once at the passenger-side door, she opens it for me. The space between the curb and the black rubber step on her tank is at least a foot and a half high. I take a few steps back and, as if preparing for a gymnastics routine, I jump up, spring forward, and then, using the passenger seat as the top of the pommel horse, catapult myself into the vehicle. I hope

this will be the hardest part of the date. Propelling myself into this thing has caused me to work up quite an appetite. When I ask Sal where she wants to go for dinner, she confidently responds, "I've already taken care of it."

I've given up on the idea of sleeping altogether. I am currently obsessed with the red flags that make up the fabric of our relationship, like:

Red Flag #2: Sal conceals information.

Red Flag #3: She prefers *not* talking to talking.

Red Flag #4: Sal's intimacy policy: Don't let anyone in, because when they leave, which they *always* do, you won't get hurt.

Red Flag #5: Her father is insane.

Red Flag #6: She believes Armageddon is coming in 2005, so she's a bit tentative about making long-term plans.

Red Flag #7: I'm the first Jewish person she has ever met.

Red Flag #8: She's a devout Catholic.

Red Flag #9: She calls herself a drummer but never actually drums.

Red Flag #10: the gifts

Sal is a focused driver—so focused, in fact, that when I

casually ask her the usual getting-to-know-you questions—
Do you have siblings? Any dietary restrictions? Have you
been to therapy?—she answers in a quick, stiff manner,
"Two, no, and definitely not."

At least we won't get into a car accident.

The restaurant is an homage to the eighties set directly on
the beach. Nagel prints displaying girls with names like
"Rio" and "Hungry" adorn the walls in this odd '80s
Disneyland. When a gay guy in a Hawaiian shirt seats us,
I'm not sure why Sal brought me here. Didn't I mention I
was an expensive culinary date? I look at the menu to find
the most incongruous cuisine: filet and potatoes gratin:
$23; chicken stuffed with spinach and cheese: $18. It goes
on. That's why gay restaurants never seem to make it—
they can't get the camp-to-cuisine ratio figured out. I easily
decide on the lamb (sorry, vegetarian sisters), while Sal
selects the chicken. We settle into our spaces, but Sal is
still not engaging in conversation.

"So, how do you know about this restaurant?" I try to
spark something.

"I've been here before," Sal says, focusing intently on the
little gold pats of butter in front of her.

"Oh, is this where you bring all of your dates?" I joke.

"No." Sal is not joking, and now she is intent on arranging
the gold pats in a perfect line in front of her.

"Sorry, I didn't mean to…"

"I'm sorry. I'm just a little nervous," she says, completing
the buttery barrier between us.

We drink. Drinking is a good first-date activity. Sal begins
to loosen up as a result of too much alcohol and first-date
adrenaline. Her pale Irish face becomes flush as she allows

herself to talk. I mean, really talk. I can't get her to shut up. Don't get me wrong, I love it. It's actually in this moment of Sal's effortless verbal eruption that I decide it would be all right for us to kiss at the end of the date, and if she is inclined to feel me up, that would be all right too, but that means...the Speech. Which one should I use tonight?

How about the organic one?
Sal, if you touch my breasts, which I strongly encourage, you will find that I do not, in fact, have a right breast. The left one, however, is in great repair and really loves being touched!

Then I could segue into the after-school-special version of *Why Tania Doesn't Have a Booby.*

Or I could go with the surprised speech.
WHAT? No breast? Are you sure? Shit! I've got to go.

There's always the McDonald's explanation.
Yeah, see, I ordered a cup of coffee at McDonald's, and you know how hot their coffee is. Well, it spilled and...it burned right off!

I wait for Sal to provide me with the perfect opening.
"...and I said, 'I'm sorry, but I can't, sir.' And the guy says..."
Thank you, Sal. "Cancer? Did you say cancer?" I ask.
"Oh, no, I said, 'can't sir,'" Sal says, placing her hands together in a praying position and rubbing vigorously. "Sorry, it sounded like cancer, which reminds me of a story

that goes a little something like this: When I was twenty-one years old I—"

Sal stops rubbing. "Look, Tania, I have to confess something…"

"You don't wear panties? Neither do I! That's always a hard topic to broach."

"I Googled you," she says, now sitting on her hands.

"You Googled me?" Google? Oh, my God, she's trying to relate to me in Jewish terms. That's so sweet! "Oh, Sal, it's kugel. You made me a kugel? With raisins?"

"No, Google. It's a search engine. When you told me you were a playwright I decided to look you up online, to Google you. I know all about the breast cancer and your plays and—"

"Why would you do that? Why wouldn't you just ask me about my playwriting? I would have told you."

Sal clams up. She reaches into the pocket of her dark brown corduroy peacoat, which is draped on the back of her chair, to retrieve something.

"I have a gift for you," she says, sticking her baseball-glove hand into the slit on the side of her coat. The gift is a stick in the spokes of our conversation. An overt redirection. After tugging and struggling to retrieve the gift, her hand emerges from the pocket holding a tiny, black velvet box. A box too fancy for a first date, or a second date, or even a third. If it's a ring, I will scream, then laugh, then run out of the restaurant as fast as I can.

"Thanks." I cautiously lift the lid, the hinges creaking to a slow open. "Wow, it's a…Well, it's pink, but what is it exactly?"

"It's an angel. As a devout Catholic, I believe angels have

healing powers. I don't mean to sound too…out there, but I just came back from this retreat, and when I read about you, and your plays, I just thought that, well, that everyone can use an angel. I hope I didn't offend you. I know you're Jewish. I just care about you."

I'm not offended, I think. *Maybe a little freaked out. I mean, first of all, you Googled me, which is duplicitous and icky, and second, how can you be a devout Catholic and a homosexual at the same time? But on the other hand, I am ready for a relationship, and how exciting to have someone take the initiative to find out about me, albeit indirectly, but still. And the gift: What a thoughtful gesture. Sure, it's an angel, I would have preferred a gift certificate to Starbucks, but you took the time to give me something that had meaning to you, and if your religion allows you the space to be open and thoughtful, then an angel is OK by me!*

"Thank you for the angel, Sal."

How come I never noticed that her copy of the Dalai Lama's *A Simple Path* is covered in dust and cat scratches? At 4 A.M. one notices many things, like the pile of gifts she has given me in place of language and conversations. It started with the angel, to avoid the *Sal, I want you to know that I had breast cancer* talk; then the bottle of champagne, to eschew the *Sal, why do you hate my loving family?* discussion; then the fancy steel commuter mug, to dodge the *Sal, why is it that you only open up after a couple of cocktails?* remark; and finally the plastic dreidel filled with chocolate coins, to avert the *Sal, why aren't you supportive of my writing?* query. As the pile has grown, I have grown less interested in stuff and more interested in talking, in sharing, in something that is not gift-wrapped.

Sal has asked me to come over today so she can tell me something. Sal and I have been together four months and seven days, but it feels longer, and not in a good way. Yesterday was my cousin's wedding. Sal was my date. It was her first Jewish wedding—hell, it was the bride's first Jewish wedding. My cousin is the only Jew in the equation, and he's not the most religious guy, but he and his fiancée agreed to be married by a rabbi. When I come to pick Sal up at the designated time, she is not ready. Not only is she not ready, but she seems to be angry, and she's wearing a dress. Now, let's stop right there. Sal might have been born a woman, but that's merely a formality. Her usual style is akin to that of an adolescent boy: grubby sneakers, baggy jeans, and oxford collars sticking out of thrift-store-purchased Bing Crosby sweaters. It's most often the case that people mistake Sal for a boy rather than a man. And much like people who look like the dogs they love, Sal's body type resembles that of her cartoon hero: SpongeBob SquarePants. A dress? I address the issue with sensitivity.

"Wow, I've never seen you wear a dress before. Are you going to wear that to the wedding, Sal?" The vague anger I felt from her earlier feels directed now, specifically at me. "It's Sally," she says, "and I like wearing dresses. I used to wear dresses all the time. Do you have a fucking problem with it, Tania?" She aggressively lifts up her dress and notices that her tight, taupe stockings are twisted. Much like a middle-aged man in the middle of a potato-sack race, she yanks and jumps until her stockings are in the winning position.

"No, I want you to feel comfortable," I tell her. "If a dress makes you feel comfortable, then wear it. It looks great." It's hard to muster up sincerity when your girlfriend looks like Arnold Schwarzenegger in a dress.

Sal then proceeds to apply makeup. I pray quietly to God that she'll look more like one of the boys from 'N Sync than a drag queen. But now she simply looks weird.

"Let's fucking go already," she says, so defiantly that her lipstick almost smears.

At the wedding, as soon as the rabbi announces, "You may kiss the bride," Sal turns to me and snarls, "Can we fucking go?"

Huh? We just drove fifty-five minutes to get here, we've been here only twenty-five minutes, and you want to leave right this minute?

"No," I tell her. "I'm sorry, but this is my family and I'd like to hang out with them. Is everything all right, Sal?" I seriously don't know what's going on with her.

"Jews. Everyone here is a Jew. I don't fit in. I wanna fucking go."

That's when I feel toxicity emanate from her body. In a few seconds I can see the toxicity oozing out from the pores on her face. The lipstick and eye shadow, which she took so much time to apply, are being forced down her face by sweat and anger. Streaks of eye shadow, lipstick, and mascara stream their way down to her chin and drip off her like she's a human candle. I want to tell her makeup doesn't suit her, but instead I say, "We're going to stay until we are both ready to leave. I'm going to go say hello to my aunts and uncles now. You're welcome to join me."

Sal follows me through the reception, sulking and saying nothing to the various people I introduce her to, until we decide to leave. On the drive home I turn NPR up as loud as I can stomach. I want to hear about conflicts that don't involve Sal or me.

Today we have been together four months and seven days. Sal has invited me over because she wants to talk about something. I'm happy to let her talk. I am finished initiating conversations with her.

I cut to the chase: "What's going on?"

"Um…I have to tell you something, but why don't you open this gift first?" She shoves at me a small, rectangular package wrapped in a paper that's not reserved for any specific holiday or event.

"I don't want the gift. I want to know what's going on," I say, surreptitiously trying to push Bob off Sal's decaying futon.

"OK, open the gift, then I promise I'll tell you." She stares blankly at the package. Not blank like she's thinking about nothing, but blank like a serial killer, blank like she's capable of doing something she can't be held responsible for. Blank.

"Tell me first and then I'll open the gift," I say, having successfully removed the fleabag from the flea bed.

"Well…I was thinking about the wedding last night and…the reason why I acted the way I did was…well, it's because I'm scared."

Bob pounces onto Sal's lap. Her attention immediately turns toward him as she methodically strokes his over-

33

grown matte-gray and worn-out-orange pelt. Bob meows with pleasure.

"Scared of hanging out with Jews?" I ask, sending Bob psychic messages to go outside and play or get into a fight with a Land Rover or something.

"Will you please open the gift? It'll help explain!" Sal's hands are shaking like crazy.

I tear open the package to reveal…*Not Just One in Eight?* It's an anthology of stories of how breast cancer survivors and their families have coped with illness. My story, as told from the twenty-five-year-old Tania Katan perspective, is in this book.

"How did you know about this book?" I ask.

"Google," she says, avoiding eye contact.

"Did Google tell you it would be more cost-effective to ask Tania Katan about the Tania Katan story?"

"Tania…I'm not sure how to say this."

"Try words."

"I'm scared you're going to get cancer again."

"Huh?!"

"I'm scared you're going to get cancer again and then…and then…die. It's my biggest fear."

Whoa! Why don't you get your own fears? Why don't you give reality-based fears a try—like dogs, heights, or guns? Why don't you read *Codependent No More?* Sal has never asked me about my one-night stand with cancer, and whenever I bring up the subject she disengages.

"Thank you for your concern," I tell her. "But I've been cancer-free almost ten years now. I'm happy, healthy, and not about to drop dead anytime soon, so don't cancel any dinner reservations."

"I'm just concerned," Sal says with a new confidence, like

if I do get cancer again, she could take care of me.
"I'm concerned too."

If Bob bites me one more time, I will bite him back. Ouch!
I bit him. It is now 5:30 A.M., two hours until breakup.
Having the idea to break up with someone is very different
from actually breaking up with her. It can take months from
the moment of inception to the actual execution, like you're
gathering momentum, repeating in your head all the reasons
why you should break up with her, so that one day, with all
the force of Dr. Phil, you can say, *It's over!* That day is upon
me. It's funny that I didn't break up with Sal after she gave
me *Not Just One in Eight.* I guess I wanted to give her one
more chance; or I needed one more ounce of momentum.

Sal and I have been together four months and fourteen
days. She has invited me over for dinner tonight. If Sal is
nothing else, she is a good cook with a savvy sense for the
art of cuisine. I arrive to find a rather romantic dinner setting for two, a zinfandel from Paso Robles, a huge slab of
evenly seasoned red meat, a mélange of colorful vegetables;
it's perfect. Except for the silence. It's as if we both know
that if either of us says something, it'll be the wrong thing
to say, so we say nothing. After a few bites and several sips,
the silence is broken by, guess who, that's right, me. "This
is really nice meat, Sal. What is it?"
"Prime rib," she replies with no intention of saying anything else. Soon, though, we're engaged in a conversation
about world-renowned chefs. And then something goes
wrong—maybe it's the little crush I have on super-cute,
scooter-driving TV chef Jamie Oliver, or Sal's disdain for
nouvelle cuisine—but we have a miscommunication

about: (a) nothing, (b) something, or (c) all of the above? I don't want to make war tonight, and with the robust zinfandel almost finished, I suggest to Sal that we make love. Why not? We have nothing else to say. She acquiesces. So, my wrists are tied together with a soft but sufficient necktie and hoisted over my head. Sal is finally communicating in a way I can understand. Her fingers trail over my nipple, her hand cups my breast, and…and…she stops. She is frozen. She reaches behind my neck, frees my hands, and carefully places them on my remaining breast.

"Tania, do you feel that?" she asks, her hand enveloping mine, firmly pushing it into the soft skin of my small breast.

In that moment, with a curious lump beneath my fingers and an even more curious lump pointing it out to me, I know what the body knows before the mind has time to glean it. The lump hits a nerve that releases all of my history.

What if your girlfriend feels like a stranger? What if your girlfriend's biggest fear is *you* getting cancer? What if the above-mentioned girlfriend finds a lump? You've got to wonder, right? I mean, if the lump turns out to be cancer, does that ensure that you'll never leave her? Red Flag #87: Toxic girlfriends equal lumps. It's 7:30 A.M. Time to break up with Sal.

print-o-rama
(left breast—2002)
I'm sitting at my less-than-desirable job thinking of ways to quit, while surfing the Web for a more desirable job and

simultaneously e-mailing my friends about how undesirable my job is. I am, in fact, a hard worker.

I always swore to myself that even though I earned a degree in theater, I would never work at a place with "O-Rama" in the title. No Frame-O-Rama, Skate-O-Rama, or Som-O-Lama-Ding-Dong-Rama! *Rama* is not even a word in the dictionary.

I started at Print-O-Rama as I always start a day job—like it's a sociological study. As a writer who has never made a living writing, I approach all day jobs as an opportunity not only to pay my bills—and get health benefits—but to study the habits of the strange and nomadic people known as the Work Force or Nine-to-Fivers, in hopes of taking my notes and someday turning them into a play or book or something that could win me the Pulitzer and get me out of my day job.

For almost four months now I've been studying the natives of Print-O-Rama. Their social mores seem to be a combination of passive aggression and blatant disrespect. It is time for me to pack up my gear, gather my notes, and leave the jungle.

I've never executed such a highly technical and dangerous mission before, just quitting, up and leaving, not saying goodbye. Every day for the past 110 days I've had thoughts of going to lunch and never coming back. Today I'm gonna do it. Yeah! Screw Print-O-Rama! This always happens. I get all of this gratuitous adrenaline, like not only am I going to quit but I'll machine-gun my way out of the office, mowing down a few superfluous employees, while screaming, "This is for writers everywhere!" And then, when my machine-gun dreams relax into weighty realities like having health insurance, I'll slowly drop my action-hero persona and have to reevaluate my position.

When I was twenty-one years old I had health insurance. When I was twenty-one years old I was diagnosed with breast cancer. One might draw the conclusion that health insurance equals cancer. Not until last week, when my boss overheard me making an appointment at the Breast Clinic and decided to activate my benefits, did I have health insurance. For more than nine years I've been cancer-free, as well as health insurance–free, and I've been fine. Maybe it is OK to quit today. But just to play it safe, I'll wait until I get my biopsy results. It's Wednesday, and the doctor is supposed to call either Thursday or Friday, only two more days to wait. Once I'm deemed free and clear, I'm out of here.

It's time to get to work. Surfing the Web is so much fun; riding the waves of information is soothing, even Zenlike. My job isn't so bad, until the phone rings.

"Hello, Print-O-Rama, where we say, 'Four colors, four presses, four reasons to give us your business.'" Actually, that's only two reasons, but my boss won't let me change it. "How can I provide you with excellent customer service?"

"Hello, may I speak with Tania Katan?"

The voice sounds unfamiliar; it could be a customer. I answer cautiously. "Uh, this is Tania Katan."

"This is Dr. Milkin." *My primary care physician? Does she need four-color printing?*

"Miss Katan, it's Dr. Milkin and I'm calling to, well, what did Dr. Comack say when he saw you?" I'm having difficulty breathing. See, the only time doctors have called me in the past was when they were delivering bad...

"He said I probably had a junky cyst, nothing to worry

about, that I'd get the pathology report Thursday or Friday."
Oh, God, it's Wednesday. I'm finding it increasingly difficult
to breathe. I mean, they never call you early, they barely have
time to see you, they even forget your history. The lump in
my breast has leapt into my throat and I can't…breathe.
"Well Miss Katan—" Thick mist oozes from the phone.
I'm stuck in smog, choking.
"At least it's a small malignancy. If you need anything, feel
free to contact me."
I hang up the phone; my breath is still suspended. It's 2:17
P.M. What just happened? Wait, this *can't* be happening.
It's a different girlfriend that found the lump. This is a different story. You can't have the same story twice in one
lifetime. It just doesn't happen. Lightning NEVER strikes
twice in the same place. I mean, statistically speaking, having cancer twice and having it discovered by two toxic
women cannot happen. Can it?
Now I'll have to keep my undesirable job to maintain my
health insurance benefits. Health insurance *does* equal cancer—wish that theory of mine could have stayed a theory.
I need to call Mom—she's gonna cry, she's gonna die.
What if she's not home? Dad will flip out; he's never really
dealt with the death of his sister who had breast cancer. It's
only 2:19 P.M. Sal just e-mailed me; she feels like since she
found the lump she's entitled to know what's going on
with it. Shit, I'm gonna cry. I didn't expect cancer; I
thought it might be cancer, but I'd hoped it wouldn't. Can
people get cancer twice in a lifetime and survive? Great, I
got tears all over this work order, which will probably
prompt my boss to fire me, which would have been cool
three minutes ago, but now I need to wipe the tears with-

out smearing the ink. I need to breathe.

I walk over to my alcoholic, inconsistent, emotionally dis-tant manager, Katie, to ask her if she'll please cover the phones because I need to make a few calls. She barks at me: "I'll try!"

Come on, Katie. I know you heard me crying. You had to. You listen and comment on all of my personal calls daily. You don't have your radio on. Fine, I'll give you the benefit of the doubt.

"Listen, Katie, I was just diagnosed with cancer again."

Oh, no, Tania, DO NOT cry now! Katie thrives on vulnera-bility! "And I need to make some very important calls." I can't stop the tears.

"I know, I overheard your conversation with Dr. Mc— something, and like I said, I'll try. I don't know why you're crying, Tania. I told you when you first got here that I'm direct, no bullshit. That's just the way I am. Don't take it personally." She waves her pen around like it's a magic wand that'll make me disappear

Why couldn't Katie have gotten cancer, or at least a painful venereal disease? I go back to my desk and call my mother. Her archaic answering machine picks up: "Bonjour. I'm not in right now. I'm probably out walking my puppy." (Kiwi, Mom's shar-pei, and fourth child, barks excitedly in the background. Mom forgets she's taping an answering machine message and starts chatting with Kiwi.) "Kiwi, who's the cutest shar-pei? Who's Mommy's velveteen puppy? Kiwi-Cutie, Kiwi-Cutie, wanna go for a W-A-L-K? Oh," she says, remembering now that she's taping a mes-sage, "so, I'll be back soon. You know what to do. Be well—"

"Mom…please call me as soon as you get this message. It's Tania. I love you. It's important. Really important. Call me. Please."

Why did I leave such a cryptic message? My mother will come home from the dog park, play the ambiguous recording from her breast cancer–survivor daughter who's been waiting for a pathology report, and easily surmise that I've been diagnosed with cancer. I should call Dad— no, I'll tell him when I get home. I'm losing it. I feel like Pigpen from the Peanuts gang, like a large dirt cloud is surrounding me. I start up my mental viewfinder, clicking through images of me with no hair. *Click:* me with an IV stuck in my arm. *Click:* me on my way to surgery. *Click:* me with no breasts. *Click:* me puking. *Click:* me looking like I've been here before.

Record-speed gossiping must have taken place, because it's now 2:23 P.M. and Liz, stressy graphic designer and fellow breast cancer survivor in the office, is hovering over my desk.

"I know what's going on, Tania, and I want to tell you it's going to be all right. We're lucky. You know, we're sur- vivors, which means we can survive anything, even cancer again. OK, so, if you need anything…"

Liz hugs me. This is what I need. Slowly, the entire cast of corporate characters encroaches my cubbyhole. There's Ron, fifty-year-old Republican Queer Boss, who wears his thinning blond hair spiky to detract from his neon-pink scalp, drives an expensive blue convertible, and comes to work drunk. His tagline: "The client is only right when he's in my office."

Victor, Latin Towel Boy and Boss Ron's "partner," is twenty- nine, wears tight V-neck T-shirts, drives a more expensive convertible than Ron, and comes to work drunk. His tagline: "Shut the fuck up. We need to be professional here!" Valerie, Hoochie-Mama-Grandma Secretary, is a forty-one-year-old grandmother who flirts with every man, gay or straight, who walks into the office. She wears short tight skirts, drives an expensive convertible, and comes to work drunk. Her tagline: "I can give a blow job like no other grandmother!" Katie, Alcoholic Inconsistent Supervisor, thirty-three, fights with her boyfriends on the phone then calls her children to verbally assault them. She wears short tight skirts, drives a Jeep, and comes to work drunk. Her tagline: "Shut up! I'm just being direct." And finally, there's Fred, forty-three-year-old Slightly Askew Accountant. He has a wife and one teenage son and wears whatever will fit over his stomach–by–Hungry Man; he reads romance novels and drives a Gremlin. His tagline: "I've seen the numbers…We're on the *Titanic*."

All of them have formed a half circle around my cubbyhole. They sniff, they stare, they smile awkwardly. I'm an unfamiliar tribe to them.

Ron, their chief, addresses me first. "Tania, ummm, so what's…? Are you…? Can you tell us how…?"

Victor, his Boy Robin, lends a hand. "Tania, we know that you're sick, so what's the problem? Will you need a lot of time off work?"

"I-I-I, well, when I was—" *Stop. Relax. Breathe. Please don't cry, OK? Continue.* "When I was twenty-one I was diagnosed with breast cancer. I had surgery, went through chemo, and called it a day. Fast forward almost ten years later: I found a lump in my remaining breast, went in for a biopsy, and today my doctor called to tell me I have breast cancer again. I have cancer, that's the problem, Victor."

Ron speaks on behalf of the entire corporate cast and crew.
"Wow, we're really sorry. We had no idea. Take as much time
off as you need. It won't be paid, of course, but we'll keep
you on our insurance plan, and if you need anything, please
let us know."

One by one they leave me in peace.

Wait a second, you forgot one thing guys! "You can go home
now, Tania." What good is having cancer if you can't leave
work early?

Screw work. What I need more than anything right now is
to e-mail my friends.

E-mail to: 200 of my closest friends
Subject A Touch of the Cancer
I'm sorry to send you guys a mass e-mail, as everyone on this
list is very important to me, but right now I'm in need of
good vibes en masse. As many of you know, I had breast cancer about ten years ago, recovered beautifully, got a cool tattoo, and wrote an autobiographical award-winning play on
the subject. The End…or so I thought. Recently I found a
lump that turned out to be malignant. The good news is that
it's small and we're going to act quickly. I don't know all of
the details, but I'll be meeting with an oncologist soon and
probably scheduling surgery so…I'll keep you posted. In the
meantime, what I would LOVE from all of you (other than
money, sex, and a high-profile writing gig) is GOOD
ENERGY. Please feel free to send any current info you have
on breast cancer, procedures, etc. I am blessed to have good
buddies, fabulous family, and my trusty journal.

Lots of love,
Tania

Within seconds, e-mails deluge my Hotmail account, putting me at about eighty-seven percent capacity and nearly forcing me to purchase additional storage space.

From: Mikey
Why do bad things happen to great…

From: Bruce
Harmless…

From: Molly
Strong people?

From: Daniele
I'm surprised…

From: Paul
Angry…

From: Lisa
Sorry you have to go through this again. That's why I'm sending you…

From: Scott
The biggest hug ever…

From: Barbi
Cancer-ass-kicking mojo…

From: Julie
My good vibes, which are the singing sort, so if you find yourself humming, you'll know why.

From: Megan
Why don't we want to fly you up to San Francisco to get some love from The Gang?

From: Jackie
If you end up doing chemotherapy, I'll be your chemo-buddy.

From: Amy
I'm going to have drinks with a friend tonight, so we will drink to your health, and if Bombay and tonic pulls any weight in the world of healing, you'll be all set.

From: ALL
Peace and love, lots of love, tons of love, healing energy, positive energy, extraordinary energy, call if you need anything, something, nothing, just call, we love you so much.

I adore my friends. Their good vibes reach me just in time. It's 5 P.M. I made it. Now I've got to tell Dad.

woozy, groggy, dazed…my first date with cancer (right breast—1992)

The paper beneath me keeps tearing as I shift my weight trying to get comfortable. I've been stuck on this examination table, in this sterile wasteland, for what seems like days. When is the doctor gonna get here? I've got to get back to school. I can't miss another dramatic analysis class. Shit. I didn't write my paper for class. Fuck. I didn't even read the play I was supposed to write the paper about. There's a pen over there, I'm sitting on paper, maybe I can just write it now. Wait, I don't even know the name of the play. I can bullshit about the content, but I at least need to know the title. Oh, *As Is*, that's it.

As Is, by William M. Hoffman, who will be a visiting play-wright next month—that's why I read the play so quickly and with such enthusiasm—is a very interesting piece.

Brevity, that's good.

Although this play seems to be better understood in Europe, making it difficult for Americans, like myself, to fully interpret its nuances, As Is *explores relationships, hardships and…big ships?*

Humor. Nice, Katan.

This play tells the unflinching story of people who have difficulty seeing things the way they are until an outside force gently/harshly/firmly reminds them to see things…as is.

To-the-point, succinct bullshit. Perfect.
The doctor finally arrives. "Why don't you take off your shirt so I can feel the lump?" he says without any introduction.
"OK..?" I go with the anonymous flow, slowly taking off my shirt, like I'm a tittie dancer and the doctor paid me five bucks for a lap dance. He paws at my right breast.
"Mmmm?" he says, raising his one bushy, continuous eyebrow.
I've heard this "Mmmm" with a question mark before.
Two times before, to be exact. The first time was two months ago when an anonymous doctor poked at the little

pea in my booby and told me to, "Stop drinking coffee and take vitamin E." She gave me a sheet of paper with the title "Fibrocystic Breasts and You" and sent me on my way. Then, a month ago, caffeine-free, hopped up on vitamin E, and sporting a marble-size lump, I went to see another doctor. He pushed on the marble in my breast and recommended that I ignore the lump unless, of course, it really bothered me. This month's featured doctor is dealing with the now–golf-ball-size lump protruding from my skin. Three doctors, three months, three sets of hands on my breast; this is clearly more action than it has ever seen. The doctor shapes his icy white hand into a duck's bill and shoves it into my breast.

"Is it painful when I push here?"

"Yes!" It's painful and poking out and… "Yes."

"Perhaps we should take it out for cosmetic reasons," he offers.

Cosmetic reasons? That sounds fun, a little booby nip-and-tuck. Clearly having a huge lump nudging my skin to expand beyond its comfort zone is aesthetically undesirable, not to mention the fact that it's extremely painful to the touch, so I say, *YES*, cosmetically remove my unsightly lump.

"That sounds great, doctor." That was easy. Now I can get back to school.

"OK, Miss Katan. The surgical biopsy will be an outpatient surgery, so you'll need someone to accompany you, as you'll be in no condition to drive home. We can schedule the surgery as soon as next Monday."

Wait, wait, wait. Cosmetic procedure: fun, exciting, glamorous. Surgical biopsy: serious, painful, scary.

"This is just for cosmetic reasons, right?"

"Miss Katan, look, this is nothing. I do this procedure all the time. It's very simple. We remove the lump, give it to the lab to biopsy, and you go home with a scar on your breast that's about the size of a minor scratch."

"OK, OK," I say, "that sounds good. Why don't we schedule it for Monday." That way I won't have to go to my dramatic analysis class.

"Great, we'll see you then," he says flatly. He grabs his clipboard and studies the details of someone else's breasts.

It's Monday and we're back in the doctor's office—Mom, Dawn, and me. The waiting area consists of two torn brown-cushioned chairs held together with a metal fastener to prevent theft. The three of us sit in a cramped row, me sandwiched between Mom and Dawn. I can tell Dawn is uncomfortable because she's laughing nervously at everything my mother says, whether in English or French. The only difference between Dawn laughing and coughing is the fact that she's smiling. Mom nervously sifts through the pile of magazines on the plastic afterthought of a table stuck in the corner. Without looking at the titles, she stuffs the magazines into her saggy purple purse, which sulks on the floor in front of her. As she bends over, the front of her loose, faded purple button-down shirt creeps open to expose the enormous crevasse between her two double-D mountains. Dawn chews on her fingernails as if they were beef jerky, gnawing with such urgency that her bulky blue sweatshirt, with its white letters representing a college she will never attend, puckers in the creases of her arms. Mom and Dawn are quite a pair.

Somehow I thought my first surgery would be more spectacular than this. At least in a hospital. On *St. Elsewhere* they never performed surgical procedures in Dr. Craig's office. I was preparing for a hospital stay, you know, playing with the buttons on the arms of the bed, moving up and down while struggling to say things like, "Could you please adjust my pillow?" and "I think I wet myself" and "For God's sake, where are my painkillers?!" I imagined being served trays of bland mashed potatoes and creamed corn with small cartons of chocolate milk by a nice, slight nurse who'd say, "Here you go, honey. Now, make sure to eat all of it." I'd take the tray and violently throw it at her while screaming, "Fuck you! I'd rather eat dog shit!" Unfortunately there will be no hospital drama today. The surgical biopsy will take place here, in the doctor's office. Mom and Dawn are my companions by default. Because I agreed to stay with my mother while recovering from my outpatient surgical biopsy, she has agreed to temporarily tolerate Dawn. The only thing Mom and Dawn have in common is a vagina. Mom is French; Dawn can barely speak English. Mom is a culinary genius; Dawn loves the Olive Garden. Mom thinks of Dawn much like one thinks of a canker sore: It's annoying but eventually it'll go away; Dawn doesn't think much but wishes Mom would eventually go away.

It's funny that I'm not scared. I thought I might be scared—this being my first surgery and all—but it's kind of exciting, a new experience; maybe I can write about it in my playwriting class next semester. Yeah, that would be pretty cool.

A nurse appears from nowhere and asks if I'm ready for the

procedure. I nod with conviction, hug Dawn, kiss Mom on both cheeks, and, instead of a fancy gurney rolling me away to surgery, I follow the nurse, on foot, down the short dimly lit hallway.

Woozy. Groggy. Dazed. Oh…so…sleepy…opening eyes. Closing eyes. Can't move. Don't want to move. Mmmm. Dreamy. Where am I? Opening eyes. I'm in a bed. This is not my bed. This is not my beautiful house. Where is my beautiful wife? I'm on a couch/bed in the middle of a living room. I'm the sleepy centerpiece in someone's living room. A spectacle, like Frida Kahlo when she was bedridden. Did a Chihuahua just run by? Where is everyone? Where is *anyone?* Where's Mom? Where's my overprotective mom? Why isn't she by her favorite daughter's couch-side? Oh, I see a figure. "Dawn…?"
Dawn sheepishly approaches, her floppy hair covering her eyes. She stares at my feet.
"What's wrong?" I ask her.
"Nothing. Um…your mom…umm…I have to go now, but your mom wants to tell you," she says, still in conversation with her feet.
"Tell me what?"
"Your mom told me she wanted to tell you herself. I have to go now," Dawn says, her Doc Martens racing out the door.
"Dawn?" I say, but she's gone. Something isn't kosher around here.
Mom enters the room. My mother, who has a fondness for talking, is eerily quiet. Why are people doing the Eggshell Salsa around me?

"Hey, is everything all right?" I ask as I push myself up to a sitting position using only my feet as my arms are sore and my scar feels fresh.

"Sure." She sighs deeply as she runs her plump fingers through her wavy blond hair. A distant monosyllabic response from my mother? This is way more serious than I'd thought.

"Are you sure everything is fine?"

"Yes, Tania." With both hands she clutches her round belly, which is covered in an old stained apron.

"You don't seem your normal happy self, Mom," I tell her, just as new pain presents itself in the form of a faint throbbing in my breast accompanied by a sharp and constant poking sensation.

"I'm happy," Mom says definitively, then turns her attention to a cabinet in the kitchen beyond my head.

I finally understand absurdist theater. All of last semester when we were studying Beckett, Genet, Ionesco, I didn't get it, but now I get it. It's about characters being plopped down in the middle of a vague postwar place who are forced to communicate with each other, and if they're unable to communicate, they're doomed to a life of isolation and loneliness. There are no happy days; there will never be a happy day—that is the irony. It all makes sense now.

"Well, I'm happy too, Mom," I say, hoping the lilt in my voice will prompt her to fess up, give me some info.

"Good," she says.

This is big. It's gotta be the lump. It's the lump. I can feel it. When the lab cross-sectioned my lump they found something, I'm sure of it. It's time to play hardball.

"Yeah, I'm really happy, and now that the lump is gone I feel so…vibrant, so…alive!" I announce, using all the energy I can muster to be convincing.

"I'm glad, Tania," Mom says, now in front of the kitchen cupboard. Her ample but short body is poised to push its way up to the cupboard; she stands on her tiptoes, squishing down the faces of the shar-pei puppies adorning her slippers. She opens the chipped yellow cabinet and grabs for the rolling pin. She gets it on the first try.

Oh, my God, I'm gonna die. This is it. I'm pulling out the big guns, because if I'm gonna die, I've got nothing to lose. "Maybe we can celebrate the lump being gone by renting a movie tonight, like *Dying Young* or *Terms of Endearment*?" Rolling pin in hand, Mom faces me. A film of water covers her light blue eyes, making them look warped and gray. Bull's-eye.

"Tania, when they took out the lump…they found… Look, everything is going to be all right, do you hear me? I've raised you three kids with no help from your degenerate father and we've been *magnifique*, no? *Oui*. And just because you have breast cancer doesn't mean we're going to take this lying down. Oh no, we're going to kick cancer's ass together. You and me, Tania—"

Breast cancer? I'm twenty-one years old. Old ladies get breast cancer. "How can I have breast cancer, Mom? I'm too young. It makes no sense."

"You're right, it doesn't make sense. *Merde. Merde, merde, merde!*" My mother always defaults to her native tongue when she's upset. "This whole thing doesn't make sense. Not only are you too young, but you're a good girl. You've never been a pain in the ass. Sure, your grades haven't been so hot, but your talents lie in writing and performing. This whole thing is absurd." She grips the rolling pin tightly.

"Yes, Mom. It is, in fact, absurd." I didn't realize she understood absurdity so beautifully.

"You don't seem bothered by this information," she says. "Are you OK? Are you in shock? It's a lot to process."

What's to process? I'm going to die. That's realistic theater, with a dash of the morality play. I am Everyman, or Everywoman, as the case may be.

"Mom, let's say I've got a few months to live, big deal. I'll call the Make-a-Wish Foundation and meet Sandra Bernhard or Björk!"

"We'll go to France and visit my family!" she exclaims. "We'll go skydiving. We'll swim with the dolphins. We'll run away together!"

"Cool!"

"Yeah! You and me, Tania. We'll skip town, leaving cancer—and Dawn—far behind!"

Mom and I practically high-five each other. Cancer ain't so bad. I start to fantasize about hanging out in Iceland with Björk and the polar bears when I realize my mother is crying.

"What's wrong?" I ask her. "Why are you crying? I thought we were gonna swim with the dolphins."

"Right. It's just that… It's just that… It's just that I don't have the right bathing suit to swim with the dolphins. That's all." Mom unintentionally drops the rolling pin; it hits the ground and rolls slowly over the warped, yellow linoleum. My short, round mother looks flattened, vulnerable in a way I've never seen before—like a little girl and an old woman at the same time. I want to assure her everything will be all right, but that's her job, and if my mother can't assure me, how can I assure her?

elliot richards's one-bedroom boarding house for wayward breast cancer–surviving daughters (left breast—2002)

I find my father, Elliot, sitting at his makeshift desk—a card table—when I arrive home from work. How do I tell him I have cancer again? Aren't there any singing telegrams for this kind of news? Singing mammograms? Maybe I don't have to tell him—not until I go bald and he starts asking questions.

"Hey, Dad." My tone is light, insouciant.

"What's wrong?" His gruff New York tone is a bit more direct. I'll have to reevaluate my strategy.

The card table is the only piece of furniture in his apartment. It's the kind of table one might see at a garage sale shelving tchotkes, or hidden in a storage shed behind the unused bikes and dust-covered stuff once designated for art projects. The top of this three-by-three table is covered in a brown faux-wood plastic veneer. It's as if the door of a 1970s family station wagon has been ripped off and given legs. On top of the table my father has placed a plastic tablecloth, which is covered with multicolored flowers, coffee stains, and pastry droppings. Plastic to protect the plastic. This table is the center of activity in my father's world. It's his desk, his den, his best friend.

Precariously placed around the table are piles of napkins and scraps of paper: Dad's urban filing system. There's also an array of remote controls. In an effort to simplify his already simple life, he collects remote controls. I think the theory is that if he can control several remote areas in his life, he's got a fighting chance at controlling his entire life.

Remote Control #1 turns the television on and off.
Remote Control #2 changes channels, raises and lowers volume—the most sophisticated remote in his arsenal.
Remote Control #3 turns the screen blue in preparation
    for Remote Control #4.
Remote Control #4 turns on Web TV.
Remote Control #5 seems to have no function at all. It's
    merely decorative.

The rest of his apartment is like a poor man's museum of modern art. Inside POMMOMA you'll find the show "Stuff I Can't Throw Out Because My Parents Were Russian Immigrants." POMMOMA is home to the Elliott Richards Collection. Mr. Richards's collection includes such gems as a drawer full of broken Kojak sunglasses, a tin can filled with dried-out Bic pens, and a large glass bowl overflowing with origami dollar bills. That's right, cranes and planes, pinwheels and wheelbarrows, all constructed from dollar bills by an ex-cabbie friend of his. I'll write him a note. Perfect. I'm a writer; I can think of a clever, sensitive way to tell him.
"Hey, Dad, can I borrow a pen?"
He hands me a Bic circa 1985. I grab a napkin with a doughnut shop advertisement printed on it and scribble. The pen is dry.
"This pen doesn't work," I tell him. "Do you have another one?"
He takes the pen away from me as if to say, *You don't*

understand the nuances of a Bic, and conducts the same
scribble test I've just conducted. There's no proof of ink.
He carefully places the pen in a Yuban coffee can and
hands me another one. I scribble. No luck. I guess I'll have
to tell him.
"Dad, ummm…" Oh, man, talk about missing a step. I
never even told him I had a lump! This is a giant leap. "So,
last week I found this lump in my breast," I say. "I went to
the doctor to have it checked out, and it looks like I've got
cancer again. Crazy, huh? Who would have thunk it? So,
how are you doing? How's work?"
My hands are trembling harder than my voice. I want him
to say something, but he's a man of few words, unless he's
telling a joke or yelling at someone. His hand leaves the
pile of napkins it's resting on and moves toward my hand.
He takes my right hand and squeezes it tightly. One, one
thousand; two, one-thousand; three… He holds my hand
for three seconds. He's never held my hand longer than
two seconds. This is worth noting.

how to put a family member to sleep
(right breast—1992)

When I was twelve years old our family dog, Kooshka,
named after the only horse my father had ever bet on that
actually won, was diagnosed with cancer. Kooshka, a soft,
fawnlike German shepherd, had been around longer than my
brother, my sister, and me. She was fourteen years old when
Mom received the news during a routine vet visit that
Kooshka had cancer. By the time the vet had caught it, the
cancer had metastasized throughout her body, thus explain-
ing Kooshka's daily aches and pains and her difficulty walk-

ing and playing. Kooshka had taken to lounging in a frail half-circle in the corner of the living room. The vet said Kooshka's departure would probably happen sooner rather than later and that we should consider putting her to sleep. But how do you do that? How do you put a family member to sleep? Kooshka was our friend, our sometime babysitter, and occasionally our method of transportation.

Mom waited until Kooshka could no longer walk smoothly. When Kooshka began to wobble and yelp in pain, Mom decided it was time. The date and time were scheduled with the vet: Thursday at 8 A.M.—that way all of us could spend time with her before we had to go to school. On the morning of Kooshka's eternal nap, Mom presented her with an extravagant-looking pastry. It appeared to be a large cupcake with pink frosting and multicolored sprinkles, but in actuality it was a rock-hard replica of a pastry. Kooshka could barely eat the pink rock, but she enjoyed a few minutes of licking the frosting. On that Thursday we simply said the word "Walk." We leashed her up and headed out for her final stroll, making sure to gently rub her ears and scratch her butt all the way around our apartment complex.

Once in the vet's office, all of us adorned Kooshka with kisses and wishes for a good afterlife. We told her how much we loved her and enjoyed having her as part of the Katan family, remembering the good times, like when we would ride her around Central Park like a pony. The vet reinforced our decision by telling us we were doing the right thing, even though it felt gravely wrong to all of us. Paul, Kim, and I were escorted out of the tiny room into the waiting area, where our preteen attention deficit disorders kicked in. Within minutes we had forgotten why we were waiting and focused on finding the shoe, scarf, and hat in the trees, window frames, and pant legs of the pictures in *Highlights* magazine.

Mom exited the office carrying a more compact Kooshka. The look on her face suggested she had done something terribly wrong. Kooshka had been reduced to a jar of gray confetti.

Nearly a decade later I'm sitting in front of a large double mocha with extra whipped cream and dark chocolate shavings. Life is good. Mom sits in front of a yellow legal pad and a thirty-two-pack of cheap see-through pens for us to compile questions for the surgeon. Before the café and expensive mocha, we took a lovely stroll around the Mill Avenue shops, stopping at a store that sells lucky silver charms called milagros. Mom bought me two milagros, one that looks like a heart set aflame and another that looks like breasts welded together. Milagros are supposed to protect and heal whatever part of the body they represent. The heart and breasts are good investments, probably as much luck as I need and Mom can afford.

"OK, I think we should start off by asking him what kind of cancer it is exactly. Is there more than one kind of breast cancer?" Mom knows what she's doing—that's why I'm going with her, not Dawn, to see the surgeon. Dawn's potential for a flare-up isn't something I want to add to my list of things to deal with.

"Question number two," Mom says. "Is surgery the only option? Are you sure it is cancer? Have you ever seen someone as young as my Tania with breast cancer? How

come a twenty-one-year-old woman has breast cancer?"
"Whoa, Mom, question number two seems to have a lot of
parts."
"I'm sorry. Hey, do you want a little treat to go with your
mocha? I saw some fancy looking cupcakes up there."
"Sure, thanks." Mom hands me a five. I'm living large.
The cupcake is amazing: light golden brown and four
inches in circumference, and when I lick the fluffy pink
frosting, it licks me back.

My surgeon's name is Dr. Cutter. Talk about getting to the
point. He greets Mom and me with an abrupt salutation:
"Hello, Ms. Katan. Here's what's going on: Your cancer is
very invasive. It's stage III, so I recommend you get either
a lumpectomy with radiation or a mastectomy with
chemotherapy. And I'd like to schedule surgery for next
week."
Next week? That's Thanksgiving break! I don't want to
waste my vacation recovering from surgery. And these
words: lumpectomy and mastectomy? I've never even
heard of them before.
"Dude, I'm 21 years old. I don't know anything about
these procedures. Which one do you think I should get?" I
ask quietly, assuming Dr. Cutter knows more than I do
when it comes to surgery
"Legally," he says, "I can't recommend one over the
other. But both are effective forms of dealing with your
cancer."
Mom pipes in with legal notepad question number fifty-
five, which has three parts, of course: "What alternatives
are there to surgery? Could you explain the difference
between a lumpectomy with radiation and a mastectomy

with chemotherapy? Have you ever seen a girl this young with breast cancer?"

"No," Dr. Cutter says, "I haven't seen anyone as young as your daughter with breast cancer. As far as alternatives to surgery, well, you can do whatever you'd like, but if we don't operate soon I'd say Tania has a pretty good chance of having metastatic cancer, which we don't want to have happen. A lumpectomy involves removal of the lump and a small amount of tissue surrounding the lump. That way Tania can keep three quarters of her breast and her entire nipple."

I start to feel a little sick to my stomach, but Dr. Cutter launches into part two, barely taking a breath between words: "But because there'll be tissue left in the breast there's a chance some cancer cells will remain in the tissue, thus the radiation to wipe them out. But even after radiation there's a significant chance of cancer reoccurrence in that breast because of the tissue remaining. With a mastectomy the entire breast is removed—we get about ninety percent of the tissue, making it extremely difficult for cancer to resurface in the breast. We then take out a cluster of lymph nodes, just to make sure that the cancer hasn't spread, because based on the stage and the invasiveness of your daughter's cancer there is a chance that it has spread. We use chemotherapy as a final blast to make sure any stray cancer cells are annihilated."

"Mom, what do you think?" I need guidance from some- one over the age of twenty-one.

"Well, this is your decision to make, Tania." She takes my hand in hers and rubs it.

I don't have time for her liberal, Euro, feminist, empower- ing-young-women crap—I'm drowning here. "Mom, if it were you, what would you do?"

"I'd get the mastectomy, because if less tissue equals less chance of reoccurrence, then the mastectomy makes sense, but then again my breasts are droopy and in their forties and yours are perky and young, so you might want to consider saving them."

OK, options: No breast equals the chance of no cancer. Three quarters of a breast and an entire nipple equals the potential for more cancer. No breast equals living. Three quarters of a breast and an entire nipple equals potentially dying. How often do I really use my breast anyway? And my nipple? Actually the nipple would be nice to save; she is an erogenous hot spot, but then again, should I reserve my right to be sexually aroused at the expense of my life?

"Dr. Cutter," I say, "I'd like to go with the mastectomy/chemotherapy, I think. Yeah. I'm pretty sure. Yes. That combination."

"That's what I would have recommended if I were permitted to recommend one over the other. Now let's schedule your surgery." He clears papers from his desk in search of a calendar.

We all look at Dr. Cutter's desktop calendar. Wow, this is real now. This is cancer. We're sitting here, setting a date like I'm going to get married or something, when really we're scheduling the death of my breast. This is not what other kids are doing during their Thanksgiving break, I'm certain of it.

"Uh, excuse me, Dr. Cutter," I ask, "how long will it take to recover?"

"Probably about a month. You'll get your drainage tubes out in about two weeks," he casually adds.

"What drainage tubes?"

"They're called Jackson Pratts, and then you'll start chemotherapy—"

"How long will I have to go through chemotherapy?"

"Your oncologist will decide that, but I'm guessing about six months."

"What's an oncologist?"

"An oncologist is—"

Too much, it's too much, I need to leave, I need to get out of this office. This hot office. This office is hot and beige and small and suffocating. I need air. I need to breathe.

"Uh, Mom, Dr. Cutter," I say, "I'm going to step outside for a second."

Gray stones with dead weeds in between them surround me. In the middle of the courtyard is a crumbling, dried-out fountain that has reached artifact status. The only difference between this courtyard and a cemetery is that here the gray stones are used to walk on rather than denote the length of time that the dead have lived.

I'm looking for a pay phone so I can call Alexander Billingford III. He'll know what to do. He'll offer me a funny anecdotal queer nugget, something. In the pocket of my faded baggy boy's dungarees I can feel my heart and breasts. I gently rub them in hopes of releasing the good luck and protection I'm going to need. Right now I feel really alone. In my twenty-one years of life I've never felt truly alone.

"Alexander?" I ask in a soft voice, brushing my short but temporarily overgrown dark brown strands of hair out of my wet blue eyes.

"Hey, Miss Katanalicious!" Alexander says as if he's in the middle of a cocktail party.

"Listen, I'm at the surgeon's and—"

"Are you crying? You never cry, Tania. Is everything OK?"

"The surgeon wants to cut off my booby and there might

be more cancer in my body and I have to have drainage tubes and go through chemotherapy and I'm freaked out, Alexander, totally scared," I tell him, trying to sniffle so hard that I'll stop my tears from coming out.

"OK, here's what we're gonna to do. We're gonna make fun of everything having to do with cancer, boobies, and chemotherapy. Got it?" Alexander says, invoking the spirit of a gay drill sergeant.

"I'm not sure. I—"

"All right, say it's your birthday. I'll send you a card that reads, 'Breast Wishes!' Or we're at a bar and we encounter someone who's a needy boundary-crosser—we'll refer to them as being 'chemo.' Like, 'No, we don't want to hang out with you because you are SO chemo!'"

"That's the breast idea I've heard all morning." I can't help but get caught up in Alexander's levity.

"Are you going to be all right?" he asks sincerely.

"As long as you're my breast friend!"

"You know it. Keep me abreast of things!"

"You got tit!"

Even though the dial tone is whining for me to hang up the phone and go back into the surgeon's office to make plans, I can't let go of the phone. Wrapping my hands around the cold black plastic handle of the receiver, I pull it close to my chest, pressing the earpiece into my heart hard enough to break it.

how to become a nuclear family with no prior history (left breast—2002)

Mom's flying into LAX today, Dad's out purchasing a bed for Mom, and I'm debating whether to have a mastectomy.

Is this what they mean by a nuclear family? The architectural blueprint for the next couple of weeks looks something like this: Dad will place Mom's bed next to his bed in the living room. My twin brother, Paul, who is coming tomorrow, will sleep with my father in my father's bed. I will maintain my "guest room status," because I have cancer. My sister, Kim, will join us next week, at which time she will sleep next to my mother, in my mother's bed, which will be next to my father's bed. And I will be in the next room refraining from masturbating and praying that we can all get along. It's like we've created a dormitory for down-and-out divorced parents and siblings dealing with their sick daughter/sister.

The last time our whole family spent more than a day in proximity was Thanksgiving last year. We arrive at my mother's house in northern Arizona every year for Thanksgiving, somehow forgetting about the year before and how much therapy we needed in between. It is amazing how easy it is to knock on your mother's door as a twenty-nine-year-old and, as soon as you enter, regress to the age when you last lived at home: seventeen. Mom is wearing black stretch pants, a dark purple sweatshirt, and a stained pink apron with white writing that says QUICHE THE COOK. She delegates the Thanksgiving duties to Kim and I, who have both arrived the day before and for the last twenty-four hours have fought over everything from who gets to check her e-mail first to who has better taste in music.

"Kim, I need you to turn off the computer and help me make the stuffing. Tania, put down your journal and start grating the Gruyère."

"Mom, I can't get off the computer right now, I just got an IM from J Dates," Kim says, flipping her long brown hair off the shoulders of her pink, fluffy, low-cut sale-sweater, made to look fancy by the addition of a dangling yellow-green jeweled necklace that stops at her cleavage.

"I don't care if you got a BMW from J Dates—help me make the stuffing!"

"FINE," Kim says, quickly typing, laying the groundwork for another dissatisfying date or even worse, a mediocre one-night stand.

I drop my journal, roll up the sleeves on my snuggly red-striped Brooks Brothers men's pajamas, grab the grater and block of cheese, and start grating. Paul drifts into the house at around noon. His crazy long strawberry-blond hair dances around his bearded freckly face like the audience at a Dead show.

A hand clutching a bunch of carrots sits in the middle of Paul's FOOD NOT BOMBS T-shirt, which peeks out from under his motor oil–stained overalls. The stains came from hours of working on his, "1966 VW Non–Pop-top Westy." Neither the VW nor Paul have worked in years. "Hey, Mom, it smells like meat in here—did you remember to make something for me, like tofurkey?"

Mom is frantically mixing, whipping, beating, stuffing, and pounding. Kim has eaten more of the stuffing than she has stuffed and is now back on the computer. I'm finished grating the cheese and have moved on to removing the tiny green veins from the insides of garlic known as the germs.

"I need some help!" Mom screams, almost crying, as her strong forearm throws her flabby underarm around the bowl containing something that will need to be baked. "Mom, relax, breathe. You don't want anger going into the oven. You don't want to bake anger, do you?" Paul says, placing his hands together as if to say, *Namaste.*

Mom stops mixing and stares at Paul. "Baked? I know what baked means. I was a hippie in the sixties. You're stoned, aren't you, Paul?"

"What do you mean by stoned?" Paul asks, as if her question is some transcendental trigger.

"I mean, put down the bong and help your mother!"

Mom throws down the bowl containing the batterlike substance, covers her face with her hands, and begins sobbing.

"Are you all right?" I ask, rushing to her rescue, rubbing her back.

"No," she says, still sobbing, "I need help and your sister is online trying to date another Jewish loser and your brother is high and I…"

The doorbell rings and my father appears bearing flowers.

"Yello! Where is everyone?" Dad looks relaxed—like all of us might look if we hadn't spent the last several hours with each other.

"Elliott, help me with the carrots," Mom says, extending a knife toward Dad.

"Nah, I didn't come here to work. I came to relax," Dad says, plopping down on the couch. As if Dad's ass hitting the cushion flipped a switch in Mom's psyche, she starts screaming, "You can relax outside! Get out!"

Dad starts to laugh. We all know the cardinal rule of arguing is that if a person is angry and yelling at another person, the other person should NEVER laugh at the angry person.

"Joëlle, relax. Do you wanna kiss? Is that why you're upset?" Dad asks, leaning back on the couch, giggling. Mom begins to yell indiscriminately. Her yelling becomes so loud that Kim is forced to get offline and make a declaration: "You guys are fucking crazy! No wonder I always end up dating freaks! Look at my role models!" She storms outside, and through the window I see her lighting up a cigarette and pulling out her cell phone to three-way-call her two best friends so they can complain about their respective families long enough to justify smoking, which they never do, ever. Paul, standing in the hallway, holds up a joint and motions quietly for me to join him in the bedroom. This offer is much too tempting under the circumstances. As I leave the room to get high, Dad leaves the house to go for a walk, and Mom is left in the kitchen surrounded by half-finished dishes and dirty utensils.

It was the coconut custard cream pie that got 'em. On that fateful day she emerged from the subway, looking like a younger, sexier, and less theatrical Barbra Streisand. At approximately 5:55 P.M. she entered the bakery where he stood behind the counter. He looked to be about six foot one, and exotic, like a Jewish Mel Ferrer. She liked tall men. She was actually living with a tall man at the time she approached the bakery counter. In a thick French accent the radiant strawberry-blond twenty-year-old asked the tall, exotic man for a piece of, "Coconut custard cream pie. It's my favorite, and I've had a very difficult day. My boyfriend is out of town and…" Whatever she said after that was background noise. He was in love with the young French woman with a penchant for pie. He cut her an extra large slice.

"We're closing in a few minutes. Do you mind if I join you?" he asked her in his direct New York way.

"*Bien sur*. OH, *je m'excuse*. Yes, of course," she told him, charmed by his foreign accent while self-conscious of her own.

He untied his stained, once-white apron and stepped down and around the counter.

"Oh! I thought you were taller?" she said, checking him out without moving her head.

"Nah, I stand on a block back there. Most people think that, though. What's your name?" he asked, now sitting across from her and the enormous slice of pie.

"Joëlle," she said while smiling and simultaneously wrapping her lips around the fork that held a sweet white dollop of pie.

"I'm Elliott," he said nonchalantly, but the fact that he was blushing canceled out any air of coolness.

She wasn't sure if it was the sweet, coarse coconut dancing around in her mouth, or the dense, effortless pudding coating her tongue, or that her possessive boyfriend was out of town, or that she was sitting with this warm and beautiful stranger, but she felt happy. Genuinely happy. To her, the man sitting across the table was six feet tall.

Joëlle invited Elliott back to her place, where they played guitar, drank red wine, and wrote and read poetry to each other. Elliott told Joëlle stories about his late-night cab-driving job and all the amazing fares he'd had—like Warhol and Jagger. Even though it was 1970 in New York, they didn't sleep together. They did, however, kiss softly on the lips several times and give each other massages. Their night turned into morning, which turned into Joëlle breaking up with her boyfriend and making room in her apartment for the handsome thirty-year-old cabbie-by-night, purveyor-of-pastries-by-day Elliott.

By 1971 the poetry, massages, and red wine stopped flowing. Shortly after Joëlle and Elliott moved in together they got pregnant, and shortly after they got pregnant they got married, and shortly after they said "I do," Joëlle had a miscarriage, and shortly after the miscarriage, she started stuffing her feelings with food, and shortly after the stuffing began, Elliott started keeping his feelings inside until he exploded, and shortly after the explosions they decided they didn't have much in common, and shortly after that my twin brother and I were born. With one parent stuffing and one exploding, our family was a lit cannon. Daily arguments inspired by everything from children crying to lack of money to my mother looking at my father the wrong way went something like this:

Dad: Fuck you!
Mom: Fuck you!
Dad: I'm going for a fucking walk!
Mom: Oh, that's a fucking surprise! You always leave when you can't handle something.
Dad: Fuck you!
Mom: Fuck you!

In 1972, in between Dad's emotional explosions and Mom's profound outbursts, my parents somehow managed to stop saying "Fuck you" and actually fucked each other. And in 1973 the cutest of the Katan kids, Kim, was born.

She looked like a gushy Jewish Gerber baby. Now, in the midst of my parents' intense dislike for each other and their propensity toward disagreeing, the one thing they agreed on was that they truly adored us kids. Mom was always snuggling, cuddling, and kissing us until our faces hurt from smiling; Dad would take us to the Museum of Natural History, Chinatown, and Coney Island. We loved our parents, just not together. Their fighting escalated.

Mom: Maybe if you got a fucking job!
Dad: Maybe if you went to a fucking shrink!
Mom: Maybe if you dropped dead!
Dad: Maybe I'm already dead!

1973–1976: The Wondering Why Years. At the end of each year, what some people refer to as an "anniversary," my mom gathered up us kids, told my father she was leaving him, and stepped out into the coldest day ever recorded in the history of New York. My father would go after her with a coconut custard cream pie, luring her back for another year. Happy anniversary!
In December 1977, after my parents' "anniversary," my mother and father got into a much bigger fight than usual. Mom ripped the shirt off Dad's back, literally. Dad said Mom was, "Fucking insane!" There was screaming and crying and then the sounds of making love. In the morning he opened his eyes to find her gone. Her body was still there, but her eyes were cold and far away. She stared at a point beyond him, beyond the walls, beyond the buildings, and her mouth was trembling like she was going to say something, but nothing came out. She got up, still in this trance, wrapped all three of us kids in blankets, and left my father.

Just in case you ever end up in Arizona, there are no Indians wearing feathered headdresses riding around on horses, shooting arrows at pedestrians on Scottsdale Road. At six years old I was disappointed to discover this fact. Also, there is no stagecoach that takes you from Brooklyn, New York, to Phoenix, Arizona, as my kindergarten friends from PS 197 had suggested: You have to fly on a plane. A total bummer. We ended up in Arizona because my mother wanted to be as geographically far away from my father as possible while maintaining proximity to her wacky French family, who had settled in Scottsdale a few years prior. Right as we set foot on Arizona soil my mother proclaimed, "I don't ever want to see your father again!" and meant it.

Eventually Dad relocated to Phoenix to be closer to us kids. As he'd been out of the parenting loop for a little while, his approach to caring for children was slightly unconventional. At his squalid studio apartment on Thomas and 40th Street he created an indoor playground with his decor; nothing was off-limits. At age eight, my brother and I relished the moments when my father handed us a BB gun and said, "Go ahead, shoot," pointing at the enormous pyramid of beer cans stacked on top of his dirty refrigerator. And then, after several failed attempts by my brother and me to hit the cans, Dad would grab the gun from our little hands and shoot the crap out of the aluminum mountain, forcing the silver and gold cans to explode into the air. Why would any child need to go to the park with this kind of action in the kitchen? My sister, being six years old and less of a tomboy than me, wasn't interested in our target range. Instead she'd delight in the theatrics that the Incredible Jewish Hulk provided. Dad would put on a thin green robe and sit on a stack of moving boxes, which had become his temporary—and later on permanent—couch, acting like a mild-mannered scientist type. He'd chew on the end of his Bic pen as if in deep thought, perhaps coming up with a serum or cure or new flavor of beer. That was our cue to get him upset, really provoke him. My sister, drawing from her six-year-old knowledge base, would start: "Dad, I scribbled on the bathroom walls with a marker." Dad would roar, "What? You what?" We would all giggle in unison.

"Yeah, and I told Mom you still love her," Paul would chime in.

"LOVE HER? I don't know from love!" Dad would yell, standing up now, clawing at his robe like it was holding him back from becoming who he truly was. His hazel eyes looked red and scary, and his skinny legs looked larger, more muscular, as they planted themselves firmly on the brown shag carpet.

"Why don't you pay Mom child support?" I asked, really wanting to know the answer. And that was it; that was all Dad needed in order to begin the transformation.

"CHILD SUPPORT? I CAN BARELY AFFORD TO BUY BEER!!!!" His deep voice was fierce as he feigned rage, ripping off his green robe like it was paper.

"I am the Incredible Jewish Hulk! THIS is what happens to you when you've had too much Hebrew school! SHALOM!" The three of us would laugh louder, so hard that hiccups and red faces always followed Dad's pretend rage.

Once Dad had put on some clothes he would begin the process of preparing lunch. He'd rub a brown, stained cookie sheet with vegetable oil and ask one of us to retrieve the bag of frozen wedge-cut fries from the freezer. He'd rip open the white plastic bag, which offered a photograph of piping-hot fries, with his teeth, still in Hulk mode, and empty the contents evenly over the cookie sheet. Fifteen minutes later we had our main course, which Dad doused with salt and butter. Immediately realizing vegetable oil was not enough vegetables for children, he grabbed another frozen sack from the freezer, which displayed little yellow nuggets on the package. The four of us sat on boxes eating salted fries and frozen corn and begging Dad to, "Ple-e-e-ase do the Incredible Jewish Hulk again!"

Even though we only saw my father on the weekends, we had so much fun with him! We had so much fun with him, we thought it might be a good idea for our parents to get back together; either that or we'd watched *The Parent Trap* one too many times. I think I planted the seed when I was about ten years old, "Mom, how come you and Dad don't get back together?"

"No way! First of all, NO, and second of all, even if there was one redeeming quality about your father, which there isn't, the fact remains that your father is frigid—he's completely nonsexual."

"But you and Dad had to have sex to have children, right?" I retorted.

"Right, twice: once for you and Paul, and once for Kim, and the only reason we did it was because the heater was broken and your father was cold."

"Really?"

"Why do you think you were born in September and Kim was born in October?"

73

This wouldn't make sense until I was in my teens and had mastered the idea of conception as well as the order of the seasons. The only reason Mom ever spoke to Dad was to ask for child support, and Dad only spoke to Mom to tell her he couldn't pay child support, and then Dad moved to Long Beach, California, which allowed Mom some room to breathe.

1992: The Year of the Mutual Parental Spontaneous Epiphany. Maybe it was the distance between them or that they were moving forward in their respective lives, or that their daughter was dealing with cancer. I can't pinpoint the exact time of day or place or event that set the mutual epiphany in motion, but at some point my mother and my father talked. They talked about their collective history, and the beautiful children they created together, and the fact that they would always care for each other. It seemed like the twenty-year-old French woman with a penchant for pie and the thirty-year-old exotic cabbie with a penchant for French women had grown up.

They developed a relationship over the phone. Dad would call Mom out of the blue to say, "Oh, Joëlle, I saw a special on channel eight about *Juniors!* You would have loved it." Mom would call Dad to say, "Elliott, you're not going to believe this, but I saw your cousin Saul at Basha's!" Their dialogue progressed from one-liners to paragraphs to entire conversations. They enjoyed talking to each other so much that they decided it would be fun to spend some time together in real life. They were both single, after all, and…who knew?

Who knew my father could be so easily frustrated by Mother's indecisiveness? Who knew my mother could cry so easily when my father freely dismissed her ideas and dreams? Who knew my father and mother had about a twenty-four-hour threshold for being in the same room with each other? Who knew they did better on the phone because gestures such as eyes rolling, veins popping, and arms folding could not be seen?

It's 1:30 P.M. Time to pick up Mom, and I'm thinking that maybe having my entire family together, under my father's 875-square-foot roof is not the best way to fight cancer.

going-out-of-booby sale!
(right breast—1992)

"Hello, you've reached the House of Cancer. Dawn's father was just diagnosed with an inoperable brain tumor and I've got a dash of the breast cancer. Please don't feel sorry for us, but feel free to leave your name, number, and personal tragedy after the beep. Have a great day! *Be-e-e-p.*"
"Aaah, Tania? It's Steph. Is everything OK? That's kind of a fucked-up message. I'm worried about you. Listen, I'm calling to see if you guys are going to the blowout lesbo extravaganza tonight. Hope so. And if you need to talk or something, I'm here for you, buddy. OK, bye."
The outgoing message was so much funnier when Alexander and I came up with it a few days ago. I guess it is a little fucked up, huh? But then again my life is a little fucked up right now. After I decided to get my breast removed, Dawn's dad was diagnosed with brain cancer, so Dawn's been flying back and forth to the East Coast. Our relationship was pretty crappy before everyone got cancer, so now it totally sucks. I've been really busy with school

and hanging out with Alexander and shopping and filling out forms and reading presurgery instructions and worrying about my mom and dad having to be in the hospital together and sneaking away to that little South American store to buy hordes of milagros and stick them in the pockets of my jeans and jackets. Other than that, everything's fine.

Stephanie's call couldn't have come at a better time. A party is exactly what Dawn and I need at this juncture in our lives together. We love parties. Partying is what Dawn and I have in common. We drink, we look good together—well, she looks good and I'm with her, so—and we share a love for drama. Let's party!

Annie Lennox assures us that "Sex can't buy it...baby," but looking around at all the hot lesbians on the prowl, I can assure Annie that sex can at least put a down payment on it. These women can't be Arizona lesbians; they're too cool. It's as if a busload of L.A.-bound lesbos broke down and walked to the nearest prefab home they could find.

"Hey, girls!" Michelle greets us by anchoring a joint behind each of our ears. I have a secret crush on Michelle; everyone has a secret crush on Michelle. She's dangerous enough to be interesting but not edgy, smokes enough to be cool but not addicted, and sleeps around enough to be friendly but not a whore. And she was the first woman I ever kissed and subsequently slept with. And when someone has the power to make your panties wet with a kiss, no matter how many times they dump you, you still desire them. Her pale white skin and pulsing red lips always seem to be asking the question, "When?" When she walks, her thin body sort of leans back like she's ready to lie down and take a nap, or pass out. And that accent! No one can place it, which makes it so intriguing. I think I asked her where she hailed from once and she said, "Here…and there…and other places too." Dawn gives Michelle the cool head-nod of acknowledgment. I practically jump up and hug her. "Hey, Michelle. This looks like a great party! Thanks for inviting us."

"Are you kidding? We're glad to have you," she says. And when she says "Have you," she looks me up and down as if to say, *I have and I will again.* Dawn grabs my hand and leads me through the crowd. "Whoa, slow down," I tell her. "We just got here."

"Michelle was checking you out. Come on," Dawn says, almost yanking me out of my oversize black mailman shoes. Dawn's jealousy makes me feel like I'm the most popular girl in school.

At the "bar," which is really a yellow tiled kitchen counter with an array of alcohol bottles and sticky surfaces, Dawn mixes our favorite: kamikazes. Tonight I'm trashing the American Cancer Society's dietary guidelines: Instead of eating plenty of fruits and vegetables I'm going to drink as much alcohol as I can stomach, smoke as much dope as I can inhale, and get as many women—and gay men—to touch my breast as possible. This is it, my going-out-of-booby sale! Come Monday this little gem will be gone, so I want her last voyage to be spectacular. I want her to experience laughter, affection, and drunkenness. I want her to chat with total strangers, to have unprotected sex, to climb every mountain; my little booby is going out with a bang! Now, how am I going to inform my jealous girlfriend of my booby tour de force?

Luck is on my side tonight. Dawn has weaseled over to the new nineteen-year-old girl du jour. She's doing the cool silent thing that she did with me where she stares intently into your eyes, sticks her awkward hands uncomfortably deep into her pockets, and says...nothing. "Hey, Dawn, who's your friend?" I ask while stirring my kamikaze with a butter knife—I couldn't find a stirrer.

"Uh, what's your name again?" Dawn asks the doting girl in a strong whisper.

"Megan." The girl giggles while keeping her gaze on Dawn.

"Really nice to meet you," I say. "Dawn, umm, I just wanted to let you know that if you happen to see women groping my breast, it's because I've asked them to. Since she's leaving and all. OK?"

"Ah, yeah, sure. Fine." Dawn's too distracted with Megan's girlish charm—what other kind of charm can a nineteen-year-old have—to really hear what I'm saying.

Stephanie is the first customer in the going-out-of-booby sale. She doesn't haggle.

"Wow, Tania, you've got a nice breast. Had I known, we could have been more than friends," Stephanie says, her eyebrows bouncing up and down à la Groucho Marx.

Once upon a time I had a crush on Stephanie; she quickly moved into the friend category because she didn't have a crush on me. And once that inequality is created, and territories are drawn—the Crusher and the Crushed—everyone feels fine and can move along with their respective lives but still flirt shamelessly with each other.

"Steph, thanks for the touch, but I've got other customers

waiting," I say, removing Stephanie's warm hand from my eager little booby.

I move in and out of crowded rooms, my right breast leading the way. I offer kind and cute strangers an opportunity to "Touch my booby," and people oblige with a gentle pat, or a purposeful pinch, or total disbelief that someone is offering up a breast for the taking—no strings, free of charge, an invitation to the sacred mound. After customer number sixteen or twenty-six, it hits me: I'm going into surgery in three days. This thought is a medicine ball hurled at my chest, forcing me to fall down. I land on a blood-red velvety sofa next to a double-headed blur of chicks kissing and wonder about my fate. Did Hamlet feel this way? Before I have time to launch into my mental soliloquy, an older woman approaches me.

"Hi, I'm Fran," she says, sinking into the soft velvet. She looks like a professor or maybe the owner of some kind of business; she looks professional.

"Hi, Fran. I'm Tania."

Fran looks over at the two entwined bodies to the left of us. "Pals of yours?" she says, flashing a cute smile.

And instantly we are friends. Our conversation easily weaves through things we have in common: We both play tennis, and we're both Jewish, and we both have a sense of humor. We can't stop talking—not until Dawn enters the picture, places her distrustful arms around my neck in a sort of affectionate choke hold, and asserts her rank within our relationship.

"What's going on, honey? Who's your new friend?" Dawn asks, now rubbing my shoulders and kissing my neck.

"This is Fran. Fran, this is Dawn," I say, expecting them to shake hands and become fast friends. Fran extends her hand to Dawn, whose focus has shifted from wanting to meet my new friend to kissing me on the cheek, working her way up to my lips, and briskly moving toward my mouth. "Dawn...DAWN, um, there's someone else here: Fran. I'm trying to have a conversation with Fran."

"Come outside with me, Tania. Come on, it's cold out there, and I need you to keep me warm," Dawn whines, tugging on the sleeve of my tight black ribbed V-neck shirt.

"No, Dawn. Maybe later, OK?"

"No. Now. Come on, she'll be all right by herself," Dawn says, now standing and literally yanking me up into the air.

"Fran," Fran says, asserting the fact that she has an identity beyond "she."

"Right," Dawn says, "Fran will be fine without you." When pulling me up doesn't work, Dawn continues to hug on me like I'm a teddy bear she threw out weeks ago but suddenly desires again, seeing the value in her furry discard now that the neighbor girl has expressed an interest.

"You go outside," I tell her. "I'll be out in a minute. Love you."

Dawn plants a huge, messy, assertion of ownership on my mouth and leaves.

"How long have you and Dawn been together?" Fran asks.

"About two years. You know, on and off," I answer awkwardly, looking at the four-inch cuffs at the bottom of my loose-fitting cream-colored pants, hoping that if I stare at them long enough I can erase Dawn, or the fact that I would choose to be with someone like Dawn.

"You don't look old enough to have been with anyone two years. How old are you?" Fran asks, assessing her chances of our dating.

"How old are *you*, Fran?" I say, not wanting my age to dictate the nature of whatever relationship we might have.

"Thirty-two. And you?"

"Less than that. Twenty-one…chronologically, but emotionally forty-five." I smile. I think I'm flirting with Fran. The freckles on Fran's face are calm and mostly blend into her peach skin. And when she laughs, she chuckles, and her chuckles send these pleasant tremors throughout her body, which result in her neck tilting back, mouth flying open, arms gesticulating. She can't hide her happiness. This is not a bad trait. She doesn't seem to fit into a butch or femme category; she has more of an androgynous look, a combination of the best traits of both camps. Actually, she reminds me of a Muppet, not Gonzo or Animal—I'm not sure who yet, but one of the Muppets. Her chin-length reddish hair looks like it's been blown dry and redirected so it won't go astray; it looks soft, and when the light kisses her head it exposes deep burgundy and shiny orange strands of hair.

"So, do you want to play tennis sometime?" Fran optimistically asks, leaning toward me, but her stiff black blazer holds her back from getting too close.

"Sure," I tell her.

"How about next week?" she asks, this time more pointedly, unbuttoning her blazer to reveal a black-and-white argyle sweater vest resting on a white cotton T-shirt.

"I'd love to, but I'll be having my breast removed next week."

Is there really a subtle way to convey a mastectomy to a new friend?

"Gulp," she says. "Are you serious?"

"Yeah." I sense her pulling away, as if I'd told her I was really seventeen. "But I'm expecting a speedy recovery, so maybe next month?"

"OK," she says, not wanting to pry, playing it cool, not twenty-something cool but adult-cool, like the *cool* in cool, calm, and collected. I want her to pry.

"I was just diagnosed with breast cancer. That's why I'm having a mastectomy. But I can kick your ass in tennis next month if you're up for it."

"Oh sure, pull the cancer card so I'll take it easy on you when we play." Fran smiles. Her right hand looks as if it wants to touch my right hand, but it doesn't.

She reaches into the back pocket of her pleated blue jeans to retrieve a receipt. A hidden pocket inside her blazer holds a fancy pen, like the ones given to bat mitzvahs. She twists the gold base of the pen and asks for my phone number. Dawn must have heard the pen squeak open, because now she's hovering over Fran and me.

"Hey, cutie!" she says in someone else's enthusiastic voice. She says nothing to Fran but immediately drapes her entire body around mine, kissing my face, nuzzling her head under my arm, trying to prevent me from writing down my phone number.

"Tania, come outside with me. Ple-e-e-ase," Dawn says.

"OK, after I give Fran my number."

"*Our* number," Dawn asserts.

"After I give Fran *our* number. We're going to play tennis when I get better. Isn't that great?"

"Yeah. I'll meet you outside. I love you so much," she says and makes that cute face where she smiles and looks up into the sky like she's a puppy watching food pour down into her bowl. Then she leaves.

"Does your girlfriend always pee on you?" Fran asks.

"Huh?"

"You know, mark her territory."

"That's funny. I've never really thought about it. Yeah, I guess she is a pee-er. Well, I'd better go outside, make sure she hasn't urinated on anyone else."

"Would it be OK if I came to visit you in the hospital?"

"I would really like that, Fran."

"All right. But as soon as you get out I'm gonna kick your young ass at tennis."

"Yeah, yeah, I'll see you on the seniors tour."

"In all seriousness," Fran says, "if there's anything you need, please give me a call, OK?"

"OK."

Outside, surrounded by drunk figures and future ex-girl-friends, I light up the joint that's been tucked behind my ear and inhale deeply, shoulders rising then relaxing. It's not that cold out here. I take another hit and stand on the periphery, hoping that Dawn doesn't see me, that no one will notice me, waiting for the smoke to work its magic. I'm waiting for the magic. I'm waiting. I don't feel anything. Shouldn't I be stoned by now? Maybe it's the kind that creeps up on you: *creep weed?* Is that Dawn making out with the young girl from earlier or am I just stoned? Wow, my right breast feels freaky; it's pulsing and shaking and a light is emanating from my nipple! I hope no one can see this! My booby has become the burning bush, and I am Moses. What are you trying to tell me? Booby? What is it? She speaks in a low, rhythmic vibration that only I, and maybe the neighborhood dogs, can hear: *Tania, it is my time to go. Release me, your booby, and everything will be all right. Oh, and free the slaves from bondage. Peace.* A wave of warmth rushes through my body like an exclamation point. God has come to me, come through me, to assure me that everything will be all right. God, I wish I were stoned. I think I'll take another hit.

morphine...the other white meat (right breast—1992)

Arizona is a resort town; it's all about easy living here. If you're wealthy and from someplace other than Arizona, you might find yourself here someday eating cactus candy and driving a golf cart as a main source of transportation. Another distinguishing feature of a resort town is the fact that all businesses, regardless of what service they provide, sound like relaxing resort destinations. Take, for example, the Coffee Plantation—the name alone evokes images of affluent white folks lounging around a porch while slaves braid their hair and serve them lattes. Or how about Zorba's Adult Shop—why go to Greece when you can fly to Arizona for an afternoon of grape leaves and orgies? There's even a commercial that Arizona has thrown together showing a neon-pink sunset—inspired, no doubt, by the Palo Verde nuclear plant—with a voice-over of a man singing "AR-i-zo-NA!" over and over and over again; why would he need to say anything else? That's why it's no surprise to me that Scottsdale Memorial is my surgical destination. It sounds like a resort, doesn't it? Not Scottsdale General, too vague, but Scottsdale Memorial, a place established in memory of a person or an event, a sanctuary. Now that's resort living.

I hope they give me a robe, like the ones advertised in catalogs addressed to "Current Resident." Bulky combed cotton with shawl collar and monogram. Yeah, T K L. And maybe after surgery Scottsdale Memorial will provide me with my own golf cart, you know, to cruise around the memorial in, check out the sights. And maybe my nurse will really be a cocktail waitress with the authority to dump strawberry daiquiris into my IV bag, and maybe, and maybe, and maybe, and maybe being in a hospital with Mom and Dawn combing through piles of papers that ask whether or not I want to donate my organs, prolong my life, allow surgeons to remove further tissue and extra parts if the cancer has spread, has really put a damper on my powers of imagination. Really.

I'm lying on this skinny, cold table, rolling toward surgery. I'm totally awake. And there's all of this commotion, these frantic figures moving quickly, talking loudly, and hovering over me. Oh, no, this is just like the "dream" sequence in *Rosemary's Baby* where all of Rosemary's freaky devil-worshiping neighbors are dancing around her in preparation for Satan to come down and get his devil on; I don't want Satan to hump me.

An enormous man peers down at me. Does he have green wolf eyes? Is he hairy? "Are you ready, Ms. Katan?" he asks. For what? A baby? Then it occurs to me: "Surgery?" I ask, slowly losing my ability to think clearly.

"Yes, for surgery." The calm voice almost laughs.

"But I'm still awake." He must be a new surgeon and
hasn't learned that patients need to be asleep before you
cut into them.

"Not for long. Why don't we count backwards from ten to
one," he suggests.

"One… Don't start, I'm still awake. Two…I mean it.
Three…wait, wasn't I suppose to count backwards? Ten—"

I'm surrounded by light, a stark white light. Where am I?
Am I dead? A tall man with snowy hair in a navy-blue suit
is standing on a stage. God? He turns off the light. There's
a moment of silence and then, out of nowhere, at full volume, "Beat It" by Michael Jackson is playing on some
ethereal stereo system. Now red and blue strobe lights are
on the scene, spinning around like Linda Blair's head in
The Exorcist. The faint smell of cinnamon fills the air. This
isn't heaven; this is the Tonto Elementary School cafeteria.
I'm in sixth grade again, about to embark on a magazine
drive where I'll be forced to sell thousands of periodicals to
uninterested aunts and difficult doctors in hopes of at least
winning a five-pound box of Hot Tamales, or, if I sell the
most magazines, winning the amazing red-and-blue strobe
light that flashes in time to songs by Def Leppard and
Billy Idol. This is horrible. Black out.

Lights fade in and out. I feel like I'm on the inside of a
strobe light, spinning, queasy, drowning. Two figures float
above me. "Satan?" I ask, still not sure where I am.

"It's Dawn," one of the figures says, but I'm suspicious.

"And who are you?" I ask of the other shadowy figure.

"Tania, it's Mom. You've just finished surgery. You're in
your room now," she says.

I see a hazy figure in back of Mom; it seems to be a man with green eyes. "Who's that?" I ask.

"It's Dad," Mom says.

"Hi, Tania." Dad tentatively approaches the left side of my bed as the right side is weighted with wires and tubes and blinking machines. He takes my left hand, which is IV-free, and squeezes it as if to say, *It's gonna be OK, kid.*

"Are you and Mom here together?" I ask innocently.

"Yeah," he says, smirking. "But not *together.*"

My parents in the same room not fighting: I must be dead. He releases my hand almost as quickly as he takes it. I feel a surge of pain. A pain that feels like someone has taken a knife, stabbed it into my chest, then dragged it in a half circle all the way up into my armpit. There's this raw throbbing, like your worst menstrual cramps times eighteen, like exposed meat being pecked at by crows or torn apart by hungry lions. My body feels like the prey on *Wild Kingdom,* the gazelle that couldn't run fast enough, the albino bunny who stopped to crinkle her nose a little too long. I just hurt really badly.

A nurse hands me what appears to be the joystick for a video game. Somehow I don't feel like playing Super Mario Bros., but she assures me that it's not a video game, that it's morphine and whenever I feel pain I'm to push the button on top of the joystick to release a stream of morphine into my body. I feel pain. I push. The morphine sounds like a librarian telling someone to be quiet, *Shhhh,* and along with the *Shhhh* comes a rush of warmth that fills my body and temporarily takes the pain away. And for five whole minutes I feel amazing, no pain whatsoever. But shortly after those five decadent minutes there's this feeling

of nausea so intense and urgent that I puke. It's a toss-up:
Do I endure the sensation of a knife cutting into my flesh
or do I brave the worst gastric turbulence I've ever experience? Pain or puke? That is the question. Before I have
time to answer I feel simultaneous nausea and excruciating
pain. I push the joystick button, puke, and pass out.

I awake to a disembodied voice stating "Visiting hours"
while a young woman in all white stuffs ice chips down
my sore throat. My throat feels like Melissa Etheridge's
voice sounds, scratched and shaky.

Rene, a French friend of my mom's, glides into the room,
"*Bonjour*, Joëlle!" She kisses Mom on both cheeks, and
without looking at me asks, "How's Tania doing?"

I try to assert my presence but find I have a very small
voice right now. "I'm OK," I say, but neither of them hear
me and now they're engaged in conversation in French,
which I can barely understand when I'm sans morphine, so
now that I'm bathing in it I really can't string together the
la's and *je*'s of an exclusive conversation.

Finally Rene speaks to me. "Hi, Tania. I just had a mastectomy last month. Your mom wanted me to show you my
scar. Would you like to see it?"

What's the etiquette around this situation? "Sure," I say.
Rene unbuttons her blouse like she's about to embark on a
one-night stand. "So? What do you think? It's not so bad,
right?"

Oh, my God! The left half of her chest looks like a pastry
chef has piped red frosting from under her armpit to just
below her throat. Like a giant red winking eye. This is the
grossest image I have ever seen in my twenty-one years on
this earth, grosser than ugly people French-kissing, dirty

fingernails, and stepping in dog shit.

"You're right," I tell her. "It's not so bad."

People begin to pour into the room, and Mom becomes the host of this unofficial party. She bosses Dawn around while muttering in French under her breath about how inept Dawn is. Dawn begrudgingly takes orders like, "Dawn, why don't you get a couple of chairs so people have places to sit?" Waves of people entering this tiny sterile room coincide with my waves of nausea.

"Hey, Tania. How're you doing?" asks Alexander, and before I have a chance to answer he practically runs to the other side of the room.

My sister Kim arrives with two friends; they're all carrying fast-food bags and digging for the extra fries that surely reside on the bottom of the bag. "Hey, I brought Joan and Samantha with me," she says. The two girls, focused on finishing the last bites of their burgers, nod in my direction. "Remember them from my eighteenth birthday party? Umm… So…where's Mom? Oh, there she is." Kim and the burger girls join Mom and Alexander in the corner of the room. Paul comes with Jim. Jim is my brother's friend and is known throughout the Southwest for smoking copious amounts of dope and lip-synching to the Stones while wearing only a rainbow afro wig and droopy stained underwear. Both Jim and Paul look stoned. "Fuck, this really sucks, Tania. Is Mom here?" Paul asks.

Jim spots the burger girls. "Dude, your sister and her friends have food." They join the party forming in the corner. Dawn makes her way back to the room, manages to avoid me completely, and reports to my mom for more assignments. Dad had to catch a flight back to Long

Beach, so he's not in attendance for this spontaneous party. Soon the room is loud with talking and laughing; *my* visitors are visiting with each other, but what about me? I want to scream, *Shut the fuck up!* I want to remind them why they're here, in the hospital. I want them to tell me that it's gonna be OK, that I look really good for someone who's just lost a breast. I want visiting hours to be over. About twenty minutes into the party, a random nurse sticks her head in the room to inform us that we need to be quiet, that this is a hospital and there are sick people here who need their rest. This request is the light that shines on a gang of cockroaches, making them scamper into cracks and down drains. In a matter of seconds everyone leaves. The room is empty. Except for me.

There is a light tapping on the door as it is deliberately pushed open.

"Tania?" Fran's bright face peeks into the room. Talk about follow-through. I can't tell you how many times I've exchanged phone numbers with people at parties, said, "I'll call you," and then promptly did not call. Fran endured Dawn urinating on me, said she would come visit me in the hospital, and here she is. That's commitment.

"Hey, Fran. Come on in. It's really nice to see you."

As she comes closer to my bed I realize which Muppet she looks like: Fozzie Bear. With her burnt-orange coloring and now-curly hair all she needs is a funny homemade bow tie and a light-brown fedora and she's a dead ringer for Fozzie. I don't think I'll share my discovery with her, not yet anyway.

"I can't stay very long," she says. "I have to get back to work, but I wanted to give you this." She hands me an envelope. "And to remind you that I'm still going to kick your ass on the tennis court when you get better, so hurry up and get better, OK?" I want Fran to climb on the bed and spoon me, but how would I explain that to the nurse, to Mom, to Dawn, to Fran?

"OK," I say.

"On a more serious note, if you need to talk, I'm a good listener. You could say I'm a professional listener."

"Oh God, you're a psychologist?"

"Yep."

"Are you here trying to drum up business?" She seemed like such a nice woman.

"No, I don't practice anymore. I'm here because…because I like you. I liked talking with you at the party; it was easy and you're funny, not as funny as I am, but you're younger, you have time to catch up." Fran shoots me a mock-patronizing look while patting my head.

She is so adorable. Maybe if I send her telepathic messages to cuddle with me, she will.

"So give me a call when you're up to it, OK, Tania?"

OK, Fozzie. "OK, Fran."

She gives the bunched white blanket at the bottom of the bed a firm squeeze and leaves. I rip open the envelope like I'm Charlie in *Charlie and the Chocolate Factory* looking for the golden ticket. A photograph of two Nordic lesbians, barely clothed, drenched in water and seemingly engaged in a sex act, is on the front of the card. Inside, Fran has written a novella:

Inga and Binga were hiking that morning when out of nowhere it started to rain. Inga, being the smarter of the two, suggested they seek refuge in a nearby cave. Once sheltered, Inga had another idea, "So, Binga, I know we are best friends and best friends do everything together, so I think we should..." Inga whispered something into Binga's ear. "So? What do you think, Binga?" Binga, stunned, cautiously responded, "Well, Inga, I'm not sure what you mean by 'Carpet Munching,' but I would like to fuck you, ya?" And it was at that very moment that I, Fran Troy, was hiking past Inga and Binga's cave with a camera and captured the photo you see on the front of this card. I told Inga and Binga about you, Tania. They said that as soon as you feel better they would be glad to take you on a hike, or hike up your shirt, I'm not sure which—Swedish is a difficult language to understand. In any case, the girls and I wish you a speedy recovery!

I prefer the pain caused by smiling too hard to the pain caused by a mastectomy.

Connie, the traveling social worker, enters my room and in all of her Midwestern goodness offers me a helping hand. "Hi, Tan-ya. I'm Connie, a social worker who helps women in your situation. Now, I hear you just had a mastectomy, which can be a very difficult thing to cope with. That's why I'm here, OK? Great. I'd like to take a few minutes to talk with you about three different areas that will help you with your recovery. Those areas are: prosthetics and you; support groups, like Bosom Buddies and Y-Me; and finally, how to deal with the physical effects of a mastectomy and chemotherapy with the help of organizations like Headwear for Hard Times and Cosmetics for Cancer."

Connie can't be for real, can she? This Connie smells a little bit like Alexander Billingford III, like maybe he hired her to mess with my mind. She looks like a drag queen. Wait, I think I see an Adam's apple. Connie retrieves a taupe stocking filled with cotton from her bag. "Now, this is only a temporary breast; eventually you'll get one with more weight to it. If you'd like, you can remove the stuffing and fill it with rice; a friend of mine taught me that trick."

Yeah, a friend of mine taught me that trick too—he was a drag queen getting ready to perform at the Tranny Shack. "Now, Connie," I say. "What would you suggest I use for the nipple, a pinto bean?" It seems logical.

"I, I hadn't really thought about that, but that sounds like a fine idea, Tan-ya."

Sure it does, Connie, or shall I say Conrad? I can definitely make out an Adam's apple. Connie is a fraud. Now it's time to mess with Alexander.

"Now, I would like to talk with you about support groups. There's a wonderful group called Bosom Buddies—" Connie begins.

"Do you know Alexander Billingford III?" I cut her off.

"No, I'm sorry, I—"

"Come on, Con. Can I call you Con? Your secret is safe with me. I won't rat you out to Alexander."

"I'm sure I don't know what you're talking about."

She's good, but not that good. "Do you expect me to believe there's actually a support group for breast cancer survivors called *Bosom Buddies*?"

"Well there is—"

"And *Y-Me*, that's absurd." This is so much fun. I'm not even in pain anymore.

"Listen, Tan-ya, I—"

"How much did Alexander pay you to come here?"

"I'm not paid for this service. I volunteer because I want to help women dealing with breast cancer."

"Wait a minute, didn't I see you in *Paris Is Burning*? You were in the House of LaBeija?"

"If this isn't a good time to talk, Tan-ya, I can come back tomorrow."

"This is a fine time, Con."

"You know what, I have an idea, I'm going to leave you with the stocking and I'll come back tomorrow," Connie says, cautiously placing the cotton-filled ball by my bedside.

"I have an idea too: Why don't you tell Alexander that he can suck my big fat cock, OK, Con?" Good one, now she *has* to fess up.

"OH," Connie gasps and leaves. Drag queens: drama, drama, drama.

Mom and Dawn are back on the scene looking like they've spent one too many minutes with each other.

"Did the social worker stop by yet?" Mom asks.

"When you say 'social worker,' what do you mean?" *Shit!*

"Tania, don't play games. The nurse told us there would be a social worker stopping by to talk about prosthetics and support groups—"

Oops. "Yeah, *she* stopped by."

"And?"

"And we had a very nice talk." I hold up the taupe mound for Mom and Dawn to see. "She gave me a new breast."

"Where's the nipple?" Dawn asks. She knows what she likes.

"In the bulk-food section at the grocers," I say.

"I need to go for a walk, get some air," Dawn says, pacing back and forth.

"Great," Mom says a little too cheerfully.

As soon as Dawn leaves, Mom looks concerned, sits next to me, and strokes my hair. "I just saw the surgeon and he said he'd have the results of the biopsy on your lymph nodes any minute."

The lymphatic system, as I have visualized it, is like the inside of a pumpkin: a damp, stringy highway of contorted roads running the length of your body, leading ultimately to the seeds, or the lymph nodes. Because the seeds or nodes are attached to this continuous web, if the node has cancer in it, then the stringy highway has cancer in it, and if the stringy highway has cancer in it, then the entire body could have cancer in it. Clear lymph nodes are the difference between a succulent pumpkin and a rotting pumpkin. I'm hoping my pumpkin will survive another October without being carved into.

Mom's chin rests on my forehead, and even though I can't see her face I can feel her lower lip tremble, then moisture. The doctor doesn't hesitate when announcing, "You're all clear, Tania. Our of nine nodes, all of them are negative. Congratulations."

Mom's chin rests on my forehead, and even though I can't see her face, I feel her lower lip tremble, then moisture. And soon I am covered in my mother's tears.

young lesbians with breast cancer trying to have sex in their mothers' homes…on the next *phil donahue show* (right breast—1992)

Two clear turkey baster–esque bulbs dangle from the out-side of my carefully wrapped bandage: Jackson Pratts. How would you like your name associated with postmastectomy drainage? Granted, Jackson Pratts are more than just two see-through plastic bulbs; they're also several feet of tubing coiled inside of my body, suctioning up all the blood and guts a mastectomy leaves behind. Like a Neiman Marcus window display gone awry, the sludge is transported to the external bulbs for everyone to see. Personally, I can think of a lot of items I might want my name associated with: for example, a double-sided dildo. "Honey, strap on the Tania Katan. I want to make sweet love to you." Or really cool urban sneakers that could be worn for bumming around a cultural center or having dinner at a trendy restaurant. "I think I'll wear the Katans with my black leather pants and chic sleeveless T-shirt." And even if I were going to foray into the medical community to gain notoriety and recognition, I'd put my name on a drug, something fun the club kids would catch wind of and cook up in obscenely large batches. "Dude, did you score any Tania Katan from your mom's hospital room?" During my forty-eight-hour stay in the hospital, every two hours a nurse would drop in to take my blood pressure, give me a shot in the ass—I'm not sure what for—and empty out my Jackson Pratts.

The contents of the Jackson Pratts were then evaluated; much like an episode of *Star Search*—well, in my case, *Scar Search*—the light yellow to dark red fluid and chunks are judged on originality, appearance, and that special *something*. My nurse was the Ed McMahon of *Scar Search*. "Oh, it looks so good, Tania! A lot of fluid, dark red, but getting lighter. You're draining just fine." Her gloved hand would squeeze the thick, toxic-smelling concoction into a measuring cup and she would chart her findings on a rather unofficial looking piece of paper. If she wrote down "scant," it was like getting fours stars on *Scar Search*; it meant there was so little fluid draining from my scar that it could not be measured.

"Now, Tania, watch what I'm doing, because you're going to have to do this at home for about a week."

Are you insane, lady? I am, how do you say, squeamish. I can't kill cockroaches for fear of…THEM. Whenever blood is drawn from my arm, wrist, or hand, I turn the other way, start to sweat, and realize that passing out is a viable option. Mayonnaise, mustard, ghee, basically anything slimy and on my sandwich, plate, or seat grosses me out. Before I sit down on any unknown surface I take a napkin, dip it in water, and wipe vigorously. So the thought of not only watching but also having to execute such a disgusting act, well…no. "Mom, will you watch, please?"

My mother jumps to attention. "Of course, my baby," she says, grabbing her legal pad and a pen.

My mother's house is the obvious choice for my three-week recovery: My mother will change my drainage bags, cook amazing meals, and drive me to all of my appointments without complaining. Dawn, on the other hand, can barely take care of herself, drives me crazy most of the time, and is busy dealing with her father's illness.

Welcome to Week One. Edith Piaf cries out in French, my mother is clanking around in the kitchen, and I'm lying in my high-school bed popping Vicodin. I'm sick of being sick. I want to have energy again, to regain my strength and bust out of this joint. But first...a little nap.

I wake up to a room full of posters from the eighties: Bronski Beat, Culture Club, and Erasure. Did I take poppers instead of Vicodin? Surrounded by this obvious display of homosexuality, it's a wonder I ever thought I was straight. "Mom—" I scream over Nana Mouskouri.

"I'm coming!" she screams back. She arrives with a tray full of food, a pair of rubber gloves, and a bell. "I made you your favorite: fresh pumpkin soup with shallots, and nine-grain bread, to keep you regular. And here's a bell to ring if you need something. I don't want you to strain yourself, so if you need anything, just—" She picks up the bell and shakes it furiously. "Ring."

"I'm not going to ring a bell. If I need something, I'll get it myself. I'm fine, Mom."

She snaps on the rubber gloves.

"Rectal exam?" I ask.

"No, Tania. It's time to drain your Jackson Pratts."

There is a distinct sound associated with draining the Pratts, a sort of squishy sucking sound, like that of my brother inhaling from a six-foot water bong, punctuated with a large splat. I turn away, hoping my mother won't comment on her findings.

"Ooh, Tania. There's little clumps of blood, but the liquid is a light pink, which is good, and it's not very much, not *scant*, but not bad. I'll be back to check on you right after

Phil Donahue. I love that man." Mom has a love for
American pop culture that borders on, and sometimes
teeters over into, obsession. One would think my mother,
as a French citizen who has lived in America for twenty-
nine years, would be interested in filling out the paperwork needed to become an American citizen, but that
would cut into her television-watching and *People* magazine–reading time. At age forty-two, my mother knows
more about movie stars, rock stars, and what's *HOT!* than
she does about senators and state capitals. She's always
finding innovative ways to get a quick fix too, like reading
an entire magazine while waiting on the checkout line at
the grocery store. By the time the clerk asks my mother,
"Do you have any coupons?" she's caught herself up on all
the latest celebrity weddings, commented on whether she
thinks they're going to "make it," placed the magazine in
its proper rack, and said, "Can you believe people read
that crap?"

Things will be fine around here as long as I don't interrupt
Mom and Phil and I don't have sex. The only rule she has
while I'm staying with her is, NO SEX. In stating this rule
she's really preventing Dawn from coming over to visit,
because she knows Dawn and I communicate best with
our nonverbal language.

Whoever said pain is a state of mind has never had their
booby removed. Every time I twist at the waist to reach
something—like the bell on my tray—I feel the yards of
tubing coiled inside me, straining to find room among my
ribs and random organs. And then there's the throbbing
pain that runs the length of my scar. Even after I've taken
Vicodin, there is no position that I feel comfortable in.

You know what I need right now? I need sex. That's right,
something sweaty and emotionally removed to remove the
pain for just a little while. How can my mother keep me
from having sex? I'm an adult. I'm twenty-one years old.
Mom told me I could ring the bell if I needed *anything*.
Maybe I could ring the bell and tell her I *need* to have sex.
My predicament is so absurd and contemporary.
Sneaking Dawn into my room is pretty easy. The window
by my bed has no screen on it and is large enough to
accommodate one adult body, perhaps two. The base of
the window is approximately three feet off the ground,
allowing Dawn to easily lift her five-foot-four, 123-pound
frame into my room. I feel like I'm in high school again,
only this time I'm doing drugs and having sex.
"I so-o-o want to fuck you," Dawn says with a fierce
intensity that is so hot and flattering, but a little loud, and
I don't want to get busted.
"Shh!" I say, grabbing the collar of her faded blue Mickey
Mouse T-shirt, pulling her on top of me.
Negotiating tubes and see-through drainage bags is a little
tricky at first, but soon there's no talking, just heavy
breathing, light restraining: It's like a made-for-TV rape
scene. Pain and discomfort interspersed with elation and
arousal. There's something about knowing that at any
moment my mom could walk in, tubes could be ripped
out, my scar could be torn open, that's incredibly exciting
to me in a way I've never known. Is this what S/M is all
about? I think I get it.
Dawn's warm body is lying next to mine, and for a second
in the dark I don't feel any pain. *Knock, knock, knock!* The
door is practically opening from the force of the pounding.

"Tania, is someone in there with you?" Mom asks.

"No! I'm trying to sleep, Mom. I just had a mastectomy and I'm a little tired right now!" I try to transform my heavy breathing into a regular breathing pattern.

"I'm sorry, I thought I heard someone in there with you. I'm sorry, honey." She begins to retreat.

"It's all right. No one's here. You can go back to sleep now."

Mom leaves. I instruct Dawn to leave.

"This sucks, Tania. You're twenty-one years old. We live together, for chrissake, she can't tell us that we can't sleep together," Dawn says as she pulls up the sheets in search of her T-shirt.

"I know, but that's my mom's one request, so…could you please leave, for me?"

"Fine," Dawn says, now fully clothed and angry, "I'm outta here."

Week Two. Even writing in my journal has become an arduous task: Feeling like shit and writing about how much you feel like shit really makes you feel like shit. I've taken to looking through my high-school yearbooks and calling all the people who innocently wrote "K.I.T." I can't reach anyone—thank God. Dawn is out of town visiting her dad, who's not doing so well; apparently his cancer is spreading faster than the doctors anticipated, and now his prognosis of six months to live has been shortened to two. *Scant* has been the by-product of my drainage for the past three days, which means that my tubes are coming out tomorrow, Friday. To celebrate, I have scheduled a tennis date with Fran for Saturday and Trash Disco tonight with Alexander. I lied to my mom about my plans for this evening, telling her, "Alexander is picking me up at 8 P.M. and taking me to that breast cancer support group the social worker in the hospital told me about, Bosom Buddies. Isn't Alex great?!"

"Eight P.M.?" she asked, expressing concern about a support group that would meet so late at night.

"Right," I tell her, "women recovering from mastectomies find their mobility to be at its peak at around 8:30 P.M."

An a-ha tape had been hiding under my bed since 1984; dusty but preserved, those cute Norwegian boys were ready to dance, so I popped them into a nearby tape recorder to begin my dance therapy. As I imagined my life in half cartoon and half reality, I extended my right arm, moving it around in time to the music. "Take me on, take on me." I discovered dance moves I didn't even know I had. It's like the surgeon removed my boob but gave me more rhythm—an OK trade-off. I practiced dancing all day long, only breaking to write in my journal and eat a gourmet lunch. The only thing left to do before going out is to try on my booby. My favorite going-out outfit consists of a tight black V-neck T-shirt, which borders on butch except for the fact that its poly-blend cling really shows off my womanly body, and jeans in a shade of green my mother refers to as *caca d'oie,* which means goose shit. In real life, I am a men's size 32 x 30; in cool-dyke wear, I'm a 36 x 32, which ensures a baggy and cuffed look, much like an auto mechanic minus the grease and proficiency with tools. Footwear is almost always my chunky black postal shoes. And lastly, my lucky socks. As a collector of socks, not something I usually admit to in public situations, I always have a pair that feels lucky on any given night, and tonight it's my…orange argyle socks.

After putting on my jeans, socks, and shoes, it's time to try on my new boob. My bra is perched on top of a bandage that wraps around my chest several times. I slip the very light disfigured baked-potato stocking into the right cup of the bra. I try a few dance moves with my new boob, but whenever I move my arms the cotton-stuffed stocking follows in that direction. It's under my arm, next to my belly button, at my throat. And even when I can keep it in its proper place I can see the lumpiness of its form through my shirt, looking like a breast full of tumors. Using my right elbow, I'm able not only to push the boob down, should it slide up on the dance floor, but make it look like a dance move, like the Running Man or something. I'm ready for fun! Wait, what about the Jackson Pratts?

The dance floor is more crowded than ever. I've safety-pinned my see-through sacks onto my belt loop so people will see them and not bump into them. I wonder if my Jackson Pratts will prevent girls from checking me out? Alexander and I push our way onto the dance floor. As the music instructs, "Rock the boat, don't rock the boat baby." Arms and elbows swing all around us. I feel like I'm drowning, scared someone will knock into my scar or, worse, rip out my tubes. Alexander can sense my uneasiness. "Hang with me, Miss Katanalicious!" he says as his hips begin to sway with more purpose, direction, and intent, bumping people out of our way, creating a dancing human barricade between me and the masses. If he could see his hips swaying right now, he would say, "You want some fries with that shake?!"

We have claimed our space on the dance floor. Alexander continues to surround me, extending his arms, snapping his fingers, bumping and grinding people away from us. Even though my breast is working its way up to my clavicle, it feels so amazing to be dancing, to be out of the hospital, out of my mother's house, to be twenty-one and dancing with Alexander feels like what life is all about.

Far away from the image of Joan Crawford repeatedly slapping Christina, demanding the respect that she deserves, on the large-screen TV hanging over the dance floor at Fosters last night, I'm now sitting on the edge of yet another exam table. Mom is frantically scanning the office for any sign of pop culture, preferably a magazine. We wait ten minutes, fifteen, then twenty. Mom finds a magazine called *Cancer and You*—I wish it was called *Cancer and Them*. Sitting in a paper gown in a cold office for more than twenty minutes can feel like an eternity.

"Hello, Tania. How is everything going?" Dr. Cutter asks, "Are you ready for us to take off the bandage and take out the tubes?"

Without giving me an opportunity to answer he paws at my bandage, peeling up the white tape attached to blood-stained gauze. This action, this peeling, makes me think of my chest and the fact that in a matter of seconds the results of my surgery will be revealed. I will see a scar, my scar, a place where my booby should be, a place that is holding the place of something else. I will be lopsided, weighted down. The speed with which the surgeon peels the bandage away from my skin parallels the rate at which all of this has happened, is happening. I don't even remember being given a choice, not a real choice anyway. I mean, having to choose between your breast or living is not a choice. It's like having to choose between a high-paying job or being homeless.

Instead of collecting the gauze in his hands, the doctor allows it to unravel and drop into a loose wrinkled pile on the floor. The whole time he assures me that, "It's looking good." When there is no more gauze to be pulled away and I am exposed, he stares at me and says, "I must say, I did a fine job. It really looks great, Tania."

I'll take his word for it. Mom looks at my chest and proclaims, "Oh, it doesn't look as bad as I thought."

Dr. Cutter nudges around my chest for a few seconds. "Everything looks good. Now, let's get these tubes out of you."

I could not even begin to imagine how much clear tubing could be tucked away in my body. Not until the doctor starts pulling and pulling and pulling and the whole thing starts to feel like that old trick with the never-ending multicolored handkerchiefs coming out of a clown's sleeve.

"All finished," he says as both he and Mother exit the room, allowing me to get dressed. The door closes behind them to reveal a full-length mirror attached to it, staring at me. Black sticky stains from medical tape left on too long, dried sepia blood, and what's that? It's longer than I thought, more jagged, not a line drawn from point A to point B, but more of a zigzag route, nonlinear. I look up from my scar to see a face that also looks slightly uneven, like something has shifted. That face is far to be sad to be mine. She's kind of a bummer; I'm a good time.

Rounding out Week Two is tennis. I have played two years of college tennis at a division—three, four, five?—school. Despite my lack of division-one talent, I love the sport. I've got a forehand like Steffi's, a volley like Martina's, a serve like Arantxa's, and a mouth like John's. If my opponent hits a ball that I can't get to in time and it's close to the line, I simply call it "Out." My backhand, well, my backhand, for lack of a better word, sucks. But I'm fast enough to run around it, making it a forehand instead. I'm a trash-talker too, especially if I'm losing. The harder I'm going down the faster I'm yelling, "I'm gonna kick your ass!" Today, two weeks out from surgery, with my right arm more than sore and extremely tight, I will wield my tennis racket like a sword and kick Fran's ass.

Who knew how exhausting a one-mile bicycle ride could be? I've ridden my bike to Arizona State University every day for the past two years, but today when I arrive at the tennis courts on campus I'm exhausted. Fran is already there and looks ready to play; she's even wearing a wristband.

"Are you sure you want to play? I mean, it's only been two weeks since your surgery. Did your doctor say it was OK?" Fran's looking at me like I'm a baby bird with a broken wing.

"Are you scared to play with me, Fran?" I ask, puffing up my chest, holding my racket in a *ready* position.

"No I—" She doesn't quite know how to respond to my tennis bravado.

"Then let's play!" I proclaim.

"OK."

"But first, can we just sit down? I'm a little tired."

"I didn't really feel like playing tennis anyway. I'd much rather grab a bite to eat and get to know you. How does that sound?"

"Perfect."

Our Dunkin' Donuts waitress conjures Lily Tomlin's character Trudy from *The Search for Signs of Intelligent Life in the Universe.* When she asks if we'd like some coffee, I half expect her to offer us *art* and a brief explanation on how *art* and *coffee* are indistinguishable from each other. We sit on black swivel stools with metal stems. With Fran's legs hanging over the stool, her feet barely touching the ground, I can see she has strong legs. Indentations on the sides of her thighs and her calves are perpetually flexed. I like that. She's thick, but soft, very much a woman, but a woman who could help you push your car to the side of the road if it were stalled in the middle of an intersection. When asked to make our doughnut selection, Fran doesn't hesitate. "Buttermilk bar, please," she says.

"Those are my favorites!" I say with a level of enthusiasm usually reserved for really great theatrical productions. The dense beige bars appear along with two cups of light brown coffee. I couldn't be happier.

"What year did you graduate from high school?" Fran asks cautiously, wiping a small piece of yellow cake from the corner of her mouth.

"Uh..doy! Class of '89: GO CHARGERS!" I say in my best adolescent tone while pretending to chew a piece of gum loudly.

"I have sneakers older than you," Fran says, beginning to chuckle. I love it when she chuckles.

Watery coffee and greasy buttermilk bars seem to facilitate getting to know someone. We banter, exchange stories from our pasts, talk about our dreams; basically we talk about everything unrelated to the fact that I have a girlfriend. Fran's company is a calm and focused addition to my reality.

mental mastectomies and IHOP
(left breast—2002)

"*I go through this, before you wake up, so I can feel happier to be safe up here with you…*" Björk is blaring through my failing stock speakers. A cup of crappy corner-store coffee, vanilla nut, is stuck in the cup holder. The torn black canvas top that usually adorns my 1997 Toyota Paseo convertible is down. I'm on a road trip. Yeah. Good times! All right, I'm pretending I'm on a road trip, because if I weren't temporarily delusional, I'd stop the car, turn around, and go home. If I were in my right mind, I would never drive to Lakewood, California, to meet the man who will dismember my member. So I'm turning up the tunes and kicking in the cruise control. Lakewood or bust!

The streets of Lakewood are lined with liquor stores and scenes from *Rescue 911*. Apartment buildings are separated by mini strip malls, each containing a pawnshop, porn shop, and corner store. Lakewood is basically anywhere, where popcorn ceilings explode leaving debris of drugs and people struggling behind. This is where my surgeon's office is.

All medical waiting areas are identical, like *Queer Eye for the Sick Guy* showed up and said, "We're thinking *sick* plus *waiting* equals…*brown!*"

Everyone seems to be running late today. Dad's stuck at

work; Mom and Paul are stuck at the Asian market trying to find lemongrass; and the surgeon is stuck in traffic. Now I have time to think about why I'm here, to survey the sick crowd around me. I might have cancer, but I'm not sick. I don't live to cough or complain or hunch over and struggle with movement. I don't use a walker or oxygen tank. My salubrious constitution is counter to everything in this dank brown waiting room. To be lumped in with this group seems really unnecessary. The guy next to me, the one that looks like an old pair of socks, just coughed and didn't cover his mouth—great, now I probably have consumption. What would Thich Nhat Hanh do if he were here? Meditate. Breathing in, I am light, breathing out, I am a smile. Breathing in, I am scared, breathing out, I am freaked out. Breathing in, I am… Forget enlightenment and maturity, I'm going to hold my breath until the cancer goes away.

The young woman behind the Plexiglas hands me a stack of forms along with a brochure. Multitasking always puts me at ease. After years of filling out forms and navigating my way through the bureaucracy of HMOs, I know how to take care of business. I'm like the Martha Stewart of the medical world. *Today I'm going to show you how to expedite your charts, get free copies of your medical records, and make a festive holiday chapeau with this tri-fold "Mastectomies and You" brochure, all before the young woman behind the counter asks for your insurance card!*

The nurse calls my name from the frame of the door, "Tanne-a Kae-ton?" Where's my support team? I thought that everyone was in town to help me? I need help. Help!

I follow her back to a small room, which displays a prominent poster of what happens to your internal organs when some disease ravages them. Couldn't they think of a more upbeat visual, like a kitten hanging upside down from the monkey bars with caption that says, HANG IN THERE!

If the nurse pumps that black turkey baster one more time, my arm will explode. I wonder how many arms she's lost this year?

"What do you think of Dr. Allen?" I ask the nurse, having learned that nurses will always give you the skinny on the doctors.

"If I was gonna get a lumpectomy or mastectomy, I'd have Dr. Allen do it," she says solidly.

I like that answer.

"One hundred over seventy. Good. How much do you weigh, Tania?"

I love it when they cut out the middleman—the scale— and simply ask you your weight. I lie, of course, but only by three pounds. They'll weigh me before surgery. I mean, they won't just guess at the amount of anesthesia to administer, will they?

"I'm sorry, I lied. I weigh 132 pounds." Actually I weigh 133 pounds, but what's one pound when we're talking about a positive self-image?

Mom, Paul, and Dr. Allen arrive simultaneously. Although I love my brother, he's not—how do you say?—*down* with the concept of Western medicine, so he stays in the waiting area, as per my request. His overtly political and vegetational agenda might prove to be a bit much in the small representation of Western medicine known as the doctor's office.

The surgeon looks like Ryan Stiles from *Whose Line Is It*

Anyway? I decide that because he looks like a funny guy, he must be a funny guy. But in reality his most exciting feature is that he makes eye contact, which is the surgeon equivalent of congenial. Dr. Allen skims through my chart. "It looks like this cancer is slightly different from your last cancer, which is good news, much better prognosis. How old are you, Tania?"

"Thirty."

"Wow, and you were how old when you had your right breast removed?"

"Twenty."

"Are you Jewish?" he asks abruptly.

Odd line of questioning, Dr. Barbie. "Are you anti-Semitic?"

"No, no, I'm sorry. I'm asking if you're Jewish because there's a breast cancer gene that we've discovered in women of Eastern-European Jewish decent."

"In that case, I am Jewish," I say.

"But we're Sephardic Jews," Mom says.

"What about your husband?"

Mom tilts her head forward in a playful manner, looking up at Dr. Allen with her blue eyes and long eyelashes. "I'm not married," she says.

He clearly isn't picking up on Mom's flirtatious cue.

"Your father, Tania, is he of Ashkenazi decent?" Dr. Allen tries again.

"Yes."

"My guess is that you do have the gene, in which case I'd recommend that you get a hysterectomy. I'm not sure, but we could probably schedule it at the same time we do the mastectomy. That way you'll only have one surgery."

Hey there, hi there, ho there! A hysterectomy? First of all, I

111

came to get my breast removed, not my ovaries, and if it's a breast cancer gene, why do I need to worry about my ovaries? Could I get ovarian cancer? Doesn't ovarian cancer equal death? If I don't have ovaries, I can't have a child. Did it occur to you that at thirty years old I might still want to have children? And what about menopause? Can someone who still watches MTV go through menopause? I don't like you, Dr. Allen, and I can't believe Mom was flirting with you! Relax, Tania, breathe, and understand where Dr. Allen is coming from. He's a surgeon. His line of products includes Sedating, Cutting, Pulling Stuff Out, and Sewing.

"Dr. Allen, I'd like to deal with the matter at hand," I say. "You're right," he tells me. "Let's deal with one surgery at a time. So, what are we going to do about the breast? Do we want to go ahead and take it off?"

Using the royal "we" at this moment is really not the most appropriate way to be inclusive. We aren't going to have *our* breast removed; it will only be me, Dr. Allen, not *we*. I take a moment. I can't believe I thought this guy was Ryan Stiles. I take two moments. I look at my mother. She looks back. Dr. Stiles is waiting, as it is my line anyway. I go with the tried-and-true,

"Fine, let's do a mastectomy," I say.

The deal is sealed; hands are shaken, are shaking, are shook up, and ready to leave.

Mom and I meet Paul and Dad in the waiting area. As we leave the brown office feeling beige, Dad asks what I decided to do. "Um, I decided to have a mastectomy. You know, less tissue, less chance of reoccurrence."

My father hugs me tightly and doesn't say anything. He

grinds his teeth together and shakes his head. I can tell that he wants to save my breast. He wants to punch the surgeon. He wants to grab cancer by the balls, or the breasts, as the case may be, and swing it around, beat it unconscious, beat it out of our consciousness. He wishes he had some pull with someone who could help. God? The Jewish mafia? He can't protect his little girl from this one. Dad puts his arm around my shoulder and continues to shake his head no.

International House of Pancakes. This culinary choice is made more out of necessity than conviction. It's near the surgeon's office, and being of Jewish faith we need to eat, now. Whether we're marking the birth of a child, the death of a loved one, a marriage, or a mastectomy, food is an integral part of any Jewish occasion.

An effeminate Native-American boy seats us. Out of sheer nerves and low blood-sugar, we each verbalize our internal monologue, starting with my mother: "Look at all the syrups! They've got blueberry, boysenberry, loganberry, strawberry…Tania, what's that one on the end called, I can't see it?"

"Vaginaberry," I say, because being at IHOP right now is so surreal that I wouldn't be surprised if they offered that flavor.

Mom continues as if I said raspberry.

"And look at all the maples. There's walnut-maple, almond-maple, pecan-maple, plain maple. I need some protein, but I also want a pancake or two…or three. My blood-sugar is so low. I want sweet *and* savory. I want a stack of pancakes, an omelet, a pork chop, and fries. Yep, that's all. I wish they'd come take our order already. I need to eat. I'm hungry."

Dad is next: "I want a steak. A Lundy's steak. When I was driving the cab in New York, when the kids were little and Joëlle and I were still married, I always used to stop at Lundy's for a London broil. I loved Lundy's. Sometimes Joëlle and I would take the kids there, but they were babies. They didn't appreciate the beauty of a good cut of meat. I wonder if they have decent steaks here? Seasoned fries? What the fuck are seasoned fries? I want authentic. I want New York. I want a steak and some fucking fries."

Paul's food concerns start with a moral monologue: "IHOP: Inconceivable Homeless Oppression Perpetrated. This menu brings nothing but pain and disillusion. Where is the macrobiotic section of the menu? How about a vegan section? What about the…OH, MAN, check out those Monster Waffles! Those look so good. Do you think they have egg in them? Nobody's gonna notice if I have a waffle. Tania's pulling focus with the cancer. If I'm mindful of each ingredient and where it comes from, then I can truly enjoy the Monster Waffles. Ooh, strawberry topping. That comes from a can, right? Cans come from aluminum, aluminum comes from the earth, and the earth comes from God. Cool."

I stare at the pictorial representations on the menu, like food photo option #7, the Tandem: two pancakes, each with a small scoop of butter in the middle and dark red strawberry topping drizzled all over them. I'm not hungry.

Dad drives an old cop car, which he bought at an auction years ago. The car has been painted white to cover up any state seals that might have appeared on the doors. He has two operable spotlights on either side of the car, which he uses to intimidate people who think they're above the law. Paul rides with Dad in his stripped-down cop car. This is not the first time Paul has ridden in a cop car. Being a political activist means spending a lot of time naked and getting arrested.

Mom comes with me. Somehow I believe I can escape my reality by driving fast, so I accelerate through potentially uncomfortable moments and future fears. Mom tries to slow me down.

"Tania, honey, slow down, you're going to cause an accident, do you want to die?" As soon as the question escapes she wishes she could take it back.

"No, I don't want to die, Mom. That's the problem."

Tears burst out of my ducts. I've never been a crier. I've always admired those who can spontaneously burst into tears when they are moved to do so through fear, sadness, and joy, but I'm just not wired that way. And there's the fact that tears take time to manage. They slow you down. How can I possibly navigate my way through a medical labyrinth if my eyes are blurry and my mind is reeling? Mom strokes my face as the Cowboy Junkies croon, "I'm so lonesome I could cry." Everyone's crying today. I sniffle through my list of fears, "Mom, what if I have this breast cancer gene? And what about having children, or going gray, or being able to take life for granted without any cosmic ramifications, or just living a little bit more than thirty years? What's gonna happen, Mom? I'm scared, Mom. I'm scared."

"My Tania." Mom squeezes my left arm. "Well…at least

you're cute," she says in all earnestness.

What else can a mom say? I catch a glimpse of my swollen eyes and damp cheeks, and realize that maybe there is a certain cuteness to vulnerability.

We drive past a woman leaving a liquor store on the corner of Redondo and PCH. She is drinking from a bottle in a brown paper bag. Her stomach is distended and she wears all black as if she's going to meet Death for happy hour. This shriveled and jaundiced woman can barely make her way across the parking lot without the assistance of a swig; I bet she's never had cancer. I bet she never gets cancer. I bet she outlives me.

death...a treasure hunt
(left breast—2002)

Why should I keep you around, huh? What have you done for me lately? When I run on the treadmill or get going on the StairMaster you flop about, causing a low to high level of pain. You have a propensity toward developing deadly diseases and you're kind of scrawny. On the pro side, you are very sweet: small and pink and innocent in all of this. And let's not forgot all the compliments, huh? You've been told by many, well, not that many, but enough, that you are "so pretty" and "perfect" and "beautiful." You are extremely sensitive when touched in the right way, immediately sending a message to your pal, vagina, to go ahead and get wet, and when touched harshly, you flinch and wish to be touched softly again. When your bosom buddy skipped town in '92 you pulled focus toward you instead of the long scar to your right. You've kept me company for the past ten years, and now it's time to say goodbye? I look at you, this vibrant little breast, the only one I have, and I think, *How could you be leaving so soon?*

In jumping to the quick and seemingly logical conclusion of a mastectomy, I'm now having doubts. Maybe I can still save you? We could run away together. We'll go to Vegas. We'll elope. After our seven-minute ceremony performed by Elvis, we'll cram into a photo booth, I'll lift up my shirt, and we'll make silly faces expressing our love for one another in six black-and-white frames. Or maybe the surgeon will open you up to discover that your tumor is, in fact, a benign growth that looked like cancer. The surgeon will remove the benign lump, pat you on the nipple, and say, "Well, kid, everything's gonna be OK." Maybe everything will be OK, and maybe it won't. Maybe getting cancer twice before our thirty-first birthday is more than just a medical anomaly. Maybe it's a sign, a premonition about our fate. Maybe everything is all wrong. Maybe I will need to let you go in order to save my life. I know it's selfish, but I'm scared. I'm sorry. I…I'll miss you. Goodbye. Sure, it feels very matter-of-fact when you tell yourself that having a part of your body removed, that you don't really need, *unless you want to breast-feed, be aroused sexually, or be accepted by society*, in order to save your life is the right thing to do. When your only option is keep a breast and lose a life, it all makes sense. But what if I have my breast removed and the cancer is still there, hiding in lymph nodes and bloodstreams, in places that can't be detected until it's too late? What if I die anyway? And if I'm going to hypothetically die, then why don't I just kill myself before I get my breast removed: That way I can rest assured that I won't die from cancer?

This time around I kind of want to kill myself. I mean it. I'm really scared. Worse than first-day-of-school scared, worse than speaking-in-front-of-a-large-group scared, this is a kind of scared I've never felt before. This is the kind of scared I've only seen in the faces of people on the news who have lost a brother in a drive-by shooting, a child in a kidnapping, a mother in a fire. And when the funeral is over, when the candlelight vigils come to an end, when there's nothing left to do but pray, they must feel like I do, like crawling into the smallest space available, closing their eyes, and never having to be confronted with bad news again. But the irony in me wanting to die is that I'm scared to die. I have my mother and father to thank for that fear.

"Tania, Paul, Kim, come into my room, I need to talk to all of you!" my mother would yell in an ominous tone from her bedroom, which was at the end of a very long hallway. From the time Paul and I were nine years old and Kim was seven, inspired by a particularly gloomy day, Mom would call us into her room to explain where she kept her valuables and what to do in case of her death. "Are you dying, Mom?" was the top question on all or our lists. My mother's answer was always vague: "No, but you never know what could happen, and I want all of you to be prepared." At which point she would present us with a handful of keys. There was a small gold key that opened the safe-deposit box at the bank; in the box we were to find some old francs, my grandfather's ring, and a watch or two. The five smaller silver keys would open five corresponding metal shoeboxes. On some occasions, depending on my mother's level of impending doom, the contents of these metal shoeboxes were revealed to us: our baby teeth, all in little envelopes with our names and ages marked on them; journal entries from our twenty-three-year-old mother documenting her pregnancies; her tarnished wedding ring; and some other small but seemingly important things. After we learned what the keys opened, Mom would take us over to the distressed white antique postal cubbyhole formation in her bedroom, a pyramid of partitioned spaces that used to house people's mail. She carefully explained how in each one of the fifty-five units she had hidden more Katan family memorabilia.

"Make sure to look in ALL of the sections. Don't miss a section because you could be missing a section of your lives," she would say.

Whoa, that's a lot to take in at nine, ten, eleven, twelve, twenty-two, even twenty-nine years old. Then she'd gaze into the distance like she was mentally preparing her eulogy and say, while placing a record on the turntable, "I want you to play this at my funeral."

She placed the needle on the spinning record, which hissed and crackled, and then, in my mother's dimly lit room, we heard, "La la la la la, la la la la la, la la la la la, la la la la la la, do do do do do do, doooo EIEIIIIEE!"

"It's 'Loving You' by Minnie Riperton," she'd tell us.

And as Minnie hit notes never meant to be hit, our mom cried and told us the story of Minnie's untimely death from cancer. Later in life, as a teenager, when my peers discovered Minnie and her high-pitched antics, they'd fall over in hysterics, while I'd picture my mother's unexpected death.

This premature-death scavenger hunt only succeeded in

freaking me out about death. Not only was I scared my mother could die at any given moment, I was terrified I wouldn't be able to remember all the secret nooks and crannies that housed her valuables, thus missing out on important sections of my own life.

My father's living will came into existence only recently, in the form of a handwritten poem titled "Treasure Hunt: a Poem." He assembled the three of us at his card table, which was used as a meeting table that night, to read his poetic death request. He invoked the spirit of a dead pirate with one eye who has just come across a tattered yellowed scroll in a musty cave that no doubt holds the cryptic instructions to finding a trunk full of riches! Dad squinted his left eye and shifted his weight, pretending to be a peg-legged Irish pirate with a slight New York accent:

Hello, my children, one and all
Here's a little poem to help you so you won't fall
There are bits of treasure here and there
This little poem will show you where
Go to the kitchen, look high and low
The drawers and cupboards will give you a show
Don't forget the shoeboxes with my many collections
Squeeze the tubes of ointment for my many infections
Lift up the floorboards, look behind picture frames
I want all of you to share, don't play any games
When you find the loot, I hope you'll think it's funny
Or maybe you'll all scream, "Where's the rest of Dad's money?!"

Love, Dad

To me, death has always been associated with fear, high-pitched singing, and instructions. I think I'll opt for surgery.

At the hospital, filling out pre-op paperwork, I'm confronted with death again, and again I'm overwhelmed by the instructions and options that potentially dying offers. The first form I'm handed is the "Advance Health Care Detective." This is the first form that's made sense to me. Of course becoming a health care *detective*, uncovering the clues to solve the case of why I'm here, literally and cosmically, makes so much sense. I imagine my advance health care detective is a gritty young lesbian sleuth who bears a striking resemblance to me. She pops out of the pages of a Raymond Chandler novel, leaning back on her squeaky worn black leather chair while propping her feet on the heavy brown desk in front of her. She chain-smokes and speaks aloud to herself.

"I was sitting around reviewing the facts of Tania's case, the broken fax machine, *The Facts of Life* to see if Jo Polniaczek's propensity for auto mechanics was a hobby or a blatant sign of homosexuality, when she walked in. She had the kind of androgynous good looks that made straight women blush and straight men question their sexuality; I knew why she was here. I could smell it a mile away. It smelled like pork medallions smothered in a mango-jalapeño chutney, or maybe I was just hungry. In any case, she was about to do something, something big, something real big. She was about to lose…a breast."

OK, so upon closer examination the title of the form is "Advance Health Care Directive," not detective. In actuality, these six stapled pages will determine the fate of my body should I become a human eggplant, asking questions like: *Who will approve or disapprove diagnostic tests, surgical procedures, and programs of medication? Who will select or discharge health care providers and institutions? Who will direct the provision, withholding, or withdrawal of artificial nutrition and hydration and all other forms of health care, including cardiopulmonary resuscitation? Who will make anatomical gifts, authorize an autopsy, and direct disposition of remains?*

Wait a second. Anatomical gifts? So, potentially my appointee could bring my vagina to the company Christmas gift exchange? I wish I had someone with me to bounce ideas off of, but today I'm flying solo: Dad's at work, Mom's back in Arizona, Kim's not in town yet, Paul's at a rainbow gathering, and I wasn't about to invite the ever-persistent Sal.

After the questions, there are sections like Part 1: Power of Attorney, in which they ask me to "Designate an agent." How cool is that? This will be the first time in my writing career that I have an agent. I need to be strategic. Do I know anyone at ICM? How about William Morris? Shit, I can't think of anyone; I guess I'll list my mom and, like, five of my best friends. Moving right along…Part 2: End-of-Life Decisions. To prolong or not to prolong? That is the question. Is it nobler to burden your friends and family with your drooling existence or to merely die? Die. Part 3: Other Wishes. This section provides me with two blank lined pages to be filled with my wishes. I take my time on this one and print legibly:

If I should become unconscious, my five best friends are to

choose the hottest nurse in the oncology unit to give me a sponge bath while playing "Big Time Sensuality" by Björk. If, after my sponge bath, I am still unconscious, I would like the above-mentioned hot nurse to theatrically toss the stereo that is playing "Big Time Sensuality" into my sudsy, serene bath. After I am pronounced dead, I want my five best friends, assuming they're in the mood, to make out with each other and, in a rather pornographic manner, make out with the hot nurse. Please make sure that all high schools, coffeehouses, and ice skating rinks are closed for the rest of the day. Thank you.
Tania L. Katan

A woman in a uniform—that sounds so much hotter than it really is—calls me back to finish the pre-op intake. In a cold room with only enough space for a desk and a scale, Megan, the pre-op nurse, decides to become my new best friend.

"Hey, Tania Katan. What a great name! It reminds me of Tawny Kitaen. Do you remember her?" Megan asks.

"Yeah, the eighties rocker chick who adorned the hoods of luxury vehicles in Whitesnake videos. She's the bane of my existence," I say, letting Megan know she's not the first one to draw the Tania/Tawny name parallel.

"You are so-o-o funny, Tania! This is so much fun! I usually get older women in here, fifties, sixties, never anyone my age. You're really young, you know?"

"Yeah, I know."

"How are you feeling about all of this? Pretty scary, huh?"

"Well, Megan, I'm sort of an expert at this. I'm ready to just get it over with."

"You have such a great attitude, so upbeat and peppy. My aunt just went through all of *this* and she was such a," she leans in and whispers loudly, "BITCH. Now let's talk about pre-op dos and don'ts, OK?"

Oh, no, not the rhetorical "OK." It's not OK, it's barely all right—doesn't she know I might explode at any moment? I don't need someone to ask me if something is OK and then not listen to my answer. I need for this intake to be over.

"First let's discuss the risks of anesthesia—" Just the word "risks" makes my body start to tremble and my brain disassociate.

"—And if the doctor goes in there and finds that the cancer has spread—" Now I'm sweating, clammy, shaking; things are not "OK."

"—And, of course, there's a risk, although slight, that you might not make it through the surgery—" That's it, Megan, I'm gonna blow.

"You'll need to have an empty stomach twelve hours before surgery. Are you OK, Tania, you look a little green—"

I lurch over and vomit on my new best friend's shoes. "Sorry, Megan."

"That's OK, Tania. We're all done. We'll get you cleaned up, and we'll see you in a few days."

subscription on the go
(right breast—1992)

She calls it "subscription on the go," which makes the act of stealing magazines from doctor's offices sound fun and upwardly mobile. *People, Us, National Enquirer,* basically any magazine whose title suggests community, connection, and concern, my mother acquires as part of her "subscription on the go."

"Slim pickings," Mom announces as she digs through a

pile of ratty magazines placed carelessly on the knee-high brown wood octagonal table. Somehow I expected the waiting room of an oncologist's office to be different, less cluttered, more sterile. I guess it's just like any other waiting room. Well, except for the people. I mean, they have no hair and look as if they are dying. In a moment of desperation, my mother opens the tiny door to the octagonal table and finds a brand new *People* magazine. She is elated. "Did you know Julia Roberts and Lyle Lovett are getting married? He's so ugly. I don't see the attraction," she announces without even looking up from the pages.

"Mom, please, I'm a little nervous," I say as I feel the palms of my hands begin to sweat; I've never felt this sensation before right now.

"Sorry." She continues reading.

I'll thumb through magazines to clear my mind: *Cancer Today. Cancer Tomorrow. Cancer Next Week. Cancer Town & Country?* Maybe reading isn't a good idea.

Even though my black-and-red letterman's jacket is baggy enough to hide the fact that my buoyant stocking breast is ascending toward my chin, I'm still self-conscious, and obviously this isn't the right setting to use my elbow dance move to bring it down. When it comes to my new physique I can't say I've studied it enough to be comfortable with it. To be totally honest, not only have I been ignoring my scar but I've been ignoring my left breast. So has Dawn. The past couple of times Dawn has climbed through my window and we've engaged in sexual activities, she hasn't touched my breast or approached my scar. When it comes to *that* region of my body her hand takes a detour to anywhere but there. Dawn couldn't make it today due to her latest hobby: starting a new job, having a temper flare-up, and being fired. Today she's starting her fourth new job in two months. It's a good thing she's cute, although I'm finding that cute can only go so far in the scheme of things. I'm starting to think "emotionally astute" might beat cute. I'm starting to think I like Fran. I'm starting to think about a lot of stuff, like going back to my apartment today, even though I wish I could stay at my mom's house, or like going back to school, or like losing my hair. Just stuff.

A nurse halfway down the hall calls out, "Tan-ee-aa Cotton? Follow me."

Mom shoves the *People* into her purse and we walk toward her. The nurse practically runs down the hall, much like an eager hostess at a local eatery. She's halfway down the hall and turning the corner; she's losing us.

"Maybe if you didn't have that *People* magazine weighing you down, we could run faster," I tell my mother as we turn the corner.

"Tania. Enough," she says, exasperated, exhausted, and just plain finished.

When we arrive in the room the nurse stands in front of a scale with a clipboard.

"OK, Tan-ee-aa, why don't you step on the scale so we can get your weight."

"It looks like…" She tinkers with the solid square weight. "One hundred, twenty-eight pounds. Now let's get your height while you're up here." She flicks the metal shoehorn up, presses it down on my spiky hair, not allowing me an extra inch.

"Five feet, three and a half inches."

Oh, God, I've been lying for years; five-foot-four seemed so much more dignified. Cancer really does force you to reevaluate your life.

"You'll want to go to room two and wait for Dr. Jones," she says, leaving as quickly as she came.

For Mom and me to get to room two we have to walk past people lying in recliners, bald, half-dead, with IVs stuck in their arms. Hanging from tall metal stands are clear plastic bags, each dripping their contents through tubes and into veins. I swear I can hear the dripping. Each IV sounds like a tin pan underneath a leaky ceiling. All ten recliners drip out of sequence—*drip*, one, two, three; six, *drip*, one, two; four, five, six, *drip*—until the sound is deafening.

Room two is small, with only two chairs and a table. I sit in one chair and Mom sits in the other.

"I cut out an article about a twenty-six-year-old woman who had breast cancer. If I give it to you, will you read it?" my mother asks while I think about the drippers and my chemotherapy fate.

"Sure," I say.

"Oh, I taped that Linda Ellerbee special on breast cancer. It had so much information. You should really watch it."

"Fine."

"But if I loan you the tape, you have to return it as soon as possible because I taped a *Phil* show on there."

"OK."

"You're very brave, you know. I don't know if I could do it. Sssss…I hate needles."

"MOM, could you please shut up? I'm scared and anxious and…please be quiet."

"I'm sorry, Tania. I guess I'm scared and anxious too." She

127

takes my hand and holds it. Dr. Jones enters the room carrying what appears to be a TV-dinner tray, only instead of a potpie and a brownie there are tiny glass bottles with liquid, long needles, and latex gloves.

"Hi, Tania," Dr. Jones says, squinting to see me. He is, like, 485 years old, so in order for him to read my chart he holds it as far from his eyes as his arm will extend. "Looks like you're twenty-one years old. You're too young to have breast cancer," he jokes.

"Yeah, tell that to my cells." I'm not joking.

"So, Miss Katan, do you have any questions?" he asks.

Yeah, Old Man River, a whole list of questions, but who can remember questions when there are needles and chemicals that kill both good and bad cells and... "No questions."

"Great. The nurse will be right in to administer your chemotherapy." He leaves.

The chemo nurse enters the room; she's old, but not as old as Old Man River. She looks like she could find a vein without holding my arm a mile away from her eyes. She sits in front of the TV-dinner trays, opening bottles, extracting fluid, tapping syringes.

"All right, Tania," she says, "what we're going to do first is find a vein on the top of your hand, preferably one that's sticking out. Then I'm going to insert a small shunt into the vein, which you'll barely feel. Once the shunt is in, I'll quickly inject two chemicals, and you'll need to let me know if you feel any burning, OK? It should take a few minutes. I'm going to see if I can find a vein now."

She taps around on my left hand like a frustrated driver

thrums on a dashboard at a red light. "OK, we've got one. Are you ready, Tania?"

"Yes. Do it." I quickly turn my head away from the action. I can't see it, don't want to; I just want it to be over. I feel a prick, then a poke, then a stab, and... "No! Please, stop! It hurts. Are you finished?"

"Tania, what happened was your vein rolled. We're going to have to do it again. I'm sorry."

I'm shaking, like Parkinson's shaking, and teary too. I turn to my mother to protect me from this. "Mom, I can't do it," I tell her.

She sits up straighter, seems stronger than ever. "Squeeze my hand," she says, taking my right hand.

"I've got one," the nurse yells. "Are you ready?"

"Just go," I tell her as I clutch my mother's hand, still facing the other way.

"OK," the nurse says as she breaks the skin and enters a vein.

The fluid moves fast, disarming me. "Mom, I feel, aah, oh, I'm...I feel...I'm gonna be...sick."

"You might experience some nausea after the initial injection," the nurse says. "But it'll go away. I'll get you some water, Tania."

After the nausea subsides she hands me a brochure titled "Chemotherapy and You." A fluffy camel-colored mountain, some hazy mint-green trees, and a couple of blurry pink figures grace the cover of the brochure. It looks like a Blue Mountain card, only instead of overt sentimentality on the inside there's a list of side effects one may encounter during chemotherapy: *hair loss, mouth sores, fatigue, loss of appetite, night sweats, loss of memory, consti-*

pation, loss of libido. And then the brochure offers some advice on how to handle each side effect: *Buy a wig. Keep your mouth clean. Rest. Eat foods that appeal to you. Change your pillowcase. Make a list. Push harder. Invest in pornography.*

It's obvious they spent more time with the graphic designer than the copywriter. The only good thing about my chemotherapy is that it's not administered through an IV drip. I found out the people in recliners getting their treatment through IVs have to sit there for one, two, sometimes five hours, allowing the chemicals to slowly infiltrate their bloodstream. Ten minutes and instant nausea ain't so bad.

Sitting next to my mother as our car curves down the concrete parking structure, I pop a pill called Zofran—my antinausea drug—which makes me think of Fran and how much I like her, which makes me think about Dawn and how different we are, which makes me think about going home, which makes me feel nauseated.

"Now, you know, Tania, if you're not feeling well enough to go home, you can stay with me."

"I know, but it's time for me to go back to my space, plus I have to get ready for school next week."

"OK," my mother says, "but if you need me to pick you up for any reason…"

"Thanks, Mom."

"And remember to take your antinausea pills and the chemo pills. Take those with plenty of water."

"Right, I remember."

"And stay out of the sun."

"Fine."

"And I will be your designated chemo driver."

"Right, thanks."

"Two weeks on, two weeks off."

"I know the regimen, Mom."

"Or if you just need to talk, if you're feeling down, or…"

My mother begins to cry. Crying is one of the side effects of chemotherapy they don't tell you about in the pastel brochure. Driving through yellow lights and close calls, we each stare straight ahead, thinking about all of the side effects they neglected to tell us about.

"Tania, Tania? We're here," my mother announces as she pulls under the aluminum parking structure of my cookie-cutter apartment building.

Maybe I don't have to get out here; I can tell her to keep driving. We could just drive until we run out of gas or pass the sign that says, YOU ARE NOW LEAVING ARIZONA.

"I know," I tell her. "I'm just feeling a little funky from the chemo. I'm leaving now."

"OK. I love you. Call me if you need anything. I love you." She pulls me into her enormous warm breasts and hugs me for as long as I'll allow her.

I watch my mother watch me until we both can't see each other anymore.

When Dawn and I signed a one-year lease at El Diablo we saw the faded white stucco apartment building with maroon and gold trim as a "good sign." I'm not sure how a poorly maintained apartment building named after the devil could be a good sign, but at the time, when we were in love or in lust or in la la land, it all looked good.

The keys flop around in my hand like a plastic red fortune

fish and drop to the floor. Before I'm able to retrieve my fortune, the door opens to reveal Dawn.

"Hey, cutie. How'd it go? Are you feeling all right?" she asks sincerely, taking my arm and carefully leading me through the threshold.

Apparently the Lesbian Stepford Community has exchanged my regular girlfriend for one of their own. "I'm surprisingly fine," I say in a trance, moving forward, slowly, into the apartment.

"You're not glowing, so that's a good sign," Dawn jokes and gives me a cautious but sincere hug. She takes my bag, ushers me to the couch. Once seated I can see Dawn has spruced up the place, taken all of her "good cartoon cells," the Daffys, the Goofys, the Mickeys, and moved them from a large closet—my design idea—to the living room. The downside to being twenty-one is that I haven't had enough time to procure *stuff*. Stuff that defines me, my space, like a funky painting, or a decoupage chair, or Christmas lights I could hang around the border of a room, illuminating all of my cool *stuff*. I know I'm capable of decor outside of the Warner Bros. lot, but I've carefully budgeted my student loan money to include: classes, books, cocktails, coffee, and a new Ford Ranger XLT with a split bench seat, stick shift, and kick-ass stereo system. So right now I have to live with decor by default.

"Do you like what I did to the place?" Dawn asks, staring pointedly at the animation cells on the wall in front of us.

"Wow." What else can I say?

"Yeah?" Dawn has misinterpreted my exclamation. "I was hoping you'd like the cells out here. They brighten up the place, huh?"

Elmer Fudd's head is bald, like chemotherapy bald, and he stands in the middle of a cell with a large rifle. Maybe he's pissed off that he has cancer too. "Yeah, Dawn, they really do brighten up the place."

"I'm glad you think so, 'cause while you were at your mom's recovering from surgery and stuff, I've been hanging out with these really cool chicks, and I wanted to have them over, so I was thinking we could have a movie night here, like tomorrow?"

Eating popcorn and entering the drama of someone else's life sounds really great right now. Oh, and I can invite my new friend Fran. "That's a great idea, and I'll invite Fran over too."

"Fran, the old lady from Michelle's party?" Dawn says, picking at the Mickey Mouse appliqué on a throw pillow like it's a scab.

"No, Fran, my new friend from Michelle's party."

"Right, the old one," she says, freeing the bottom half of Mickey from the pillow.

"She's like seven years older than you. Big deal. What's your problem with her?"

"Which makes her like, eleven years older than you. I don't have a problem; I just didn't know you liked hanging out with senior citizens."

There's my grouchy girlfriend. I knew she'd be back soon.

"I'm sorry," Dawn says, collecting herself, "I'm just having a rough time with you being sick, and my dad is getting worse. Go ahead, invite Fran. Oh, and when you call her, tell her to pick up the video. My friends will bring over the booze."

Elmer Fudd keeps looking at me, like he wants to tell me

something. I zoom in on his bald little head and disproportionately large rifle. I mouth, *What is it? What are you
trying to tell me, Mr. Fudd?*
Elmer springs to life. "You wook miswable. I should know,
I'm going thwough chemothewapy too. You know what
you need, Tania? You need a wife. That way you can bwow
youw way out of youw sad cartoon cells too."

control (left breast—2002)

Everyone in my life knows what I should do. Doctors
insist I take off my clothes, nurses demand I get on a
scale, radiologists suggest I put on a vest, and Sal urges
me, daily, to get back together with her. I think Janet
Jackson stated it best when she said, "I wanna be the
one—in control!"
The first time I was diagnosed with cancer I found that
the most effective and efficient way to maintain some
semblance of control was to drink as much alcohol as I
could stomach, eat as much nonfat ice cream as we had
in the fridge, and work out to the point of fatigue.
That's right, I was gonna show my five-foot-three-and-a-
half, 128-pound body that I had control over it by
engaging in a low level of abuse. But now, at thirty,
instead of looking for guidance in the bottom of a mar-
tini glass, I'm inspired by the words and practices of
spiritual leaders like Thich Nhat Hanh and the Dalai
Lama. This time around being in control means giving
up control. Maybe by giving up my addictions, which
only provide me with a false sense of control, I can truly
be open and present and aware of what my body needs.
But the problem is, I don't have a whole lot of addic-

tions, and the ones I have have taken me years to cultivate. That's why they're so dear to me. I write down a list of my addictions:

1. **SNIFFING:** smelling various parts of my body, my undergarments, and other scented things. *Age seven–present*

2. **THE USE OF OBSCENITIES:** fuck, shit, dick, and others. *Age nine–present*

3. **SUGAR/FAT:** cake, ice cream, cookies, etc. *Age six–present*

4. **COFFEE:** drinking, smelling, and loving. *Age nineteen–present*

5. **DOPE-SMOKING:** self-explanatory. *Age nineteen–present; approximately once every two months*

6. **SEX:** having it recreationally. *Age twenty-one–present*

In my quest for balance, it's time to relinquish my addictions. But first I must ask myself the obvious question: "What is it that really makes up an addiction?" I mean, an addiction, by itself, is nothing. It's the ritual and subsequent stories around an addiction that make it more or less important to keep as part of one's repertoire. That's why giving up dope-smoking will be easy for me. Sure, dope has provided me with lots of laughing-to-the-point-of-urinating-and-eating-too-many-soft-tacos-and-waking-up-next-to-somebody-else's-lover stories, but the ritual surrounding dope-smoking has always eluded me. Buying dope from dealers? Come on, who has time to pretend to be friends with a group of people who perpetually say, "Dude, close the blinds!" Then there's the paraphernalia involved in dope-smoking, which I've always found to be both silly and functional. I'm ashamed to report that I've wrapped my lips around so many swirly fimo penises that my lesbian membership card has almost been revoked. But I will gladly give up puffing on a hollowed-out apple for healthier cells. Buh-bye blunts, hello health!

Coffee. Oh, how I love coffee. My addiction to coffee is a bit more ingrained than the dope addiction. Not only is there a tremendous amount of ritual surrounding my coffee-drinking, but the stories…the stories aren't informed *by* the addiction but exist *because* of the addiction. The only way I've been able to write plays, essays, rants, etc., for the last ten years is with the help of *coffee*, and her trusty pal *caffeine*, and their sidekick *coffeehouse*. The four of us have spent long hours writing, laughing, and loving each other. But if giving up coffee prevents me from getting cancer again then I, Tania Cancer-Ridden Katan, relinquish caffeine forever. Goodbye to the sweet steam of inspiration twirling around my nimble writer fingers, allowing them to gently brush the pages of my journal with strokes of genius. So long, clarity and potential literary greatness. Au revoir, cute barista girl, who always knows how to fill up my cup. Adieu to you and you and you.

No more sugar, fat, or meat. No carbohydrates, because carbs convert into sugar and sugar feeds cancer cells. No fruits, because fructose acts like sugar and sugar feeds cancer cells. No meat, because animals are shot up with hormones and hormones cause cancer. No meat, because animals have fat and the American Cancer Society recommends a low-fat diet. No genetically modified foods, because, well, who knows why? No preservatives, no additives, no wonder I'm hungry! What's left? Air? That's it, I'll become a Breatharian. A few years ago, while my hairy now-vegan brother and I devoured a pile of greasy chicken nachos at our favorite San Francisco tacqueria, he espoused the virtues of the Breatharians.

"There's this woman, she's ninety-seven years old and has sustained herself for the past fifty years on air alone," Paul told me.

"That's freaky. Can you pass the guacamole?" I said.

"That's not freaky, Tania. That's Breatharian. I'm working up to becoming a Breatharian. Can you pass the chips?"

If I decide to suck all my nutrients in from the air, could I too live another fifty years? Is it possible to close my eyes and pretend to breathe in brie, chocolate cake, and mousaka? If it will save my life, I'll give it a try.

Giving up obscenities, no fucking problem. And I can wait to have sex with someone I love. And as far as sniffing—oops, sorry, I just took a break to smell the posts of my earrings. What was I saying? Oh, yeah, sniffing: I'm totally over it.

There's one slight problem: As soon as you give up your addictions in pursuit of control, that's when your addictions take control over you. You shift from wanting things that are bad for you *sometimes* to wanting things that are bad for you *all of the time.* You want them now, you want them fast, and you want as much of them as you can get. I don't want *a* brownie; I want a whole fucking tray of brownies! I want to drink a triple espresso while alternately eating osso bucco and marzipan. I want to hump like a dog in heat. I want to hump a random passerby, a blanket, a telephone pole, anything, everything.

Why is it that the minute you give up sex, your most recent sexual partner phones you? OK, based on the fact that Sal calls every day, three times a day, asking me to get back together with her, the chances of her calling right after I've had an epiphany are pretty good.

"Let's get back together, Tania. I can take care of you. When I told my boss that my girlfriend has cancer he said I could take time off of work," Sal says in a desperate voice.

"Sal, we're not together anymore, and I'm in the middle of dealing with a major illness. I need all of my energy and focus to go into my health and healing. I can't be in a relationship right now. Can you respect that?"

Sal's fury flies through the phone line: "It's always about *you*, Tania. Sometimes you can be so selfish. Did it ever occur to you that I might be dealing with a lot too? I mean, you just broke up with me, I'm battling depression, I've got no one to talk to—"

"Have you thought about getting some help?" I ask sincerely.

"Like a psychiatrist?"

"Yeah, or psychologist, just someone."

"No. I don't need a shrink, I need a girlfriend who isn't going to leave when things get rough."

"OK, I have to go now. I'm getting my stuff in order for surgery."

"I'm sorry, Tania. I just need to see you for a second. I need a hug," she says.

I got needs too, Sal, and if I come over to your place to give you a hug, well, that will lead to kissing, and kissing always leads to groping, and groping inevitably leads to sex.

"I need a hug too, Sal. I'll be over in ten minutes."

pre-op photo op
(left breast—2002)

Sex feels so good when you think you're never going to have it again. I ended up in Sal's bed because I needed pre-mastectomy sex to assure myself of my desirability. I needed to be held, I needed to come, I needed to cry, I needed to be lost in the anonymity of naked bodies and sweat. But I needed to stop Sal from calling me three times a day. I needed to lay down the law! So right after we had sex, I decided it was time to DTR: define the relationship.

"Look, Sal," I tell her. "I just want to make sure we're on the same page—I do not want a relationship with you. I want to have convenient sex with you, maybe grab a latte now and then, and that's all. What is it that you want?"

"Ah, yeah, me too," Sal says, barely believing it herself.

I should have known better. I should have pulled myself out of my postorgasmic stupor and gotten the hell out of Sal's bed. But I didn't. Instead, once again, I allowed my vagina to lead the way. And here we are now, in San Francisco, having a miserable time. My vagina, Sal, and me. It's our final day in San Francisco; tomorrow I'll be in the hospital having my only breast removed. I should be having the time of my life—considering I just signed a waiver stating that the anesthetic used in surgery could kill me. But instead Sal and I are in Good Vibrations fighting over which double-sided dildo we should purchase. I don't want to be here with Sal. I don't want to be anywhere with Sal. I don't want to be on the other side of anything attached to Sal.

Before we embarked on our six-hour drive up the coast to San Francisco, I told Sal that this road trip was a send-off to my booby. A farewell tour, a parting glance, a season finale. I needed to see my good friends in San Francisco, drink my last cup of Peet's coffee, and take photos of my booby to pictorially preserve the essence of my breast. Sal said, "Can I come with you? I can drive. You can use my new camera. It'll be fun." Now, one might think that going on vacation with my possessive ex-girlfriend to see good friends before major surgery isn't the best way to get centered, but the promise of hot sex, a chauffeur, and a Nikon camera was enough to compel me to agree to her proposal. Plus, Sal was being very kind and supportive of my pre-op/photo-op vacation. She even offered to act as photojournalist. She was actually sweet about the whole thing, until we arrived in San Francisco.

Yesterday, with the Golden Gate Bridge in the background and a scrim of fog in the foreground, Sal and I pushed our way through all the gym boys and butch girls who lined Market Street to find the Boys sitting in Peet's Coffee. The Boys are, primarily, Mikey and Paul, who have been together five years, but the title also refers to the extended group of fantastic gay men, and the few girls who think like gay men, who occupy the long brown lacquered bench at Peet's Coffee in the Castro between the hours of 7 and 9:30 A.M.

As usual, Mikey, Paul, Rod, Bruce, Scott, Melissa, and the rest of the gang were sitting, squished up next to each other, talking, rubbing each other's legs, hands, shoulders. None of this touching is done as a way to get into each other's pants; this is just what we did at Peet's, we adored each other and snuggled. And whenever someone with an ass walked by, all conversations that might have been taking place prior to the ass coming into Peet's would cease abruptly, and all eyes would land on the ass.

Mikey was the first to notice Sal and me.

"Little bunny!" Mikey called out ("little bunny" was our term of endearment for each other).

"Hey, little bunny!" Paul stands up and walks toward me. He's a big guy, six feet tall and very muscular, big, like Paul Bunyan big, and he has a propensity for lifting little people—me—off the ground until they squeal "Please put me down."

"Please put me down, big bunny!" I squealed from the ceiling of Peet's.

Paul laughed and put me down safely on the ground.

"So, is this the fabulous Sal?" Mikey asked, looking at Sal. I guess the last time Mikey and I spoke, Sal and I were on an upswing.

"Yep. Sal, this is Mikey and Paul," I said, introducing two very different parts of my life.

Sal shook both of their hands politely while maintaining her physical distance.

In a matter of seconds I was sitting on Paul's huge thigh, as if riding a horse sidesaddle, while he massaged my shoulders—I love having a friend who's a massage therapist. It didn't take long to settle into the human soup of love and limbs and lattes. Sal continued to stand and look distracted.

"Tania, tell me what you think of when you think of Florida," Mikey said as he took my hand into his strong but oddly soft hand.

"Jews," I said.

"That's right. And do you know why so many Jews live near bodies of water?" he asked me, not waiting for a response.

"Jews live near bodies of water in case we need to flee in the middle of the night. That's right, you never know when little Tania and little Mikey will be persecuted again and have to get on the ferry and head toward the false sanctuary of Angel Island. Jews aren't stupid; we're just tired. We don't want to wander around the desert for hundreds of years; we're a civilized people. We'll flee in the middle of the night, in a boat with a well-stocked bar."

Within our group Mikey is known for many things, one of which is the existential Jewish rant. Another definitive Mikey characteristic is his choice of fashion. Maybe it's because he's a graphic designer and has been invited to one too many press checks, but he's always wearing something from the gray scale. Yesterday was no exception. Mikey was sporting his baggy light gray cargo pants with a wool charcoal-gray V-neck sweater, and in the middle of the V you could see a black T-shirt. And of course he always has on his sufficiently worn black boots. Oh, and another Mikey trait: his skin, which is unnaturally soft, and whenever you tell Mikey how soft it is, which people do all the time, his stock line is, "You know what the secret is: I never use lotion, I don't drink water, I drink tons of alcohol, and I do as many drugs as I can. Seriously."

Sal continued to stand until Paul said, "Sally, you can sit down. Tania and I are going to get some tea."

The minute Paul said "Sally," and Sal heard his false earnestness, I knew the two were not going to be friends, or even friendly for that matter.

In line to refill his small white porcelain teapot with hot water, Paul said to me, "What's with Sally? She's not one of us. She's so…uptight."

"I know. We're not really together. We're just having casual sex before my surgery," I told him, feeling the need to justify being with someone not warm and comfortable.

"She's not good for you, little bunny. Even for casual sex, bunny. Plus, her face looks like it's perpetually in pain. The Goddess is telling me you need someone who smiles, not someone in pain," Paul says, as if a celestial energy has surged through his blue sweatshirt and touched his large, open heart.

Even though Paul is completely sincere when he refers to "The Goddess," I can't help giggling in his direction. I mean, if he were in a group of the toughest straight men in the world, he would be the butchest. His salt-and-pepper hair is buzzed to about a half an inch from his scalp, leading you to believe that he was, or is, in the military. Firmly implanted in his right eyebrow is a silver hoop, letting you know he's not in the military but you probably shouldn't mess with him anyway. The definition in his muscles can only be the result of many Myoplex shakes ingested before and after three-hour gym workouts. All of this is packaged in whatever blue jeans seem to be hanging around his room, the muted blue or green sweatshirt du jour, and a level of masculinity usually reserved for prisons and sperm banks. Half spiritual guru and half silly trickster, Paul is as insouciant and magnanimous as he is beguiling and deceptive. It's just a question of which side he filters you in through.

"May I please have some water for my tea?" Paul asked the disgruntled boy standing behind the counter while softly extending the teapot. "Tania, Sal's got really heavy energy. You have a lot to deal with without that heavy energy, you know what I'm saying, little bunny?"

I did know what he was saying. And when we returned to the three tables we had overtaken, Sal was chatting with this guy. Out of the fifteen or so friends of mine sitting next to her on the bench, Sal had found the one person nobody knew and chatted with him at length.

Anytime someone tried to engage her in conversation, she made sure to answer in a way that stopped all possibilities of connecting.

"So what do you do for a living, Sal?" Paul asked.

"I'm in computers," she answered.

"Oh, I'm into computers too. What do you do with them?" Paul asked.

"It would take too long to explain. Is there a bathroom here?"

Mikey pointed to the bathroom and Sal left.

"So, are your doctors hot?" Paul asked me.

"Paul!" Mikey playfully hit Paul's knee. "We don't care if they're hot, we care if they're good doctors. Are they good? Jewish? OK, are they hot?"

When Sal came back from the bathroom she started to complain, in my ear, about feeling uncomfortable and wanting to leave. I too was feeling uncomfortable and wanted her to leave; it felt like the first time in a long time that we were on the same page.

Good Vibrations should be just that: good vibrations. Yet, in the fifteen minutes we've been here, Sal and I can't stop arguing. The arguing began with Sal's interest in the army-fatigue dildo and my expressing that I didn't want to get fucked by the government any more than I have to. Then Sal stated, "It's always about you! What about me, Tania? You don't give a shit about me!" And I explained that if I didn't give a shit about her, I wouldn't be spending $120 on a sex toy. The argument has now come to a head—so to speak.
"Let's go!" Sal commands.
I carefully return a cobalt-blue dildo to her respective stand, glad she will go home with two people who are not Sal and me. Outside of Good Vibrations I notice the tires on Sal's SUV are not curbed. When we arrived in San Francisco I told Sal to curb her tires whenever there was an incline, no matter how slight. She nodded a dismissive yes but apparently didn't do it. I can't tell you how many tickets I've been issued by the City of San Francisco for not curbing my tires (because I threw them all out). The idea of curbing my tires, of swerving them into cement, always felt weird and wrong until one day I got it; I remembered that question on the driver's license test:

While driving on an icy road, your car starts to skid. What do you do?
a. Turn in the opposite direction of the skid.
b. Press firmly on the brakes.
c. Turn into the direction of the skid.

I would sit in my cubicle at the DMV using my imagination to construct the skid scenario. I'm in Iceland cruising around with Björk. She hits a high note. I'm so moved that I turn to applaud, and all of a sudden my car starts to skid out of control. Car parts, bottles, and cutlery stream out of the window in slow motion. There's a polar bear about fifty feet in front of the car. I want to slam on the brakes. I want to turn away from the potential horror of hitting a polar bear. *Turn into the skid?* How can I? It feels counter to every nerve in my body.

Sal grabs the ticket off her SUV, jumps into the driver's seat, unlocks my door, and starts the engine.

"So, what do you want to do now?" I ask her.

"I don't care," she says, and means it.

"OK, why don't we go to the hotel and relax before the party tonight?"

"Fuck. I forgot about the party. You know what, I don't know if I'm gonna go."

"Fine," I say.

"Your friends kind of irritate me."

"Do you need some alone time?"

"No, forget it." She disengages.

"It's our last night here. What can I do to help you feel more comfortable?" I engage too much.

"I want you to focus on me. I want us to be in a relationship. I'm totally depressed most of the time. You don't even know what's going on in my mind. You pay more attention to your friends than to me."

"Sal, the deal was that we were going to hang out and enjoy each other's company. We are clearly not enjoying each other's company. I don't want to fight with you. If you're not having a good time, then go home. I'll catch a plane tomorrow." Wow, that felt really good to say. Even my vagina feels good about it. Is it possible I'm allowing my tires to turn into the skid?

At the hotel room, Sal lies down on the bed, fully clothed, right hand cradling her head, left hand holding up the *What's Hot in San Francisco* hotel magazine, while I prepare for the shoot.

The photo session begins like many: I toss my shirt aside with all the abandon of a *Sports Illustrated* swimsuit model wanting to make the cover. I powder my nipple. I aim the camera. I am the photographer, the subject, and the stylist. Work it, work it, own it, own it, that's it, that's the look! *Snap.* Beautiful. Now hold still; look up, nice, nice… *Snap..* One more, pretend you're in Iceland, *brr,* that's good, the nipple looks great! *Snap, snap, snap!* Thirty-two exposures of Her Pinkness. In another two days my booby will be gone but not forgotten, immortalized in crisp color thanks to Sal's fancy camera. I thank Sal for allowing me to use her camera. She says "You're welcome," and apologizes for her behavior leading up to today's fallout. She decides she will go to the party tonight after all, and, per my request, she will be on her best behavior.

A Blaine and Jonathon Party. A way of life, a life of luxury, a luxurious introduction to how people *really* party. Blaine and Jonathon's innovative party themes have made them the toast of the Castro. I mean, who can forget "Karen Carpenter Cocktail Hour," where Blaine served celery in buckets while Jonathon talked about being "too full" in

between frequent trips to the bathroom. Not to be confused with the famed "Bend Over, It's Passover" party,
which involved strategically placed yarmulkes and matzo
balls. Tonight it's "Thanksgiving/Thanksgetting: a
Celebration of Tops and Bottoms."

Sal and I approach the apartment, and before we have a
chance to knock the door opens. Sal gasps. Blaine is standing in the doorway wearing blood-red lipstick around his
lascivious grin, to match his blood-red sequined jockstrap
and his blood-red leather cowboy boots. Jonathon stands
next to him wearing an ecru cable-knit crewneck sweater
and a black leather codpiece. When Jonathon turns around
to let us in he reveals a dildo rigged up to his ass, present-
ing a tableau of perpetual penetration. He looks like a rep-
resentative from J.Crew's S/M division.

Although this party isn't in my honor, everyone here is
aware of my impending surgery. All the cute queers I
brush past, even ones I've never met before, offer me
drinks and advice: "Tania, remember, when you're done
with surgery, they give you Vicodin…for free." The Boys
are here in full force. "Hey, little bunny! Over here!" Paul
yells from across the apartment. Mikey is with him, waving for me to come over. I ask Sal if she wants to come
with me; she sulks into the scenery and says, "No. I'll
stay here."

Paul and Mikey lead me to Blaine's room, where Paul reaches
into his coat pocket and pulls out a brownie wrapped in
clear plastic. There's a round sticker on the brownie that
shows a purple marijuana leaf swaying in the San Francisco
breeze. Underneath the leaf it says MEDICINAL.

"I got this for you, little bunny," Paul says, unwrapping

the brown nugget, "because inhaling smoke is not good for you, but that doesn't mean you can't get high."

Paul breaks off a tiny piece and hands it to me, then gives one to Mikey, and soon there are six, eight, ten of us strewn across Blaine's California king–size bed, all with tiny brown crumbs around our mouths. I am *sooooo* relaxed. This *is* medicinal. We are a pastiche of relaxed bodies in an opium den, transported into an urban dwelling.

Paul looks up, barely coherent, and notices the antique painting of Blaine's great-great-great white grandmother's stern face looking down at us. Paul addresses Blaine's grandmother, "Hey, Grandma Whitey, you wanna piece of this?" He grabs his extremely large cock—that's for Paul's benefit—and earnestly offers it up to Grandma Whitey. The entire bed of bodies erupts in laughter. I'm not sure who, but someone is massaging my legs and arms; maybe two people? It's so calming to be high and massaged simultaneously. *Surgery will be all right, right? Right.*

I can see a tight, white cloud floating overhead. "I'll have a hit," I say as my arm slowly reaches for the joint. I'm giggling even before inhale. I slowly breathe in, and, and, and I release the stream of smoke into the face of a pinched and angry person.

"Tania, I need to talk with you right now." Sal is hovering above me.

"Sal? Hey, man, where have you been? Come lie down with us," I say.

"No. I need to know what we're doing."

"Well…I'm getting totally high, you know, like floating-over-a-rainbow high, like catching-a-ride-on-the-back-of-a-unicorn high, like—"

"Are we dating or not? Your friends keep asking if we're dating, and I don't know what to tell them. Do I have any importance in your life? Do you even care about me? You like your friends more than you like me, don't you? Can we leave?" She hands me my jacket. What a buzz kill, man.

"I'm not ready to leave. I'll meet you at the hotel," I say, making no effort to move.

"You're not coming with me?"

"I'm enjoying my freedom. Tonight it's not about you, Sal."

Hurricane Sal blows out of the party.

A six-hour car ride with an ex-lover who's angry and silent can feel much like having your entire body tattooed in one sitting. As we drive down Highway 1, I stare out the window, soaking in the blue coast and making silent pacts with myself like, *If I make it through surgery tomorrow, I will tell Sal that I want her out of my life once and for all. I'd rather have no sex than sex with a toxic woman.*
After what seems like days, we arrive at my father's apartment. I practically jump out of Sal's SUV.

"So…thanks. I guess I won't be seeing you again for a while, you know, surgery and all…" I say, quickly gathering my things. Sal stays seated in the driver's seat, her Droopy Dog face reinforcing my mental pact, which I will enact now. "And because we're broken up, you know, maybe it would be a good idea if we didn't have contact for a while, OK?"

Sal nods. I'm not sure if it's a yes or no nod. I'm almost to the front door when I remember the most important part of this trip. "Hey, can I have the film of my booby and me?" I ask.

"Umm, you know what, I'll get it developed for you," Sal says.

"That's nice of you to offer, but I can take care of it. You shouldn't have to pay for it."

"It would be my pleasure. It's my breaking-up gift to you."

"All right, thank you." I'm too tired to argue, and I know this is the end of the line for Sal and me. The skid has come to a stop. I rode it out, I turned into it, and now I'm sitting in a pile of snow with Björk on my left and the polar bear on my right. All three of us are safe and laughing.

strangers in good company?
(right breast—1992)

Picture a squishy flesh-tone mound with a permanently erect nipple. This is my new booby. I picked her up the other day from the Booby Lady. The Booby Lady is a small round woman with an easy demeanor who uses a tape measure to graph the coordinates of your body. She says things like, "I've never seen anyone your age with breast cancer before," and "You've got a great breast, young lady. Me, I could put a pencil underneath mine and it wouldn't drop!" After she determined my breast size, she offered me two colors of breast to choose from: light peachy taupe or dark peachy taupe. "But what if I were a black woman?" I inquired, always pushing the envelope. The Booby Lady was a bit startled and said, "Well, you're not." Then I was issued two mastectomy bras, which are these huge cloth contraptions, much like blinkers for horses. What distinguishes a mastectomy bra from a regular bra are pouches sewn into the cups. If I slip the heavy peach mound into the sheer white pouch, it gives the appearance of a "real" booby in my bra. Prior to picking up my breast I found that clothes fit me differently. The once easy task of putting on a shirt has recently become an exploration in the study of balance. Every shirt I casually throw on, forgetting that my physique has been altered, sags down my right side, leaving me slightly askew. The fabric drips on my chest like a clock in a Dali painting. Nothing feels quite right draped on me.

All of Dawn's finest cartoon-character figurines are displayed in various tableaus throughout the apartment. Dopey and Sneezy are sitting next to each other, perhaps chatting about Brecht's theory of alienation; Bugs Bunny aims his enormous carrot dangerously close to the Tasmanian Devil's bottom; and Foghorn Leghorn, Pepé Le Pew, Yosemite Sam, and Sylvester surround Porky Pig in what appears to be a potential gang-rape situation. The stage is set for movie night, the last hurrah before I go back to school and start to exhibit some side effects of chemotherapy.

A few months ago my biggest fear about having people over was Dawn's decor, and now I'm worried about my fake booby sneaking out from its pouch and flopping onto the floor in front of an unsuspecting guest. Or what if I lose my first clump of hair tonight in the communal popcorn bowl? And what if Fran brings a movie with a main character who's dying of cancer? A few months ago I didn't worry so much, but now I worry a lot. It's amazing how quickly concerns can transform when you have cancer and a vital body part is discarded in the name of health. I decide to wear a really baggy sweatshirt and no prosthetic tonight.

Fran is the first to arrive. She is sparkly and happy and not Dawn. "Hey!" she says as she looks around for a place to set down a grocery bag. Dawn acts like she's busy, like she doesn't notice Fran is here.

"Dawn, look who's here, Fran," I say.

"Oh, hey, Fran," Dawn says as if she's in deep thought.

"Hey, Dawn. How are you doing?" Fran says, as she sets her bag on the kitchen counter.

Dawn acts like Fran has asked her a rhetorical question—if Dawn knew what *rhetorical* meant.

"What movie did you bring?" Dawn asks.

"*Strangers in Good Company*. Have you heard of it?" Fran asks her.

"No. Who's in it?"

"No one, really, no one I've ever heard of. It's sort of a docudrama. A good friend of mine recommended it, so..."

"Docudrama, that sounds stupid," Dawn mumbles audibly.

"So, what's in the bag, Fran?" I'm trying to shift the focus from Dawn's blatant rudeness.

"Red Vines, of course, because we all know Twizzlers are waxy and weird."

"I know, I hate Twizzlers."

"And I have my favorite drink of all time, Fresca—refreshing, citrus, and no calories."

"Oh, my God, Fran, I thought I was the only person in the nineties who knew about Fresca. I love Fresca! Did you bring cans or a bottle?"

"As if there is any other option." She pulls out a six-pack of cans.

"I love you, Fran!"

Why is it that bitter, jealous girlfriends always hear things out of context? After my innocent confession of love for Fran's choice in soft drinks, Dawn decides to hang out with Fran and me, not interacting, merely making her presence known.

The buzzer is pushed with such force and repetition that I'm sure if I open the door there will be a gang of angry trick-or-treaters demanding full-size candy bars.

"COMING!" Dawn screams with glee as she dashes toward the door. As she pulls the door open, the angry trick-or-treaters fall forward, in a cluster, into our apartment, and onto the floor. The three of them sit in a pile giggling, reeking of cigarettes.

"Hey!" Dawn seems to be just as excited about these three women being in our apartment as I am about Fran being here.

The three lesbian stooges stand up and start poking around the place. There are no salutations. "Um, hello," I say, addressing our new guests, playing the role of the happy wife. They say nothing, as if they've never heard the word "hello" before this moment. Instead they are transfixed on Dawn and her new pewter Tasmanian Devil. Fran and I each crack open a Fresca and make our way to the living room.

"Yo," says the tough boyish girl with short, spiky, hard bleach-blond hair. Her yellowish-white skin is peppered with blotches or bruises or something that she tries to cover up with base, or maybe it's not base but just more sick skin. She doesn't look well.

"Um, hi, uh, nice place," says the mousy girl with long, stringy, taupe hair and low self-esteem who's sitting notably close to Dawn and making very little eye contact with me.

"Uh, yeah, nice place," says the nondescript, lumpy, pasty lesbian.

And there they are, Dawn's new friends. Dawn's wearing her best embroidered Warner Bros. baseball cap backward, the one where all of the animated characters are half inside the WB and half hanging outside, waving to their fans. I don't like that hat.

Dawn and her new friends are more comfortable splayed on the floor in front of the television than sitting on the huge comfortable couch with Fran and me. This makes me very happy. When Fran offers them a Fresca, all of them, including my girlfriend, laugh and punch each other on the shoulder while repeating the question "Want some Fresca?" like Fran had offered them a rectal exam. Instead, they have their own stash. The tough girl with hard hair reaches into the front pocket of her army jacket and pulls out a bottle of Jack Daniels—I'd say a fifth, but I'm not really sure how much that is. Mousy girl reaches into her dingy black purse and retrieves a small bottle of Coke. It's a furious train of swigging from the Jack, passing it on, grabbing the Coke, swigging the Coke, passing it on, grabbing the Jack, swigging the Jack, passing it on, grabbing it, swigging it, passing it on, grabbing, swigging, passing, grabbing, swigging, passing—*choo choo!* Fran and I are two worlds away from the lesbian bar that's found its way into my living room. In between swigging and giggling, Dawn pops in the videotape. When tough girl asks what movie we're going to watch, I cringe, guessing that if the subject matter isn't sex, drugs, or murder, she'll be unhappy. She seems to be a bit drunk, and a drunk, unhappy, hard-haired lesbian with bad skin is not someone I want to piss off. "I don't know. Fran brought it," Dawn says, absolving herself of any responsibility.

The camera pans around a lush countryside. Lining the desolate dirt path are multicolored flowers that sway calmly from side to side, depending on which way the wind is blowing. A close up shows a bright yellow school bus happily bouncing down a beautiful flower-lined dirt road.

"What the fuck, dude? This is like the most boring shit I've ever seen," says the hard-haired one. "What the fuck is it called? *Boring School Bus Piece of Shit?*"

Dawn and the rest of the girls on the floor giggle and hit each other.

"*Strangers in Good Company,* that's what it's called," Fran says, focusing on the TV screen.

"I like it," says the lumpy nondescript one. And then, after two seconds of her friends looking at her in total shock, she says, "If it was fucking over!"

The yellow school bus is driven by a large, young—compared to her passengers—black woman with a cheery disposition, who sings as her unlikely cast of passengers, women in their eighties and nineties, sit quietly anticipating their destination. The bus hits something—a rock, a bump, a bad angle—and bounces off the road and into the most beautiful green meadow one can imagine. With no chance of repairing the bus, the women file off and begin to explore their surroundings. A vacant cabin with a wrap-around porch, a calm pond, and the natural beauty of their new environment prove to be enough to inspire these women to speak to each other, and themselves, about the memories that make up a lifetime. Each woman's confession feels unscripted, maybe prompted by a director saying, "What was it like being a little girl in Europe during WWII?" or "What hardships have you faced as a woman?" leaving the viewer to savor the candid answers and intimate lives of these remarkable women. This is what filmmaking is all about. At some point, when I find myself silently crying, I look over at Fran to see if she's crying too. She is, but we're both keeping it under wraps.

"Dude, did you see that old lady cry and then get a snot bubble at the end of her nose?" Dawn says.

"What about the one who's, like, half dead?" the hard-haired one says.

"Which one?!" Dawn laughs in her harsh cough-laugh way. And soon there's a fierce collective roar of laughter from the floor. I don't even know who's saying what. I mean, if there's a group of assholes, does it really matter who's the biggest? I want to save them from themselves by ripping out their vocal chords so no one will ever know how stupid they are. That's like doing a mitzvah, right? I just want them to go home so Fran and I can fall in love…with this film. Look at Fran, crying, cuddling up on the couch, inches away from me. That's what I want—I want a girlfriend who cries when watching films about tender elderly women. Yeah, I want to be with someone who's adult enough to keep a job but fun enough to indulge in Fresca, someone who loves playing tennis and is bright and who's demeanor is happy and…

"Hey, Tania, we're gonna bail, go to the bar before we miss two-for-ones. Is that cool?" Dawn asks in all seriousness.

And in all seriousness, that is so cool!

"Sure," I say.

"I mean, I know you can't drink, cuz of the chemo and all. Otherwise I'd invite you, you know." Dawn is not looking at me. Dawn tends to avoid eye contact when she's concealing information. And tonight, that's just fine. I'm concealing information too: I like Fran, and I want Dawn to leave so I can spend time with Fran.

"Go. Have fun. Drink a Dirty Dog for me!" I say, waving cheerfully at the ragged bunch as they make their way out of the apartment.

Finally I am alone with Fran.

"Did you love the film or what?!" I ask, eager to connect with her.

"It was the most beautiful and moving film I've ever seen," she says, wiping the tears from her eyes, pulling the Mickey Mouse blanket up under her cute freckled chin.

"Me too," I say, pulling the other end of the Mickey Mouse blanket up and under my chin.

"The only thing that could have made it better is if Dawn and her friends had decided to go to the bar at the beginning of the film," she says. "I'm sorry, did I say that out loud?"

"You did."

"Look, Tania, I have nothing against Dawn or her friends. It's just that…"

"Hey, I wouldn't hang out with them if I wasn't dating their leader."

"No, it's just that, well, I really like you, and I know you're going through a rough time right now, and I just want to make sure you're OK, that your surroundings are helpful to your healing process."

"Oh, right, the cancer," I say. "I'm actually doing really well. I'm fine. I start school soon and I'm doing well. Thanks for your concern, though." At the end of my sentence I look at Fran too long to look at someone who I'm not splitting the rent with, but the thing is, she looks at me too.

"Well, I'd better get going," she says, standing up. "Thank you for watching my new favorite film with me."

"My new favorite film too," I say, but I really want to scream, "Don't go! Can't we curl up on the couch and snuggle?" Instead I thank her for the Fresca and Red Vines.

"No problem. And, um, maybe next week, if you're feeling up to it, we could hang out," she says.

"That would be super cool."

Super cool? Sometimes I'm so twenty-one.

Fran leaves. I snuggle up on the couch, wrap the blanket around my body, press my nose into the part of the blanket that was tucked under Fran's chin, and breathe in.

Strangers in Good Company got me thinking: How can I be living with a woman who hates that film? Who would opt for two-for-ones over warm stories? Whose most intimate relationships are with cartoon characters? After our movie night, Fran and I call each other more frequently, talking on the phone for two, three, sometimes four hours at a time. We've been meeting for coffee too, playing tennis, hiking, developing a friendship. In the midst of my starting school and going through chemotherapy, Fran's friendship has given me a tremendous amount of energy. While the cells inside me are dying by the hundreds, I spring to answer the phone when it rings. I run crosscourt and whack the ball down the line as Fran stands on the other side pleasantly astonished. In my playwriting class I actually listen to what my professor is saying *and* read the materials she assigns. Fran feels like a primary relationship to me. And if my primary relationship feels more like a secondary relationship—well, no, actually Alexander would be secondary, which would leave Dawn in the tertiary position, which all adds up to my reevaluating the hierarchy of my relationships. Am I growing up? Is that what's going on? Is this realization part of the elusive maturation process that everyone over thirty keeps talking about? The realization that having a cute partner does not equal being intellectually and emotionally fulfilled and does not, in fact, make *you* look cuter? So why haven't I broken up with Dawn? Am I codependent? Probably. But more than that, it's just not the right time. When is the right time, Tania? The first problem is, I know how Dawn will react when I break up with her. She'll be angry, like, throwing chairs and plates and snarling angry. The second vote for bad timing is the fact that her father is dying of cancer, and then there's the reality that I'm starting to lose my hair.

Until it starts to manifest itself physically, cancer is just a word, a title, a vague concept. It's something we don't say for fear of getting it, or we whisper it because someone in our family is dying of it. But cancer has a sneaky way of demanding to be heard. I thought I was OK with the whole cancer thing until a couple of weeks ago when I ran my fingers through my hair and there was hair in my hand. Pretty soon I didn't need to run my fingers through my hair—the clumps just fell out, in the shower, under the blow dryer. Friends and family members tried to console me by saying, "It's not that bad," and "It's only temporary," and "It's not like you're losing your life, just your hair." But this cotton-candy mound on top of my head is a constant reminder that I have cancer. So I've taken to combing my hair forward now, like a sixth-grade science teacher, and I'm spontaneously crying en route to classes, and then there's the issue of the mouth sores, which are like the worst canker sores you've ever had, times two. One must see why breaking up with Dawn has taken a backseat.

surgery
(left breast—2002)

It's 5:30 A.M. In one hour and forty-five minutes I'll be checking into Long Beach Memorial Hospital. My mother, father, and sister will be my support team in the hospital. Paul is at another gathering for rainbows, learning how to make a Mercedes run on vegetable oil. Even if he didn't have to gather with the rainbows, he wouldn't have come anyway; Paul believes one should *will* cancer away rather than cut it out. Hey, I believe in positive energy, positive visualization, positive thinking, but I also believe in chemotherapy and statistics. It's a combo deal. I'll meditate *while* I'm going through chemotherapy; I'll visualize my healthy cells gently escorting the cancer cells to a nearby recycling bin. My choice is, and has always been, both methods of healing. I find it fascinating how people who have never had cancer always know how to deal with it. I'm writing in my journal now, hoping the act of writing will somehow carry me through the jitters and anxiety that Megan conveniently forgot to mention during my pre-op intake. Late last night my mom and my sister Kim molested my breast. Kim, being a preschool teacher, is very craft oriented, so it was her idea to make a cast of my breast. Apparently, during our visit with the surgeon, Mom had shifted her thievery from magazines to gauze and loaded up her purse with as much as she could get. Last night Mom and Kim dipped pieces of gauze into warm water then smoothed the dripping white squares onto my breast. As they built up the solid nest of white cement, Dad walked around uncomfortably in the background of our newly remodeled one-bedroom dormitory.

"Shit," Kim said, while fondling my nipple. "We're gonna run out of gauze!"

As I stood half naked, one breast under wraps and the other on sabbatical, Mom had an idea. "Why don't we go over to the neighbors and ask to borrow a cup of gauze?" Although this was a creative, and hysterically funny, solution, we opted to stay at home and wait for the plaster of paris to dry. And dry it did. The protective shell started to heat up and harden, pushing my breast through a condensed menopause: waves of heat, then cold, then heat, then cold, then hot, hot, and hard. Mom and Kim stood on either side of my booby, and when they gently pulled on the cast nothing happened.

My mother looked concerned. "Tania, do you remember us putting Vaseline on your breast before we started?"

"Um, no, why?" I asked.

"Well…it's going to be a little uncomfortable when we remove the cast," she said.

Mom and Kim began pulling, ripping, and tearing at my breast. Moist bits of plaster clung to my skin, turning it red and angry, but somehow the pain seemed negligible in the scheme of things. Kim yanked the last piece of plaster, the one that engulfed my areola, and said, "Hey, if we take off your nipple, will the surgeon give us a discount?"

Kim and I slept together, a presurgery slumber party of sorts. We talked until 2:30 A.M. about silly unrelated things, about high school and what we thought happened to the popular kids.

"I think April Smith became a hooker, I'm just saying," Kim said.

"And I think she became a whore," I said.

"What's the difference?"

"Hookers get paid. Whores do it for free."

"Oh, then you're right. I'm sure April's a whore."

I woke up before the alarm, which was slated to go off at 6 A.M. I brushed my teeth, trying not to get a drop of water in my throat, and listened as Mom and Dad quietly scurried around the apartment, talking in hushed tones. I packed my hospital bag with all the necessities: striped Brooks Brothers pajamas; lucky socks, which have roulette tables and dice on them; literary buddies: Anne Lamott, David Sedaris, and Thich Nhat Hanh; and, when I'm finished up with this journal entry, my journal.

When I was twenty-one years old I didn't understand the virtues of being present, of being connected to my surroundings rather than commenting on them. I don't want to write a scene in a play that borders on hyperreality; I want to write my reality as is. This time I'm going to bring my journal with me, documenting everything. I will become a reporter, a documentary filmmaker, the subject, and the object. The only time I'll stop writing is when the surgeon asks me to count backward from ten.

Mom, Dad, Kim, and I are crammed into Megan's little pre-op office as she prepares some more forms for me to sign. None of us are talking. That's how you know when a Jewish family is freaked out: They stop talking and/or eating. Surprisingly enough, I'm calm. The prospect of actually resting in a hospital bed after my horrible attempt at a vacation with Sal is comforting. Plus, I've got a good vibe about this tumor: She measures in at a modest one centimeter—the last one was four centimeters—and I don't feel any swollen lymph nodes under my arms. The silence of our Jewish family becomes too great for Kim, so she transforms into the court jester.

"Hey, Tania, wouldn't if be funny if your surgeon had Tourette's syndrome? Like he'd be cutting you open and screaming, 'Shit, motherfucker, bitch!' Hey, Tania, wouldn't it be cool if surgery was set up like Splash Mountain at Disneyland? So, like, right when you come out of surgery there's this guy dressed in lederhosen with a Polaroid camera waiting to take your picture?"

Megan hands me a piece of paper, which has a pencil drawing of a naked woman on it. *Is this some sort of lesbian litmus test? Like, if I touch the pencil-woman's genitalia and my finger turns it red, then I'm a dyke?*

"This form is very important, Tania. What I need for you to do is draw a large black *X* over the breast that the surgeon will be removing," Megan instructs.

"Doesn't he know which one he'll be removing?" I ask.

"Yes, but we need *you* to express that in writing. We've had a lot of, well, um, misunderstandings," she says.

Misunderstandings like, *When you said it was your left breast that had cancer in it, we misunderstood and cut off the right one?* "Well, Megan, I understand the litigious nature of unhappy patients, but I only have one breast, so the chances of the surgeon removing the correct one are pretty high."

"I understand, but we are required by law to have you mark the breast diagram." Megan becomes more insistent. Instead of drawing an *X* on the left breast of the pencil-lady, I draw a scar on her right breast with an arrow pointing to her left breast and a caption that reads, *Repeat Performance.*

My support system is long gone, waiting, pacing, hoping everything goes all right in surgery. I am in what feels like a meat locker. It's freezing in here. An oversize grade-school clock on the wall is ticking loudly at me, suggesting that my time is almost up. I'm lying on a gurney in some sort of presurgery holding tank. There are two other people here with me, and we're all dressed in the same uniform: powder-blue paper-thin robes with matching puffy paper hats. Lying on top of a gurney across the way is a large black woman in her sixties. She looks nervous but keeps smiling at me, like she's the next contestant on *The Price Is Right* but she has no idea which is more expensive: a can of tuna fish or a box of macaroni and cheese. A lean white man in his fifties lies on a gurney next to the nervous woman, diagonal from my gurney. He looks suspi-

ciously happy, nods at me with confidence, smiles spontaneously. I'm starting to feel anxious. I need my journal.
They wouldn't let me bring my journal with me; they said
it would be safer in my room, waiting for me. Maybe I
could get a piece of paper and a pen from the nurse.

The nurse on duty looks like she just got back from a
Fleetwood Mac concert. Her wild blond hair with black
roots, the smell of faded patchouli, and a coolness only
matched by Stevie Nicks herself makes her a prime candi-
date for interacting with pre-op patients.

The thin guy who keeps smiling calls for the nurse. He
doesn't seem so happy anymore; he seems nervous and
starts talking before she arrives at his side.

"Genetics. I mean, I run three miles a day, every day, tennis two days a week… My mother, my father, my brother
all had heart attacks by age fifty. I'm fifty-one, healthy as a
horse. I'm here for a triple bypass, but I'm not scared. You
do what you've got to do…"

A man with a straight-edge razor enters the room and
approaches the side of the thin guy's gurney. He begins to
lather up the man's long white neck.

"We'll be removing an artery from your neck. That's what
we'll use to rewire your heart," the razor-wielding guy
announces.

Somehow this puts me at ease. I mean, I'm only having
my boob removed, right? No rewiring or shaving required.
I'm gonna be just fine. It's gonna be fine. It's gonna be
more than fine, it's gonna be all right. I'm sure I signed a
form stating that everything will be all right. I am not
going to drop dead on the operating table. They are not
going to botch my surgery and leave me with scar tissue

and damaged nerves. My nerves are already sitting on edge. I need my security blanket.

"Nurse, can I have a pen and piece of paper?" I ask.

The cool nurse with the black roots dances over with a one-inch square pale pink pad of sticky notes and a white pen with bite marks at the bottom. I write vigorously until a man with a tray arrives at my gurney side.

"Hi." He reads my chart and quickly mispronounces my name: "Tan-ya Kay-ton?"

"Sure," I say.

"I'm here to hook up your IV."

"Listen, um, my veins have been poked so many times that they have a tendency to roll and hide, so…please be careful," I say.

"Don't worry. I'm really good at this."

If I had a dime for every time someone in the medical profession said that.

I feel a light prick, and then the left side of my wrist feels numb. This confuses me. Usually when they try to get a vein for an IV it's the most painful prick you'll ever encounter. That actually felt nice.

"Excuse me, but how the fuck did you do that?" I ask.

"I gave you a little bit of novocaine. I know how to take care of anxious young ladies," he says.

OK, tiger. "So, what's on the IV menu today?"

"You ever hear of the date-rape drug?" he asks with a lascivious grin.

"Yeah, why? Are you going to slip me a Roofie?" They'll let anyone administer anesthesia.

"Yep." Dr. Date Rape is starting to freak me out. "You probably won't remember anything from this point on," he says.

His face moves in toward mine, and before I know it we're making out. OK, maybe he just kissed me, or maybe there was no kissing. I'm a little foggy at this point. There's a woman wearing a pink bandanna standing over me now. Does she want to make out too? What kind of creepy hospital is this?

"Tania, I'm going to take you to the OR now," she says as she grabs the corners of my mobile bed and starts pushing me briskly down the hallway. We're now in a room with too many blues moving too fast to make out, and then…black.

"Where are my glasses? Where's my journal? Where's my family? Am I in my room yet? It's cold. Can I have a blanket?" I'm alert, multitasking even. I made it; I'm alive. A disembodied hand gives me my glasses. No one seems to be around, but I've got questions that need to be answered, like, *Where's my family? Do they know I'm out of surgery? Could someone please tell them?*

Finally a nurse shows up. "Hi, Tania. Don't worry, your family knows you're out of surgery, but it's going to be a little while before you can see them. It looks like you woke up at the wrong time. We're in the middle of changing shifts. Here's a blanket to keep you warm. See you in a little bit," she says and leaves.

I woke up at the wrong time? Are you insane? You're lucky I don't— I don't—I don't have any energy. My tenuous lucidity is being broken by morphine…dripping… slowly…through my consciousness. Blackout.

"Tania? Tania? Are you OK, my baby?"

"Mom?"

"Yeah, it's me," she says.

"Am I in my room?"

"No, they can't move you yet. They let us come in for a second."

Kim, Dad, and Mom hover over me like urban angels. I feel like I'm in a Tony Kushner play.

"I'm so cold, Mom. Can you get me a blanket?"

"Sure, honey."

"How are you feeling, Tania?" my sister asks.

"I'm fine. I can't believe how aware I am. Who are you?" I say.

"Kim," she says, about to cry.

"I was just kidding. I'm sorry. See, I have my sense of humor. I'm fine."

Dad says nothing. He's clearly uncomfortable. He scans my body for a space unencumbered by tubes and needles to give me a squeeze. He finds my foot to be a satisfactory spot. Mom returns with what appears to be an airplane blanket and tucks it around my legs.

"Here you go, my baby. Now we're going to have to leave, but we'll meet you in your room. They said it will be just a little while longer."

A young Asian nurse removes the paper bonnet from my head.

"You have great hair," she reports. "Really fabulous and thick."

"Thanks?" I say.

Two beefy guys are called over to wheel me to my room. One of the guys leans over and says, "Cute glasses." The other guy is also anxious to compliment me. "Wow, you've got pretty blue eyes." OK. What's going on here? Did surgery somehow enhance my appearance? Or do I look so fucked up and hungover from morphine and Roofies that they feel sorry for me? I choose to believe the former.

A gigantic brown television set looms over the room like a bad omen. Thick beige canvas separates me from my roommate, whom I'm told is on "vacation," which is probably medical-speak for dead. Mom and Kim take stations on either side of my bed. Dad had to go back to work but will return later, and I'm perched on a narrow steel raft, in the middle of my half of the room, holding the morphine joystick, ready to tap the button at the first sign of pain. Why do we have to urinate after a nap? Is there some sort of physiological explanation for this? Is it like needing to urinate after sex? Will it prevent you from getting a UTI? The reason I'm asking is because I have to urinate. Under normal circumstances, I'd just get up and go to the bathroom, but right now the thought of moving out of this bed seems impossible. "Mom, I need to go to the bathroom," I say. "I need to pee pee. Can you please help me?" Mom is amazing, a total Renaissance woman. She's a chef, a pop-culture expert, and now a nurse. She clicks into mode by moving tubes and gathering anything that could be ripped out of my body if snagged. Placing her hand in the middle of my back, she gives me a guiding push forward.

"I can't, Mom. I can't move. I can barely budge." I strain to lift my body from the bed.

"Breathe, Tania, and focus," she says.

I take a deep breath in, and in one fluid pilates move I lurch forward. I'm sitting up now as Mom gently moves my legs so that they're dangling off the bed, ready to be used. A wave of nausea sweeps into my stomach and out of my mouth. Being resilient sort of sucks; it means forgetting about the first time I had a mastectomy and all the puking involved. I puked when I was in pain, I puked when I took pain medication, I puked when I took anti-nausea medication, and sometimes I puked for the sheer sport of it.

I shuffle toward the bathroom, bent over, feeling the need to puke, pass out, or pee pee with every step. It's a long walk to the restroom. As I'm seated on the toilet with my head down in defeat, my mother holds my tubes and I understand why they call it a *rest*room.

"Are you finished pee-peeing, Tania?" she asks.

"Yeah, Mom."

Being sick is a very humbling experience. I slowly lift myself from the toilet and…

"I'm gonna…I'm gonna…"

I do. I vomit. Movement equals vomiting. I will sit on the toilet until I'm released from the hospital in two days. This is a good plan.

The shot always comes at three in the morning. That's how they get you. Your defenses are down, because you're sleeping and you're completely unaware of the danger that it's headed directly for your ass. And while they've got you down, and stunned, they strap on the Velcro sleeve and start pumping. So the next time you find yourself hanging out in the hospital, watch your arm and your ass, 'cause they'll get you.

Ellenmary, not Maryellen, is the first nurse on the scene. She is compact and looks efficient, like a breath mint. Ellenmary is from the Philippines and full of that exotic Philippine wisdom.

"You are lucky to have a mother lie you do," she says after talking to my mother for only a moment. She is a psychic medium.

"You, Taneea, look lie you are a genius," Ellenmary says. She's intuitive also.

It's 3:30 A.M., which seems to be breakfast time in the hospital world. Ellenmary presents me with a tray of something old, something new, something borrowed, something…I'm not hungry. I smile politely and wait for her to leave before I vomit and push the tray away.

From 3:30 A.M. until 9 A.M. I engage in flipping between the two channels offered by the hospital: That Dated Soap Opera Channel and the Hunting Network. In a very short time I have learned a lot about extramarital affairs and fly fishing.

9:15 A.M. brings Nurse Fred to my room. As a male nurse there are really only two options for your sexuality: gay or kind-of-gay. Nurse Fred is all gay. After he pricks my ass, merely a handshake in the hospital world, Nurse Fred sits on the side of my bed just to hang out with me. I love Nurse Fred. Although he doesn't seem to bring the psychic wisdom that Sister Ellenmary brought to my hospital experience, Nurse Fred brings a gay sensibility that makes me feel at home. His fondness for *Tales of the City* is second only to his fondness for *Tales of the Hospital*. My sister, my mother, and I gather around Nurse Fred as if he's our summer camp counselor and it's scary-story time. I imagine Nurse Fred illuminated by a handheld flashlight as he begins telling… *Tales of the Hospital.*

"Only five doors down from us is a man with the flesh-eating disease. You know how he got it? I'll tell you. He was playing basketball, just like you and I have done a hundred times—well, for me only once, and it was because I was trying to seduce the coach, but that's another tale, my little sickadees. So, our basketball-playing friend jumps into the air to make a—what's that shot called, a laydown or some such business—and he scrapes his ass on the concrete, gets the flesh-eating disease, and now he only has one butt cheek."

We gasp in unison.

"Do you want to hear another story about this lovely hospital?" he asks.

"YES," we all say.

"OK, about two weeks ago, during our monthly nurses' meeting, we found out that, due to an error that Betsy in pre-op/check-in made, all of us nurses have been exposed to TB."

We gasp again.

"But the worst part is, we all tested positive for TB. There is not one nurse in all of Long Beach Memorial that is free of TB! Do you kids want to hear another tale?"

If I say no, then I'm forced to focus on feeling like shit, and if I say yes, then I'm forced to focus on all the diseases I could catch while recovering in this hospital.

"Well…only if it's a good one," I say, covering my bases.

"OK, it's not really a story—it's more like a warning. First of all, do you drink from water fountains?" I nod somewhere in between yes and no, not wanting to pick the wrong answer.

"Good. Because I like you, Tania, and that's why I'm going to tell you and your mother and your sister: DO NOT drink from water fountains. We just read a study about public places and germs, and I can't even tell you how many germs and deadly diseases are festering on the tip of a fountain's spout. Not to mention the sides, where you place your hands for stability. You might as well give a stranger a rim job! Gosh, you Katans are a good time. I feel so comfortable with all of you. Can I tell you a dream of mine?"

Why stop him now?

"My dream is to quit nursing and work at a bookstore, where there are no diseases. I want to be surrounded by books." Nurse Fred looks truly happy for a moment. "Oh, God, but what about booklopheliacs? You know, those people who derive intense pleasure from licking books? I mean, once a book has been licked and subsequently dries there is no way of truly distinguishing a licked book from a germ-free book. OH, GOD. I think I'll stay at the hospital for a while."

Nurse Fred is a hypochondriac with facts to back him up. Story time comes to an end when a tentative figure ekes into the room.

"Hey, Tania. I brought you some Ben & Jerry's." It's Sal. She stands. She stares. She hovers. Just like old times. The thing is, I don't feel obligated to make small talk anymore. I let her stand and fester, which she does for a little while, until she realizes it's really not about her right now, so she decides to leave.

"OK, so, well, I hope you feel better," Sal says, cautiously moving mounds of cards and overflowing bouquets, in search of a spot on the bedside table for her Hallmark card.

"Hey, have you developed the pictures of my booby yet?" I ask.

"Uh, no, not yet, but I will, soon. Don't worry," she says. Floral arrangements and card choices are good indicators of who people are and what they want to say. Sal's card, for example, is Hallmark in nature, which means she wants someone else to speak for her. The inside of the card is filled with a very long preprinted sentiment. There is only a tiny blank space on the bottom of the card for her to express herself. She uses this space to say, "I'm glad I found a card that says it all—Sal." Paul and Mikey sent me a colorful and sweet-smelling floral arrangement; Bruce and Scott sent a sleek and stylish arrangement; other friends sent lush, overflowing forests and homemade cards. A group of friends in Jerome, Arizona, sent me a box full of papier-mâché breasts they'd painted and strung together.

"What are you still doing here?" glib Dr. Allen asks as he parades into my room.

I don't want to state the obvious, but what the fuck, I'm on painkillers. "I just had a mastectomy, remember? Actually, I think you performed it."

Dr. Allen smiles sheepishly and gets to the point of his visit. "How are you doing?"

Great, considering you severed my muscles and nerve endings. "Fine, but I can't really move my arm. I don't remember it being this difficult to move my arm last time."

"Well, you're thirty years old, this time," he says, poking fun at me.

I'm tired of being poked. "Look, are there any exercises I can start doing?"

"Sure, walk your fingers up and down the wall." He demonstrates a therapeutic version of "Itsy Bitsy Spider" on the wall. "I expect to see you out of here this afternoon, Tania."

And I expect to see you begging for change on a street corner because you were fired for being such an asshole. "OK. Bye doctor!"

Long after the phone stopped ringing, flowers stopped being delivered, and needles stopped entering my body, I went to sleep—a deep relaxing sleep, like a little puppy who passes out after gorging herself on milk. When I woke up, at two in the morning, my sweet exhausted mother was sprawled out on the plastic recliner next to my bed. She looked tranquil and heavy, like she was happy to have taken away some of my weight and incorporate it into her own.

The only reason I've been here in the hospital for four days is to spite Dr. Allen and for the round-the-clock service. After what feels like a botched surgery, ongoing nausea, and moments of crying with my mother in the stark hospital light, it's time to go home to heal.

righting your life
(right breast—1992)

The mind and body are your internal travel agents. If, for example, you're feeling distressed or uncomfortable, your internal travel agents engage in a dialogue to come up with an itinerary full of exotic scenarios, inviting images, and sweet smells that allow you to relax, have a mental cocktail, and go somewhere that's not here. My travel agents have selected the following vacation destination for me: Conscious Denial, a state in which one acknowledges the fact that one is dealing with something extremely difficult but chooses not to deal with it at this time, and there are palm trees there too. But maintaining my residency is becoming more and more difficult. I fear I must leave the island of Conscious Denial soon.

"Hey, Alexander," I say from the pay phone outside my movement class, which has become my temporary office; twenty-five cents is a small price to pay for having your own space.

"Hey, Katanalicious! I haven't heard from you since parachute pants were hot!" Alex says, letting out a high-pitched squeal.

"Sorry, I've been busy going bald."

"Bald is so hot this year. Look at Right Said Fred—he's too sexy for himself! That's hot!"

"I don't feel so hot. I kind of feel like shit."

"Have you broken up with Goofy yet?"

"No."

"Well, you know you'll have to do it in person. I mean, you can't write a letter, because she'd never be able to read it."

"OK, Alexander Bitchingford III."

"When are we gonna go dancing? I want to shake my groove thing!"

"Well…Fran and I are going dancing next week."

"Fran! Fran! Fran! Just because she, unlike your current girlfriend, can speak in complete sentences doesn't mean she can take my place."

"No one is taking your place, except for maybe Conscious Denial."

"Denial is fabulous. It's totally healthy. But shopping is better. Nine out of ten cancer patients prefer shopping to thinking about their condition. It's a fact, Tania."

"I just wish I could go one day without thinking about cancer," I tell him. "I'm over this whole cancer thing. In the movies they make having cancer seem like a romantic dance one does with illness. But really having cancer is totally humiliating—it sucks. Someone's always asking you how much you weigh, to take off your clothes, put on your clothes, close the door, I'm not finished, I'm finished for now but I'll be back later, I'll need to continue seeing you, you can't stop seeing me because you don't like me, you're in the middle of treatment, you need me to help you fight the cancer, otherwise you could get it again. All of this anonymity connected to hospitals and doctors' offices. I mean, I don't know the names of most of the people involved in my treatment, and they're always mis-pronouncing my name, or not even saying it. It's like a never-ending series of doctors flipping my chart, pricking my skin, and calling it a day."

"Oh, my God!"

"Sorry, I kind of went off."

"No, it's not that. It's that I so-o-o-o know what you're talking about. It's a one-night stand, honey, that turns into a reoccurring bad date!"

"I don't get it. I've never had a one-night stand, Alex, you know that," I say.

"Oh, Katanalicious… It starts out with Gloria Gaynor, some drugs, and the promise of anonymous sex. One night with someone: It's got to be hot, right? WRONG. I can't tell you how many times I've gone home with some guy and we're having sex, I think, but who knows, I mean, my eyes are closed and I'm thinking about getting home, hoping my mom and step-dad bought me the cookies-and-cream ice cream I asked them to buy the other day. And when he's finished—I say 'he' because I don't know his name—I find my clothes, put 'em on, and leave. On the lo-o-o-ng drive home, I feel like shit. It's always a long drive home and I always feel like shit. The end, right? WRONG. Because he calls, they ALWAYS call, because at some point in the evening I was so drunk I actually gave him my phone number. So I agree to meet him for drinks, which he pays for, and we do it again, this time a little bit better, but not much. And soon we're dating, I guess, because he keeps paying for things and telling people I'm his boyfriend. And what should have been a one-night stand has turned into a two-month relationship, and I know I have to break it off, but it's two months too late, honey, because he's got my number and knows where I live and somehow he always manages to convince me that it's easier to stay with him than break up. Like my mother always says, 'Two months in, a lifetime getting out.' It sounds just like cancer, Ms. T. You never know when he's gonna call or leave you alone for good."

"Wow, I don't think I ever want to have a one-night stand."

"Yeah, me either, until the next time I have one."

My playwriting class is super cool! The professor, who is actually a playwriting grad student, is this sassy, young, hip teacher full of really great suggestions. Sometimes she wears brightly colored short retro skirts with black boots that go all the way up to just under her knees. I've never had a teacher who wore boots like that; I've dreamed about some of my teachers wearing boots like that, but... I'm not attracted to my playwriting teacher, just sort of astounded that someone who looks and acts like the coolest girl in high school's even cooler older sister is teaching me how to write plays.

There are only seven of us in class, which makes individual consultations a luxurious reality. After reading and discussing Caryl Churchill's *Cloud 9* last week—what the fuck was she smoking?—we got to choose what we wanted to write about for the next three months. I decided to write about all the cancer stuff. That way I can turn my life into a play rather than actually living it. Pretty smart, huh? I mean, if I'm writing the script, then I have control over my fate. If I'm writing scenes where I'm kicking cancer's ass, or breaking up with Dawn, then everything is fine, right? It's fine until it's not fine. Tomorrow I'm going to break up with Dawn.

I couldn't have predicted the chain of events that would unfold when I finally decided to take care of myself. Who could have predicted that the day I broke up with Dawn would be the day her father died? How could I have known that Dawn would punch in the wall in the kitchen to punctuate the end of our relationship? And who knew it could get worse?

Dawn and I are living together like roommates. The only job she has managed to stick with, of late, is sulking on the couch. She's been on the couch, in the same Bugs Bunny flannel pajamas, for weeks. With her father gone, the wall punched in, her girlfriend leaving, I understand why Dawn's sulking, but it doesn't make me want to stay with her any longer than I have to. The other day, when Fran dropped me off from our now regular coffee meeting, Dawn yelled from the couch, "Are you sleeping with

Fran?" To which I said, "No." And then she said, "I bet she has gray pubic hair!"

I have finally moved out of Dawn's Disneyland and back home with my mom. I can't believe I was with Dawn as long as I was.
"Mom, how come you never told me Dawn wasn't the One?"
"Tania, as a social worker, there is an ethical code that prevents me from discussing clients' problems with anyone other than my client. As a mother there is a logical code that prevents me from telling my daughter why I feel she is in an unhealthy relationship until after the relationship has ended. And because you and Dawn are no more, I will say this: DSM 301.82: Avoidant Personality Disorder, Narcissistic Personality Disorder, some Delusional Jealousy, and, based on all of her cartoon friends, Arrested Development. She was socially inept, unaware of good cuisine, and didn't like *Donahue*; how could I like her, Tania?"
I'm so glad to be home.

oh, that
(left breast—2002)
Maybe I should have Itsy-Bitsy-Spidered up the wall more. As I struggle to lift my left arm, there's this feeling of ingrown chords restricting my movement. It's as if one end of a really short rubber band is attached to the crease in my arm and the other end to the base of my wrist. And when I extend, it feels like the band is going to snap, leaving my arm dangling and useless. Maybe I should have stretched more? Masturbated less? I need to cut myself

some slack; it's only been a few days since my surgery. Sticky remnants of gauze and tape remain as charcoal-gray stains on my wrist. I haven't showered since Jennifer Lopez became J.Lo, and the only reason I know that contemporary tidbit is because my mom, who is currently sleeping on a bed next to my dad's bed in the living room of this odd dormitory, told me so. I'll have to shower in about five minutes because today is the day I meet with my oncologist.

My outlook is Positive and my lymph nodes are Negative. I could never quite reconcile the idea of a Negative being a Positive. Even while working in the printing industry, the idea that you must have a Negative in order to reproduce a Positive didn't make sense. How could I ever shake the years of grade school indoctrination that stated Negative equals Loser and Positive equals Winner? I'll tell how: Hang out with Mikey and Paul before they got their HIV tests. A couple of years ago, while I was living in San Francisco, a nervous Mikey and Paul met me at Peet's Coffee before they were to embark on their HIV tests. In an effort to console my two concerned friends I said, "I'll be sending you Positive energy." To which they responded with a sarcastic, "Great, Tania, that's all we need, POSI-TIVE energy," and "Thanks for the POSITIVE energy, Tania." After their tests came back Negative, I had a true appreciation for a Negative result giving someone a Positive feeling.

Everything is new with no boobies, like there's no jiggle when I walk, and there's nothing protruding from my shirt, and there's no ledge to rest a towel on. I just got out of the shower, and as I wrapped the towel around my body, unconsciously lifting it up to the human shelf known as the breast, there was nothing there. For the last ten years I have performed the One-Boob Towel Tuck. Gently I'd mold the towel over my left breast, creating a hood for it, and then, much like a toga, I'd drape the rest of the towel down and around my right scar. But as I started to configure my booby hood today I realized there's no head to put the hood on. What's a girl to do? Should I wrap the towel around my neck, creating a terry-cloth cape? Or, because I have no boobies and by law can be topless, should I simply tie the towel around my waist and pretend to be a man in a shaving cream commercial? Wait, can I talk to my parents while half naked? What if the half that's naked is no longer anatomically correct? If men can do it, so can I.

"Hey, Mom, Dad—" Dad is stunned and Mom is flustered. Oops.

"Uh, aren't you going to get dressed?" Dad asks as he stares intently at my face.

"You look like a cute boy, Tania. Don't you think so, Elliott?" Mom asks.

"I think Tania needs to get dressed to go to the oncologist," he replies, not yet sold on my new physique.

"Yeah, you kind of look like Ben Affleck," Mom adds. As long as I resemble a pop icon, Mom is fine with my new look, and I guess if given the choice of looking like J.Lo or Ben, Ben suits me much better.

Picture a taupe-painted room with taupe furniture and taupe people dressed in taupe clothing. Now picture me, sitting, smiling, wearing blue and orange, with my extraordinarily colorful parents. Sitting in this waiting room makes me feel like a Jew in the South. I don't fit in. I never seem to fit in, not that fitting in is ever the goal for me, but it would be really nice for it to just spontaneously occur. You'd think that a group of people who are dealing with the same life-threatening illness would have more in common than medications and doctors. Alas, we don't, so we sit and wait. There's a rather flamboyant man, a very attractive man—based on health care aesthetics—wearing a pineapple-print tie, floating, maybe even bouncing around the office. He just waved at me. He's been flitting by and happily waving in my direction in thirty-minute intervals for the past two hours. Is he my oncologist? Is he some crazy gay guy on too many meds? Is he God? Periodically a smiley nurse comes over to reassure us that Dr. Moore is worth waiting for. "Dr. Moore is really fantastic. He takes a lot of time with his patients, making sure to answer all of their questions. That's why he's running a little late. I promise he's worth waiting for."

A while later we're in Dr. Moore's office. "Welcome. Tania Katan, I presume?" The guy in the pineapple tie pronounces my name impeccably while making sincere and compassionate eye contact. He shifts to shake my mother's hand and asks, "Are you Tania's sister?"

Mom blushes, and without thinking says, "Yes."

He shakes my father's hand and says, "You're a lucky man, Elliott," as he holds my mother's gaze. My father, unimpressed with the doctor's romantic antics, says, "Are you fucking kidding me? Joëlle and I have been divorced longer than you've been alive."

"I'd like to welcome all of you. Thank you for waiting. Now let's get started."

Dr. Moore doesn't even open my chart. He starts rattling off what appears to be a previously rehearsed monologue. "We're gonna treat this cancer aggressively." I almost expect to hear prerecorded cheers and laughter. "You're very young, Miss Katan. What are you, twenty-eight?" It's not flattering to have your oncologist *guess* your age. "So, what we're going to do is blast the cancer with Cytoxan and Adriamycin. Have you had Adriamycin before?"

"No," I tell him.

"Great. Adriamycin is one fierce chemical. You'll definitely lose all of your hair. We'll probably knock you into menopause, and we'll give you four months of treatment, each being administered through an hour-long IV drip. What else? Oh, yes, I want to test you for the breast cancer gene. I'm pretty sure you have it, in which case we'll talk about getting your ovaries out, and—"

My hair? I can't believe I'm crying over my hair, but the tears are running down my face at lightning speed. Last time I lost *some* hair, not *all*; there's a big psychological difference between the two. If I have some hair on my head, then I'll look like I just have thin hair, but if I'm bald, and I'm not an Irish pop sensation, then I'm just a young woman with cancer. And no matter how many times, just for fun, I've said in my head, *I wonder what I'd look like bald?* I didn't really mean it. Being a bald cancer patient is too predictable, not to mention that I'm *single,* and even though my top priority isn't dating, I'd love to know that I have the option to date, and with no hair my choices might be limited. So you can see how hair loss *is* something to cry about.

What else did Dr. Moore say? Oh, my God, an IV drip? I'm going to become a Dripper? As a writer, aren't I immune to becoming a character I've written about? Now I'm going to *be* one of those bald people in a recliner, looking like I'm courting Death, if I'm not already scheduled for dinner with him/her. People with less extensive chemotherapy regimens will hurry past me, scared that my cancer particles will infiltrate and inflame their own. And menopause? The gene? *You're* going to knock me into menopause then take my ovaries out? How about I knock you into the land of *Compassion* and get your ego out of the room? What about having a baby? Freezing my lineage? What about...

"Some other side effects you may experience are loss of libido—" Dr. Moore starts to say.

"You obviously don't know my Tania," my mother sticks up for me. "She's kind of a whore, so she'll have no problem with her sex drive." Mom's my biggest advocate.

The gene discussion is introduced into Dr. Moore's polished performance.

"You're Jewish, right, Tania?"

What gave it away? My sharp wit or my tiny Yentl-ish glasses? "Yes, I'm Jewish."

"Ashkenazi?" he asks, proud of himself ahead of time.

"On my father's side, and Sephardic on my mother's side." I won't let him be entirely right.

"I'll bet a million dollars that you will test positive for the BRCA-1 gene," he says.

I don't need my oncologist to be a gambling man.

"What happens if she has the gene?" asks my concerned Ashkenazi father.

"Since she's already had breast cancer twice, that's not an issue. However, she will have a forty percent chance of developing ovarian cancer. To give you a gauge, women who do not have the gene have a one percent chance of developing ovarian cancer in their lifetime. And as you know, we have no way to detect ovarian cancer until, well, it's too late. That's why we want to take out her ovaries."

"So, if there are no ovaries, she can't get ovarian cancer?" my mother asks.

"Well, not exactly. If she has the gene, and she gets her ovaries removed, she'll have a seventeen-percent chance of getting ovarian cancer, but because she'll have no ovaries it's called ovarian-related cancer."

Mom and Dad are tense, taking it all in, wanting to ask questions that the doctor can't possibly answer, like, *How long does our daughter have to live?* and *Can you please help her?* Instead they continue with a more rational line of questioning.

"*If* Tania has the gene, what other complications could arise?" my father asks.

"Does Tania have siblings?" Dr. Moore asks my parents.

Yes, Tania has siblings, and Tania can talk for herself now that she's all grown up.

"Yes, she has a twin brother and younger sister," Dad answers.

"If she has the gene, then there's a fifty-percent chance that her brother and sister also have the gene. I'd be more concerned about her sister, as this is a breast cancer–ovarian cancer gene. Also, if Tania decides to have a child, that child has a fifty-percent chance of inheriting the gene."

This is when my parents turn on me.

"Then she won't have a baby," Mom declares.

"That's right," Dad backs her up.

"Do you think that Tania is happy that the two of you had her? I'm sure that both of you are happy to have Tania in your lives. If Tania has the gene, then one of you gave it to her. There are always risks involved in having children, but if she wants to have a child, that is her choice." Dr. Moore finally appears sincere.

My parents are stunned. Of course they're glad they had me, and if they knew they had a fifty-percent chance of passing along this gene to me, chances are they still would have had me. And quite frankly, I'm happy to be alive, regardless of how many times I have to endure cancer. And assuming I don't go into an early menopause, I would love nothing more than to squeeze out an adorable—I'm guessing—little snugger, even if s/he has a risk of inheriting a gene I don't even know I have yet. Just when I was about to write Dr. Moore off, he came through for me; he defended my existence. That's big. I guess if you're the closest thing there is to a cure for cancer, you can be a little arrogant.

Dr. Moore has asked my parents to leave the room so he can examine me.

Half-naked, which I always seem to be these days, I sit on the frosty butcher paper, allowing Dr. Moore to stick his cold stethoscope against my chest and even colder hands where my boobies used to be.

"OK, looks good. Why don't you lie down for me?" Dr. Moore asks. One day I will ask a doctor, if she is cute enough, to lie down for *me*. He pushes his hands into the soft flesh just inside my hip bones.

"OH, MY GOD!" Dr. Moore exclaims. "What's this?!"
Oh, *that*. I forgot about *that*. It's easy to forget about
that in all of the chaos and confusion that a second
round of cancer brings; in all of the predictions about
hair loss and loss of the ability to have children, I forgot
to mention *that*.

The scar stretches from my belly button down to the top
of my pubic bone. It measures 4.5 inches in length. In
1994, while receiving a routine gynecological exam, the
gynecologist placed his hands on my belly, pushed cautiously, and exclaimed, "Whoa, there's something in there.
It feels like you're four months pregnant, Tania." After a
battery of tests that included x-rays, blood work, and all
kinds of scans, it was determined that the only way to see
if the mass was cancerous was to remove it. As the mass
was located somewhere near my uterus, bowels, and
ovaries, all of these *parts* were fair game for removal. And,
because the bowels were involved, they needed to be clean
enough to eat out of. Cleaning out the intestines is the
equivalent to pouring Clorox down a drain a hundred
times. The cleanse, which lasted for three days prior to the
surgery, was comprised of clear liquids, enemas, and laxatives. I could drink clear fluids—broth—as much as I
desired during these three days. Enemas were administered
two times a day, and laxatives were the chocolatey reprieve
I was allowed to ingest once a day. The liquid-fast enema-
laxative diet proved to be the most effective weight loss
plan ever; after four days I had lost thirteen pounds.
Waiting for me in my hospital room the day of my surgery
was a clear plastic gasoline container marked, GO-LIGHTLY.

A nurse explained what to do with the plastic jug.
"Because of where your tumor is, we need to get the intestines as clean as possible—"
"I know, I already did the three-day cleanse," I said smiling, boasting of my clean colon.
"Right," she said, "but we use Go-Lightly just in case there's any fecal matter left in the colon, because if the surgeon were to accidentally cut the colon while trying to remove your tumor and fecal matter made its way into your body, you would become contaminated and die. This way, if your colon is really clean and the surgeon cuts it, he'll have enough time to insert a colostomy bag."
"A colostomy bag?"
"Colostomy bags aren't scary, Tania. Lots of people live with them just fine. You can pretty much carry on with your normal activities."
That eased my mind...a little.
"OK, now, Go-Lightly might taste a little funny, but you can chase it with juice. Make sure to drink the entire two gallons. Good luck."
Go-Lightly: The name sounded like a request that a Buddhist monk might make of me while in attendance at a spiritual retreat: "Tania, remain present, become the whole inside of the circle, and go lightly into your meditation." Alas, Go-Lightly was not a guiding spiritual phrase but, in fact, the Antichrist. Go-Lightly didn't taste fruity or "funny" as the nurse suggested; it smelled like gasoline and tasted like water from a rusty pipe. After four hours of choking down two gallons of liquid hell mixed with cranberry juice—the reason why I can't drink a Cape Cod to this day—I was urinating out of my bottom. That's really

the only way to describe running to the toilet every five minutes to have a clear stream of water come out of your rectum.

The surgeon did not cut my colon, remove my uterus, or take out my ovaries. I gave birth to a healthy three-pound fibroid tumor. The umbilical chord, which originated at my uterus and extended to the head of the tumor, had been feeding the fibroid, supplying it with the blood and nourishment it needed to grow up into a huge benign tumor. Fran and I named the tumor Juan Valdez, as our belief was that my excessive coffee consumption created this giant coffee bean of a tumor.

Dr. Moore waits for my answer.
"Oh, *that*," I tell him. "I had a fibroid, they took it out, it was benign. No big deal."

ain't nobody's biz
(right breast—1992)
Why are all the lesbian bars in Arizona named in honor of shame? There's Secrets, Talk of the Town, Incognito, and Ain't Nobody's Biz. It's a good thing I'm comfortable with being gay. Tonight Fran and I are going to the Biz, a.k.a. Ain't Nobody's Biz, to meet up with some of her friends and go dancing. Despite my dwindling cell count, I'm ready to get my groove on. I just have to remember to bring my chemo pills and ID, because I always get carded at the Biz, and to wear a different baseball cap, because the one I've been wearing for the last three weeks smells funky. The bouncer looks like she could fulfill all of her job requirements. Even though her hair is French-braided,

with the tip of the braid reaching the middle of her back, there's nothing feminine about her. Her extra-large flashlight, used to expose fake IDs and underage optimists, seems excessive, perhaps a leftover accoutrement from her jail-guard days. The stool under her tight size-22 jeans buckles and cries out in pain.

"Welcome to the Biz, ladies," she says in a harsh tone, grabbing for our IDs, shining the three-inch radius of light at our stunned DMV photos. She examines Fran's photo only as a formality; mine she spends more time with, moving the spotlight from my face to my birthdate then back to my face several times before determining that I can, "Go on in."

The bar, which has an ample dance floor surrounded by at least thirteen tables with four chairs per table, is packed. Fran has purposefully left an extra button open on the top of her crisp mint-green button-down polo shirt. Her shirt's not open far enough to expose cleavage, but it does reveal a planned casualness that Fran could get used to. The way her jeans are free of wrinkles, her loafers always shiny and well cared for, her fashion so different from mine, from anyone I know except for a few of my professors, feels sexy and off-limits to me.

As Fran bounces around the bar, looking for her friends and anxious to dance, I follow her like a puppy dog. We move through packs of dykes smoking packs of cigarettes, searching for people we know. Oh, no. I know her.

"Hi, Tania...Fran." Dawn scowls at both of us.

Fran nods hello to Dawn, then turns to me and says, "I'll be right back."

She squeezes my shoulder as if to say, *Good luck.*

"Hi, Dawn," I say, embarrassed for Dawn, who appears to be drunk.

"You know, Tania, when you were in the hospital, having your ma*sec*tomy—"

She never could get that one right: maSTECTomy.

"—I slept with Amy, you know from movie night at our place? The one with the long brown hair. The hot one," says Dawn.

Amy, the mousy girl with stringy taupe hair? "Nice, Dawn. That's really sweet of you to divulge."

I'm pretty sure that having sex with a girl while your girlfriend is having a breast removed will not get you into heaven. I'm so glad I'm not with her anymore.

"I'd love to chat with you more about life and all the women you slept with during my first round of chemotherapy, but I've got to find Fran."

Dawn wells up with tears, looks exposed and sad.

"I'm sorry," she says, "I miss you. I don't have anyone with you gone and my dad dead. My life sucks right now. I'm sorry I told you about Amy. That was shitty. I'm sorry."

This slurred confession from Dawn compels me to give her a hug and move on.

I find Fran surrounded by her friends. She's excited to see me.

"Tania, this is Melanie, Kris, and Susan," Fran says, nervously rubbing the gold Jewish star hanging from her necklace.

"Nice to meet all of you," I say, realizing that one, or all, of these women could have been my mother under other circumstances.

"She doesn't look as young as you said she was," Kris says

to Fran in front of me.

"Yeah, I think I look at least twenty-two," I say, smiling at Kris. She smiles back as if to say, *You're one of us.*

Melanie asks if I like Chaka Khan, and when I say yes, she grabs my hand and leads me to the dance floor.

"You know Fran likes you," Melanie yells over Chaka.

"Yeah, I like her too," I yell back.

"She likes you *a lot*," Melanie says.

"Duh, we hang out all the time. I hope she likes me a lot. I think Fran's awesome!"

Melanie smiles at me, and we continue dancing until the song is over.

The neon-green numbers forming a circle on the face of my watch inform me that it's time to take my chemotherapy. I casually excuse myself to go to the pizza joint next door and grab a cup of water. Fran knows why I need to leave and decides that it's time to go home anyway, so we say goodbye to her sweet friends, who stare at us as if Fran and I are *Fran and I.*

In the pizza joint the teenage boy with bad skin and an attitude to match leans on the counter reading a magazine and ignoring my quiet request for a cup of water.

"Um, excuse me, could I please have a cup of water?" I ask with a little more *oomph* in my voice, knowing that my medication regimen is serious for a reason. The kid must be hard of hearing or have a hard-on from the magazine he's looking at or something, because he's not responding. My right eye is starting to twitch, and for some reason I've convinced myself that if I don't take the drugs within the next ten seconds, the cancer will not go away. I need my medication now. Fran, feeling my anxiety, jumps in.

"Excuse me, we need a glass of water, NOW," she says in a commanding voice. He slowly puts the magazine down, walks over to the faucet, turns on the spout, and hands me the cup. I frantically place the pills on my tongue, tilting the lip of the Styrofoam cup into my mouth and gulping the polluted faucet water. I made it with a second to spare. I *will* get the cancer out of my body.

Driving home with Fran I find myself embarrassed by the whole pizza-chemo scenario, so I say nothing. After a few minutes of driving in silence Fran places her hand over mine. She leaves it for a few moments, just sitting there, floppy and warm. Then, as if she's made the shift from idea to action, she squeezes my hand. Fran likes me. I like Fran. There's nothing wrong with things being easy, is there?

angela
(left breast and right breast)

"Hello, may I speak with Tania Katan?"

The voice sounds formal, like a prospective employer, only I haven't been in the job market recently.

"Who may I ask is calling?" I counter with my professional voice.

"This is Angela. Angela Ellsworth," the voice says.

"Angela? How did you get my number?" I ask.

"I got it from Stephanie. She told me about your cancer and—"

It was 1995 when I first encountered the likes of Ms. Angela Ellsworth. I was a professional playwright, finishing up my degree in theater and working at an aspiring coffee hot spot, Common Grounds, in Scottsdale. I was frothing milk and wiping off tabletops with a soiled rag so my recent theatrical fame wouldn't go to my head. I was, after all, a local celebrity. My autobiographical play about breast cancer, *STAGES*, was being produced professionally in local venues as well as a few East Coast theaters. Pictures of my nerdy little mug with captions like, "I don't think one can deal with cancer without a sense of humor," and "Writing this play has been a free form of therapy for me," and other wise-beyond-my-twenty-three-years comments adorned the pages of newspapers, academic publications, and magazines. I was ready to be recognized for my innovative theatrical accomplishments, or at least my kind-of-cute half-page picture in *The Arizona Republic*. But in order for one to be recognized, one must be seen. No one ever came into Common Grounds except for lost tourists and local shop owners. I spent most of my time making cappuccinos for myself and writing in my journal.

Turning skim milk into a dense froth is nothing short of a miracle; I had performed a miracle that day. As I carefully spooned the luscious froth on top of my eager espresso, the door that never opened opened, and in walked the most exquisite woman I had ever seen. I didn't even know the word *exquisite* was a part of my vocabulary until that day. Her dark hair was slicked back and stark against her pale, smooth skin, and as she walked in, those two cute clusters of hair that flipped around her ears and licked the tips of her lobes bounced in time with her stride. And her lips…the red that decorated her lips might have been described on the lipstick tube as "Sultry But Sophisticated." She was of a different era. She looked like a 1920s movie star, like Clara Bow. She was definitely the It Girl.

"Ah, hi, um, ah, what can I get for you?" I stammered. It was my job to serve coffee after all.

Although I was happy in my relationship with Fran, pretty girls in proximity have always flustered me.

"I'll have a, um, uh, cappuccino," she said nervously, but her sparkly light blue eyes were confident as they held my gaze long enough for me to turn away so she wouldn't see me blushing.

"Here you go," I said as I handed her the demitasse cup piled high with thick froth.

"Is your name Tania Katan?" she asked, wrapping her hands around the warm cup.

"Yes?" I said, confused as to how this sexy woman might have heard of the likes of little ol' me.

"Are you a playwright? Did you write a play called *STAGES*?" she asked more pointedly, her adorable little nose wrinkled in excitement and nervousness and whatever else makes a cute girl's nose wrinkle.

"Yes and yes. How did you know?" I still wasn't sure how she could have known about the play. Even if I don't possess the BRCA-1 gene, I do possess the NERD-1 gene.

"Well, my mother and I just went to see it. It was amazing, really. I'm also doing a lot of art around illness. I had Hodgkin's lymphoma. Actually I finished with chemo almost a year ago. I'm Angela." She leaned over the counter, closer to me, wanting to engage in a conversation.

"Wow, I'm glad you liked the play, Angela. I'm Tania," I said. Duh, she already knew my name.

The counter was an unnecessary formality. I grabbed my

cappuccino, pushed aside the stinky brown-and-gray stained rag—knowing that if my boss heard me refer to it as a "rag," he would say, "It's not a rag, Tania, it's a towel," to which I would say, "Would you dry yourself off with it?"—and joined Angela at a little square table with mismatched chairs by the oversize window.

"You know, my studio is right across the street from here," Angela said, adjusting her chair to be more square with mine.

"What kind of artwork do you?" I asked.

"I'm a painter and a performance artist—" she said and stopped herself, sensing a shift in my body, in my focus, as if she knew the words "performance artist" triggered images of messy food items, like liquid chocolate and marshmallow topping, being smeared rather violently on a naked body, on a bare stage. She was right.

"I know what people think about performance art," she said, "a whole lot of mess and not a lot of substance. Well, it's partially true, the mess part, but only sometimes and…"

She stopped to search her brain for an image. She did this a lot: stopped and looked off to the side as if a slide show of her memories was being displayed on the wall, and as soon as she saw the slide that accurately described what she wanted to say, she spoke deliberately, paused when necessary, zoomed in and out until she could paint a portrait so thick and vivid I felt like I could taste it.

"And I'm a painter too," she said, her right hand reaching up to caress her smooth gray iridescent pearl necklace.

"Who's your favorite painter?" I asked, not knowing anything about painting and even less about painters.

"That's a loaded question. I mean, I love Cy Twombly and of course there's…" She searched, paused, then answered, "Yeah, if I have to choose right now, I really love Lucian Freud." She unbuttoned her buff cashmere sweater, exposing a dingy paint-stained T-shirt with an image of boys wrestling on it.

I was hoping she would have said Warhol or Magritte or someone whose work I might have seen on postcards or T-shirts.

"Oh, Freud. What do you like about his work?" I asked, as if I'd been a big fan of his work for years and was merely looking for her to confirm what I already knew to be true.

"You know him?" she asked optimistically.

"No, I was just faking it," I confessed. "But I'd still like to know why you like his work so much."

Angela seemed charmed by my disclosure as she smiled and described Freud's work.

"There's a lusciousness to the materials being used by Freud. He's using paint as if it were flesh. It's thick, like frosting, so you're drawn to the paintings, like you want to lick them, but at the same time they're acutely grotesque. Because he's not missing anything, every mark on the body, each rumple in the blanket… If a woman has age spots or excess flesh, he conveys it, he doesn't leave anything out. And the figures feel like they're dripping off of the canvas, falling toward you—" She stopped to access the last image. "The luscious and the grotesque, that's why I love Lucian Freud."

"Wow, I love Lucian Freud too," I said, but you could have taken out "Lucian Freud" and inserted "Angela Ellsworth." When our conversation drifted to more intimate places, like illness and our own artwork, her fingers moved from the pearl necklace to a barely visible scar at her throat. She lightly skimmed the discolored line of skin, back and forth.

"Yeah, it's kind of odd that they went in through here," she said, noticing me notice her scar, "considering the tumor was wrapped around my heart. I've done a lot of performances around it, around cancer."

"Like what? Would I have seen any of it?" I asked.

"Maybe. There was a piece my partner, Tina Takemoto, and I did a few months ago, downtown, called *Caffeine and Carotene*. Does that sound familiar?" she asked.

Partner? Was she gay? Was she in a relationship with Tina? Did her sexuality really matter to me? Yes. I shook my head no in response to her question.

"*Caffeine and Carotene* explored the absurdity of illness and what we do to cure ourselves. When I was sick everyone kept telling me that all I needed to do was drink juice. Seriously, they sent me every brand of juicer you could imagine. And they also recommended I do coffee enemas. I wasn't ready to commit to coffee being shot up my ass, and I don't know if you've every tried to clean the filter of a juice machine, but it's almost as intense as going through chemo. So Tina and I turned it into a performance piece. We're actually performing next month. You should come." She reached into her baby-blue mesh bag to retrieve a glossy postcard and handed it to me.

"Yeah, I'll totally check it out," I said, aware that the *I'll* was really a *we'll*, but in that moment mentioning my significant other, Fran, seemed insignificant.

At some point during our conversation I swear I heard an

extraordinarily loud *CLICK.* Not a metaphorical click, but the real deal. I even checked the legs of my chair to make sure they hadn't snapped. It was so loud I was sure everyone in Old Town Scottsdale could hear it too. I remember thinking, *Wow, here's a woman who's making poignant artwork. She's articulate, funny, connected, and she's HOT. I wish I didn't have to make a latte for the guy who just walked into the coffeehouse.* And that was that.

Fran and I went to see Angela and Tina's performance, which involved Angela wearing turn-of-the-century undergarments and black flippers and tap dancing on powdered milk. Tina, who was sitting high above the crowd on some scaffolding, held a fishing pole with a strawberry on the hook. While Angela tap-danced, Tina would cast out the strawberry, into the powdered milk, swoosh it around for a bit, and reel it back in. Fran and I didn't get it. We chuckled and talked about, "Those silly performance artists with their repetition and food and no stage manager. Ha!" It turned out that Tina was not Angela's *partner,* but Angela did date women. For years after our long moment in the coffeehouse, Angela and I would run into each other at art openings, plays, and concerts. We would each smile and say hello in such a way that our respective girlfriends would be forced to ask, "Who's that?" And then, in 1999, while I was living in San Francisco and sleeping with every woman who had a vowel in her name, my good friend Stephanie called from Arizona to say, "Hey, I'm dating someone who knows you: Angela."

This meant that over the two years Angela and Stephanie were together, whenever I flew into Arizona with my date du jour for a special occasion, I would see Angela and

Stephanie. What could be better than seeing my good buddy with a woman I've *CLICKED* with? I'll tell you what: having the opportunity to talk with Angela at these events. Although our conversations about art and scars were brief, we had an ethereal chemistry that made catching up and sharing imperative and delectable.

"How are you doing, Tania?" Angela asks from the other end of the phone.

"Great!" I say, my excitement linked to Angela's voice, not really to how I'm doing. "It's nice to hear from you."

"Um, I'm calling to see if you'll be my date at OutFest next Tuesday in L.A.?" Date? Date. DATE. "I'd love to, I'd love to catch up, hear what you're doing, but…"

"If you're not feeling well enough… I know you just had surgery—" she says.

"No, it's fine, it's just that I start chemo on Tuesday." Is it kosher to reschedule chemotherapy for a date?

"What about this Saturday night? Do you have any plans?"

"No." And even if I did, I would cancel all of them!

"My friend John and I are going to have dinner—he lives in L.A.—but I would love for you to come with us. We could meet you in Long Beach. John will adore you."

It's early, too early for anyone to be up and functioning on a Sunday morning, let alone someone who has had four hours of sleep and is still trying to get the remains of morphine and Vicodin out of her body. But I can't sleep. I don't want to sleep. I want to sing and dance. I want to hug children in Third World countries. I want to create interesting architecture with my body. I want to climb the

highest mountain in all of Long Beach and scream I
LOVE ANGELA! That's right, you heard me, I said it. I'll
say it again: I love Angela! If Superman kept a journal, he
would be writing like I am, hands moving so fast that
traces of ink stain pages of paper faster than a speeding
bullet.

After a quick but specific shower I throw on my best soft-
butch uniform: faded red Massey Ferguson work jacket
with frayed collar, tight black V-neck T-shirt, too-long
dark blue Gap jeans with 1950s greaser cuffs on the bottom, and thick black leather boots. My hair is fabulous
and excited to be going out before its anticipated departure. Before I leave my father's apartment both my parents
demand to know where I'm going and when I'll be home.
Like any good teenager I tell them "Out" and "Whenever
I want," and when I leave I slam the door.

Driving to meet Angela and John, I feel like Danny Zuko
racing for the pink slip in *Grease*. Go greased Tania! I
arrive at the designated spot, a small art gallery in Long
Beach, ten minutes early. I play it cool, leaning back
against my red convertible. I look like James Dean in
Giant: hands in pockets, head tilted slightly forward, eyes
glaring straight ahead. I am cool and mysterious, or a giant
dork. A champagne-colored rent-a-car pulls up next to me,
and I start to lose what little cool I have contrived for the
occasion. It's them.

Angela and John emerge from the car. John is an adorable
thirty-something fag with the necessary gay-man mus-
tache-goatee combo, you know, like a handlebar mustache
connected at the chin. The G in the middle of his belt
alerts me to the fact that fashion is his greatest priority. As

if I couldn't glean that from his FCUK T-shirt delicately
tucked into some fancy jeans that I don't even know the
name of, they're so fancy. His soft hands embrace mine.
"It's so nice to meet you, Tania. Angela tells me many
wonderful things about you," he says.
And then…Angela. How can I accurately paint a picture
of how beautiful Angela is? Let's start with this: She looks
kind of like the love child of Annette Bening and Björk.
Her fair Icelandic skin transcends age. A perfect nose rests
on her face like a pink gumdrop. Her short dark slicked-
back bob allows her blue eyes to sparkle. I'm not making
this stuff up either. Also, there's this light that seems to
pour out of her body and surround her and whoever is
lucky enough to be in proximity to her. Oh, and she's got
a nice ass.
"Why don't you guys go on in? I'll wait here," John says,
aware of the chemicals dancing around in the air.

"This is a really great show, huh?" I say, not really looking
at the art. How can I focus on anything beyond Angela
and my trembling hands?
"Yeah," she says as she pinches and releases the collar of
her vintage brown WOMAN'S WORLD T-shirt over and over
again. "You look really great, Tania," she says, and then
feels the need to add, "for just being out of the hospital.
You're glowing."
Damn right, I'm glowing. I'm standing next to you.
"Thanks. You look really great too. Really great." There
you go, Tania, you can be flirty.
We try to size each other up through sideways glances
while we stroll too quickly past splotches of color. I'm

nervous but calm, but nervous, but calm. And for the first time in several weeks the intense pain under my armpit and down my arm has turned into a mild discomfort. Angela is magical.

"So, what have you been up to over the last several years?" I ask.

"Oh, you know, being gross and glamorous: the usual."

"Is that a skirt or a slip?" I ask, catching a glimpse of sheer, black frilly material under her T-shirt.

"A slip, but I want you to know that I was wearing slips as fashion way before Madonna was. She stole my thunder." She flashes the most adorable smile that has ever been smiled.

At the restaurant I sit next to John, and Angela sits across from me, creating a right angle. Before any of us has a chance to really study the menu Angela has a request: "Tania, could I see your scars?" She asks me this honestly, directly, sexily.

John shoots her a look as if to say, *THAT was a rude question*. But I love it. After being with Sal, the woman of few words and even fewer questions, Angela's curiosity is delightful.

"Sure," I say, "but can we wait until after dinner?"

Angela smiles. "If we have to."

I'm usually unaware of people flirting with me, especially in relation to my physical deformities, but I think Angela finds the prospect of seeing my scar a bit titillating.

I don't remember exactly what I ordered or how many glasses of that really great zinfandel I consumed, but I do know that last night changed the course of my life. I know

this because it's 6 A.M. on a Sunday morning and I'm writing in my journal at the speed of light. I'm trying to
recount every morsel that made up last night, like the mischievous way in which Angela leaned over mounds of sil-
verware and little white plates to feed me a bite of her
crème brûlée. Or when John told stories about his psychic
and her need to be surrounded by lawn gnomes inside her
home and how this year is, according to the psychic, His
Year. Or when Angela stood up to perform a thirty-second
impromptu modern dance based on lawn gnomes with
psychic powers, followed by a declaration of how shy she is
about promoting her artwork. Or when Angela told me
she was planning on moving to Los Angeles. There is
nothing more stimulating than people deftly moving in
and out of extreme silliness and complete honesty. Except
for maybe getting naked in the bathroom of a restaurant.
After dinner Angela and I headed to the bathroom for the
unveiling. I guess I was expecting the bathroom to be lit
by a few soft scented candles; that's why the austere fluorescent lights made me a little panicky. This feeling of
panic was compounded by the fact that we were surrounded
by floor-to-ceiling mirrors. So there I was, standing in
front of this woman I desperately wanted to impress,
about to take off my shirt and reveal a very fresh scar. I felt
a bit nervous, a little clammy. I felt small and unusual.
What if she thought she wanted to see the scar, until she
actually saw it? What if she liked girls with boobies better
than girls with none? So, as I unzipped my jacket I focused
on the lines around her mouth that suggested a lot of hard
laughter, and her cute concerned chin that had scrunched
up into a walnut shell, and the fact that her eyes were

allowing me the privacy to undress by looking off to the side, and before I knew it my shirt was off. Her gaze softly shifted to my scars.

"Wow, Tania. They're beautiful," she said, unaware that her hands were tilting forward and fingers extending as if she wanted to touch them.

"We're lucky, you know, you and me. We get it." She was standing in front of my bare chest, calm, focused, connecting to my body in a way even I had been too scared to do.

After dinner the three of us strolled down 2nd Street into the chilly Long Beach night. John and Angela arm in arm and me next to Angela. Maybe it was because I wanted to add my arm to the equation that I said, "My hands are really freezing." Angela, without stopping to think about her action and the chain reaction it might be setting off, took my hands in hers, rubbing my little paws for a few seconds before I withdrew them out of sheer scaredy-cat-ness.

"I've been training to run a 10K," Angela declared. "It's something I've wanted to do since I got cancer eight years ago. I've been running four days a week, I'm feeling really strong, I'm getting really excited."

"I'll do it with you! I've always wanted to run a 10K," I blurted out, getting caught up in her excitement and knowing that making a plan in advance would require us interacting—a lot. Sure, I've always been athletic, but stating that *I've always wanted to run a 10K* implies that I sit up late at night visualizing me and a couple hundred people at a starting line, wearing numbered bibs and short shorts; I've never pictured myself in that scenario.

"Great. That's so great, Tania. Are you sure you're going to be up for it?"

"Totally," I said.

"It's going to be in Phoenix on October 17. This is so great, Tania," she said, practically hugging me.

In John's rent-a-car, en route to my car, Angela, who was in the backseat, placed her hands on both headrests, pulling herself forward to begin her confession.

"Tania, do you remember when we first met at Common Grounds?"

"Yes." Like a favorite play.

"I have to tell you something... I had the biggest crush on you."

"Really?" I said, milking every second it.

"I actually had seen you in the coffeehouse before that day. I knew you were the cute lesbian from all the newspapers who wrote that amazing play and I wanted to meet you. I almost stopped in before we actually met, but the day I drove past the coffeehouse window and realized it was you, I was wearing a really awful outfit. So the next day, the day we met, I put on my fancy pearls and headed over to Common Grounds to meet you."

"Wow, Angela, some people would call that stalking, but I call it flattering. I had a crush on you too," I confessed.

"Really?" she said, astonished.

Where do you go after you've confessed a crush that has spanned seven years?

Home.

We all hugged goodbye and exchanged contact information, knowing that something spectacular had transpired that night.

I ran upstairs to find my mom and dad anxiously awaiting
my arrival.

"Mom…Dad…I'm totally in love!" I exclaimed.

"It's midnight," Mom said, as if one can only fall in love
between certain hours.

"I'm in love with Angela!" I repeated, just in case she, and
the neighbors, didn't hear me.

"That's great, now go to bed," Dad said, exhausted from
having waited up for me.

I ran into my room with the cordless phone and proceeded to
call all of my friends.

"Hello, [insert name]! It's Tania. Listen, do you remember
me talking about a woman named Angela? YES, from the
coffeehouse all those years ago, that's her. Well, I'm in
love with her. No, we're not dating. No, she doesn't know
I'm in love with her. No, I'm not a whore anymore. Yes,
she still lives in Arizona. Yes, I'll give you a call in a couple of months to let you know how it's going. OK, it was
great talking with you too. Right, next time I won't call
so late. Bye."

At three o'clock this morning I felt like starting my 10K
training. I was wired, repeating *Angela and John* in my
brain like a mantra. I want to marry Angela and have John
be our flower girl. I needed to write Angela an e-mail to let
her know that our evening of dinner and flirting that cul-
minated in an overt backseat pass was not lost on me. But
the Web TV is in the living room, which is really the bedroom of my sleeping parents. The great thing about love is
that it allows you to believe that doing something stupid
or silly is actually romantic. So I crept, on all fours, past
my snoring mother and my loud-breathing father, into the

living room, grabbed the flat black keyboard, and turned on the TV while pushing the "volume down" key as fast as I could. I wrote, deleted, and rewrote until I sent Angela the following e-mail:

Angela,
It's not often that a beautiful artist with an absurdly pro-
found spirit warms my hands while walking. Thank you for
an insightful, insouciant, in-the-bathroom-taking-off-my-shirt
kind of evening. I look forward to being friends, to warming
hands, and to continuing my crush. —Tania

The four hours I did manage to sleep were all spent dreaming of Angela, and when I woke up, I ran over to Web TV to find the following e-mail:

Tania,
You are beautiful! I went to sleep pondering my dinner/bath-
room behavior…look what you pulled out of me. Your energy
is intoxicating, and I couldn't resist. I would be happy warm-
ing your hands while walking or while you tell incredible sto-
ries. I have always wanted to know more about you. Thank
you for sharing your scars with me. I am always interested in
how the body changes and heals itself and how the medical
world leaves traces and marks. You must be taking very good
care of yourself and have a supportive environment, because
you look soooo healthy, happy, and hot. I'm sure this will con-
tinue even through chemo. Oh, I meant to talk with you
about your eggs. If you have the time to explore your egg
options before you go through chemo, do it. I wanted to have
a baby so badly, but chemotherapy put me into early

menopause. When I found out that it wasn't possible to have children, my heart was broken. It was more difficult to be told I couldn't have a baby than when I was told I had cancer. I knew that I could fight cancer, but menopause I just had to accept. Anyway, John and I had a wonderful time with you, and I feel so lucky I was able to spend time with you. Have a lovely Sunday. —Angela

Over the past forty-eight hours, Angela and I have exchanged more than twenty e-mails. Chemotherapy is tomorrow, and I'm preparing for the big day by meditating and e-mailing Angela. The last e-mail I sent to her, ten minutes ago, expressed how scared I was about going to chemotherapy, especially because of the long dripping process. She wrote back five minutes ago saying, "I say, dress up. Pretend you're a movie star. Bring someone with a camera, like your own paparazzi. I hope they don't try to stick you in one of those gang-chemo rooms. Who wants to talk to other sick people? You tell them who you are and that you need a private room so that all of your fans can go to chemo with you!" Her e-mail makes me smile and feel better about chemotherapy and my powers of imagination.

Björk is whispering "Possibly maybe" into my headphones as I lie on my bed visualizing the chemo nurse getting the needle in on the first try. I hear my mother yelling over Björk, "Tania! Tania, the phone!"

I bet it's Angela! I run over to my mom, grab the phone from her hand, cup the mouthpiece, run back to my room, lie down on my bed, and casually say, "This is Tania."

"Hey, it's Sal," says a heavy voice.

AAAAAAAAH. No. No, no, no, no, no. Not Sal. Not my ex-girlfriend.

"Hi," I say. "Are you calling about my photos? Do you have the photographs of my breast developed yet?"

"No. I'm going to get them developed tomorrow." Long pause. "So, how are you doing?" she asks.

"Great, really great." I can't stop myself from smiling, from thinking of Angela and John.

"That's great," Sal says, sounding like a freshly popped balloon. "What have you been up to?"

"Well, I have chemo tomorrow, so I'm getting ready for that, and then an old friend of mine, Angela, and her friend John, who's now my friend, hung out the other night. John is such a cutie, incredibly down-to-earth, and Angela is an artist who's totally amazing, and she's training for a 10K in October, so I'm going to train too and—"

"Angela, huh," she says. "I don't remember you ever mentioning her. Well, I'm glad somebody is doing well. I've been suffering from severe depression lately and I'm not saying that I'm going to *do anything*, like kill myself, but it's really hard right now, you know?"

I do know. I feel like at this point in my life, I do have a healthy concept of things being really hard. But I gave up my obligation to fix cracks in people's foundations when I broke up with you, Sal. "Yeah, Sal, I do know what *really hard* is all about," I tell her.

"Well, you don't seem to care very much about the fact that I'm losing it. I'm not sure why either. I think I have Asperger's disease. My dad is displaying all the signs of

Asperger's."

"What are the signs?" I ask.

I can hear the pages of the DSM crackling open.

"Asperger's: difficulty in social interactions; a lack of spontaneous seeking-to-share enjoyment, interests, or achievements with other people; lack of social or emotional reciprocity; intense preoccupation with patterns; linked to schizophrenia and obsessive-compulsive disorder."

Asperger's it is! I've never heard such an exact description of Sal. "It feels like you're on to something. Maybe now is a good time to get a therapist?" I say.

"Yeah, maybe. I just feel like killing myself," she says plainly.

"Sal, killing yourself is not the answer. It's never the answer," I say, accessing all of the after-school specials I stomached as a preteen.

"I don't know. I wake up every morning and I feel like dying. I've been thinking a lot about you and how you're the only person in my life that means anything to me. I wish we could start over again. I'd be a better girlfriend."

"You were a fine girlfriend. I think what you need right now is to get some help, a therapist or something, huh?" I'm grabbing at straws here.

"I can't believe that I'm bitching about me and my problems when you've got so much on your plate. I feel even more like shit. I'm sorry."

"That's OK. Don't worry about it. Listen, I have to go now. I'm a little constipated from all the painkillers and I've got to finish my prechemotherapy meditation, so…" I say, trying to get out of suicide-hotline duty.

"Yeah. OK. Well, I hope it goes well tomorrow. If you need anything, give me a call."
No, I don't *need*. That's *your* job. "Bye, Sal. Oh, and can you please make sure to send me the photographs of my booby this week?"
"Sure. I can do that."

a room with a view...of the parking lot (left breast—2002)

Tuesday is just a day of the week, nothing unique or spectacular about Tuesday. It's at the beginning of the week, but it's not the dreaded Monday. And there's none of that sexual energy or excitement associated with it, like Wednesday. Tuesday lacks the glamour and intrigue of Friday and Saturday. Tuesday doesn't possess the allure of sports and leisure that Sunday does. Tuesday is sort of benign, utterly overlooked, until today. Tuesday is my first day of chemotherapy.

As I sift through tapes in my glove box while driving, Mom insists that I, "Pull over and pick out a tape. Don't do it while driving. You're going to get us into an accident."
I want to tell her that I'm already in an accident, that driving with my mother to chemotherapy can't be part of a plan. This is an unexpected event, an accident. Without my losing focus on the road, my fingers insert the mystery tape into the deck. Sinéad O'Connor begins chanting in Gaelic. I couldn't have planned that one. Oddly enough, listening to my bald companion as Mom and I breathe quietly in our respective worlds is comforting for me, con-

sidering my anxiety level is warp eighteen.

The sign reads, NO PREGNANT WOMEN OR CHILDREN
BEYOND THIS POINT. HAZARD. Not exactly a welcome mat.
Seven burgundy pleather recliners line this slim rectangular
room. The recliners are optimistically positioned in front
of a wall of windows. The view, however, is of the parking
lot; there goes the optimism. On one of the walls a David
Hockney print hangs, displaying a road lined with trees, a
lively body of water, orange hills, a picture of possibilities.
But upon closer examination the print has brown water
stains on the edges and is so clumsily framed that the left
side slants down, looking like it's trying to escape. There
are two large obviously donated television sets for each
group of recliners to enjoy with signs above them that
read, FEEL FREE TO BRING IN A VIDEO FROM HOME! I am
certain they would not be OK with gay male porn, but
maybe next treatment I'll give it a try.

This is Motel 6 with IV drips. The only seat available in
the motel is next to a salty woman with moles, like black
freckles, covering her prematurely frail body. She smells of
cigarettes and the lubricant that connects hinges of trailers
together. Her security-guard husband sits on the ledge of
the window, facing her, reading *Martha Stewart Living*. He
is her view.

Nurse Alison is about my age. She looks like an Arizona
State University liberal arts major: blond, cute, seemingly
smart, but maybe a little more interested in beer busts
than Brecht. Alison approaches my recliner wearing plastic
gloves and bearing needles while my mother strokes my
hair, soothing me. What my mom doesn't realize is that
my regular fragile veins have been replaced by plump

healthy ones. All morning I've been jumping up and down, drinking lots of water, opening and closing my hand, and heating up the veins in the crease of my right arm with a hot compress. My veins have collapsed and hidden from one too many crappy phlebotomists for me to be complacent.

"Hi, Tania. How's it going?" Nurse Alison asks in a friendly, upbeat manner.

"Quite frankly, I'm a little anxious," I say.

"That's totally understandable. Do you have any immediate concerns?" she asks, assessing the level of anxiety.

"My primary concern is your finding a good vein," I say, opening and closing my hand in a final attempt to keep the veins supple and receptive.

"Mine too, Tania," she says.

I get a good vibe from Alison and trust that she will find a vein without having to skewer me. Mom shifts to sitting in front of me, next to the frail woman's security-guard husband. Alison throws the tourniquet around the upper part of my right arm, tying and pulling it, cutting off any circulation I might have had. She hands me a small red squishy ball to squeeze as she taps on my tentative veins.

"OK, Tania, give it one last squeeze and hold it."

I follow her instructions carefully. I hold the ball firmly as I turn away from the point of entry. I never watch a needle go into or come out of a vein. I don't feel her digging around. I wonder if everything is OK, if she's going to have to try again, if the needle broke inside of my arm, if...

"All right, I'm all done," she says.

I'm in love Alison, but not in the same way that I'm in love with Angela.

The antinausea drug is the first to drip in. Dangling from the IV stand is a bag full of a clear substance with a yellow hue. As the drips drop into the long clear plastic tube and into my vein, I keep waiting for some nasty chemical taste to creep into my mouth, but nothing. I'm not disappointed, just taken aback. Mom quietly reads a magazine that she will later take and periodically peers down from the glossy pages to make sure I'm all right. When I catch her, I give her a thumbs-up. She smiles a tired half-smile and continues to read. The IV bag shrivels pretty quickly about twenty minutes into my hour, leaving me feeling pretty much the same as I did twenty minutes ago. Except for a mild grogginess, which feels more bearable than pain or the taste of chemicals so it almost goes unnoticed.

The next item on the chemo menu is Adriamycin, a.k.a. the Red Devil. Alison hooks up the bag of Adriamycin, which is blood-red and imposing as it quickly drips through tubing, into my arm, leaving my veins cold and exposed. As my mother gets up, she asks if I need anything. With her eyes she follows the red liquid from its source to my arm; it looks like it could be coming out of my veins rather than going in.

"I'm fine. I'm just going to put on my Walkman and do some positive visualizations," I tell her.

Mom leaves, but before I have a chance to get my headphones on, my frail recliner mate starts an unsolicited conversation.

"I've got cancer in my bones, blood, and brain. It's all over my insides. This is my third time around. I started off with regular ol' breast cancer. All the nodes were negative, did some chemo, and thought I was all done. Then, 'bout a year later, it shows up again, this time in my lungs. So I gave up smokin' and did chemo again. Now the cancer is everywhere," she says, leaning into my personal space, lingering a little too long, like cigarette smoke.

Doesn't she know that the last thing on my list of things to hear while going through treatment for breast cancer is "it started with regular ol' breast cancer" and "now it's everywhere"?

Fortunately Alison interrupts the frail lady with an announcement. "We've got cookies and doughnuts in the waiting room if anyone is interested!" she says, like she's offering everyone a Get-Out-of-Chemo-Free card. She knows that her sincerity combined with her commitment to buying cheap baked goods is what keeps people happy around here.

This announcement is the equivalent to winning the lotto for my frail metastatic friend, who instructs her security-guard husband to "Go get us something!" He carefully places his *Martha Stewart Living* on his seat and leaves. This is my chance to listen to Enya murmur about a day without rain. Eyes closed, breathing, I am in a meadow now, surrounded by wildflowers. Dew, in all of its magnificence, sparkles from each of the flowers' petals. Angela is with me, naked of course. We are snuggling in the meadow, rolling around, while talking about art and giggling. Angela's cheek feels soft against mine. The sun is shining, but not so bright that one would call it *blinding*. Angela leans in, about to kiss me; I lean in, about to kiss her, and...

"Jesus, Carl, why did you get me a cookie? You know I love them doughnuts!" huffs my recliner mate.

"Cuz you don't need no doughnuts!" her husband shouts. The red is gone, and for the next forty minutes Cytoxan and Enya will be my companions. I'm starting to feel less comfortable in my skin, wanting to crawl out and take over someone else's body, someone who's sitting in a recliner at home sipping wine through her mouth rather than Cytoxan through her veins.

Before track eight, "Silver Inches," the last drip has dropped and I'm free to leave. I don't say goodbye to my recliner mate and hope, rather loudly, that I don't have to see her for the duration of my treatment, no matter how sweet and scared she is. Nurse Alison has done her job too long to expect goodbyes from patients who are anxious to leave, but I was so impressed with her poking prowess that I have to say, "Goodbye, Alison, and thank you very much for getting my vein. You don't know how much I appreciate it."

"I kind of do," she says.

I'm just lucid enough to ask my mother to take me to the Library Café so I can write in my journal. Sitting in the Library Café, as I write, I realize I feel kind of stoned. But it's not the kind of stoned that makes you giggle or eat too much; it's a funky, foggy kind of stoned that dulls your senses, that makes you think your dope's been laced with something not so fun. This kind of stoned makes you talk slower and your thinking is…uh…it's…ah…delayed. There's a chemical change occurring in my body, and it doesn't feel as nice as smoking a joint—that's all I'm trying to say.

Returning home in my chemo fog, all I want to do is write an e-mail to Angela. Despite Mom telling me to lie down and rest, I head over to the keyboard and start pecking.

Hey, cutie,
I just got back from chemo. My mom was my personal assistant/paparazzi, handing me Evian and taking pictures. I'll have to tell you more about the gang-chemo room, the people, etc., later as I'm feeling a little crappy right now. But I will tell you that I listened to Enya and thought of you. God, that sounds very Pollyanna, but it's true. Hope all is well with you, Angela. I hope we can see each other in person sometime soon. Do you think girls with no hair are cute? Lots of love, Tania

Minutes later, Web TV informs me that Angela is also thinking about me.

Darling Tania,
Although our cancer stories aren't the same, and our actual cancers are different, I can't help being reminded, on an emotional and physical level, of the absurd turns life takes when we go through this. Hearing from you and learning what you are going through is having a profound impact on me. We are really the lucky ones. If we allow expansion, and I think both of us have and do, our growth process is sped up and we can potentially share what is learned with others—while we're still young and hot! I don't mean in a formulated or literal way, but rather in our daily life practices and communication with others. That's why you have the potential to be an artist of the highest nature. OK, I'm starting to sound like a cancer self-help book, sorry. What I'm trying to say is, you are special

and I'd like to believe that you are going through all of this because you are one of the few that can handle it; many won't have the opportunity to experience this because it would be too much. You are my personal hero. I am finding pure enjoyment in writing to you, so please don't feel like you need to respond to my e-mails. I think you're sexy with or without hair. Love, Angela

Angela's e-mails are the most powerful antinausea drug ever. Speaking of which…I just got hit with this wave of nausea crashing all around me. The undertow is dragging me into the coral reef of queasiness. I feel like I'm going to puke, pass out, drop dead. First plan of action: Pop a Zofran and hope that its magical antinausea powers will be expressed in less than thirty seconds. Second, yell for help. "Mom, I'm gonna be sick!"

My mother rushes over, escorts me to the bathroom, and places a cold compress on my hot and clammy forehead. We hover over the toilet together, her rubbing my back and me desperately trying to hold back my puke; as sick as I feel, I'm not about to puke up a pill that costs $15 and can help me feel better. Tania, you are going to relax and allow this feeling to pass right through you. As I breathe in, my belly feels calm; as I breathe out, my belly feels happy. Breathing in, calm; breathing out, happy. My homespun Zen mantra is working. The puking has passed; the Zofran will work.

I'm in bed now, exhausted from today's activities. My calves are twitching and tight and the muscles feel like they're trying to claw their way out of my skin. My mother must have watched me writhe around in discomfort from the dark hallway, because she has arrived to massage all of the inflamed tendons and sensitive muscles with aloe vera lotion. She starts with my calves. The coolness of the lotion and the firm, circular motions that her hands make lull me to sleep.

Here's how the three weeks after my first chemotherapy go: During the first week I find it difficult to smile, not based on any internal turmoil or feelings of unhappiness but based solely on the fact that I have no motor skills. Chemotherapy has killed my motor skills. I struggle to put on my socks in the morning, finding that if they are inside out, they will stay that way. Most of the time my body is fatigued and my mind is foggy. Going to the gym is not an option anymore. Although I write in my journal incessantly, I fear that it is all incoherent. I begin to ask questions, things like, *Why do steroids make some people happy and muscular and others temporarily insane?* Eating food becomes an activity reserved for other people. I have a strong desire to start a Chemo Brain Exchange Program, where people who are going through chemotherapy can temporarily exchange brains with healthy, clear-minded folks.

After the first week I start to feel more like a human being. Mom and I take short walks to the beach, where we talk about the future and dying and how much we love each other and other stuff that I can't remember because chemotherapy strips you of your memory. Dad and I shoot a few games of pool, and even in my weakened condition I kick his ass. My relationship with Angela has progressed to writing letters and postcards, and talking on the phone all

the time. Also during week two, I start to lose my hair.
It's time to get my hands on some clippers.

I'm surrounded by hair. Becoming bald took five hours
more than anticipated. With my $14.99 blade I hacked
and shaved my way through the Mullet, the Mangy Kitty,
and the Naval Officer. And now that it's all over and I'm
knee-deep in hair, I look in the mirror to see a naked, stark
white, disproportionately small head. Wait a second,
maybe it is proportionate; it just looks funny because it's
naked. We all look kind of funny when we're naked—why
should our heads be an exception? Upon closer examination…it looks like…one fine-looking head! My head is
phenomenal. Look at it. It's perfectly round. No bumps,
lumps, or scars, and it's soft too; it feels like a flaccid
penis—I only know that because my gay male friends are
whores. This naked head needs to go outside, make some
friends, and get a cup of tea. I'm going to go to the
Library Café to try out my new head.

Dad is standing outside of the bathroom. I didn't expect to
see him, and clearly he didn't expect to see me.

"Whoa," he says, staring at my bare head like he's seen a
ghost. He looks like he's going to cry, takes a second to
collect his thoughts, clenches his jaw, and investigates the
situation a little more closely. "You've got a nice head,
Tania. You really do," he says.

I throw on some baggy ripped-up blue jeans that used to
be my brother's, a red wool sweater with flecks of blue and
green, and my camel-colored suede thrift-store jacket. As I
leave I check myself out in the mirror to find that I look
like either Vin Diesel or a diesel dyke. I hope I don't look
too cool or arty: I don't want people to think that my hair-

cut was a matter of fashion and not function. What if I got a tattoo on the top of my head that says, HEAD BY CHEMO?

As I step outside the apartment into a beautiful Southern California day, I feel something I've never felt before: the wind on my head unencumbered by hair. It feels spectacular.

At the Library Café the adorable barista girl who usually remembers my drink and always remembers my name says, "I really like your haircut, Tania." Other than that comment, my new hairstyle and me go relatively unnoticed.

As soon as I get home from my twenty-minute adventure at the Library Café, I call Angela to tell her of my new haircut. Angela invites me to Arizona for what will be our first real date. "When I was going through chemo and I was bald," she says, "I found that swimming was the most amazing sensation. There's something about feeling water around you, on your head, that I would love for you to experience. Can you come swimming with me? Naked? Oh, I also want to snuggle you up and rub jojoba on your head."

Knowing how crappy I felt in the first few days following chemo, we decided to make our date for a week after my second chemo. I tell my parents about my upcoming date with Angela in Arizona, expecting them to say, "No way." My dad is the first to respond.

"Look, Tania, I see the letters that come here every day for you, the e-mails, the phone calls… Angela obviously brings a lot of joy to your life, and right now, you know, that's good, really good."

Mom pipes in, "This Angela is so good for you and your healing. I'm so glad you're not with Sal, honey. She had a heaviness about her that was disconcerting. Your father and I will drive you to Arizona for your date."

No way! My parents are *so* cool!

Finally I look the part: bald, tired, and waiting for my blood to be drawn. I definitely have cancer. Here at Uni-Lab, there are always two phlebotomists on staff. One is fast, direct, and friendly: I refer to her as the Good Phlebotomist. The other is not: I refer to her as the Bad Phlebotomist. Whenever the Bad Phlebotomist calls my name I pretend I've left something in the car and tell her to go ahead and take the next patient. When I see, through the window of the lab, that she has taken some poor, unsuspecting schlump back with her, I return to the warmth and comfort of the Good Phlebotomist.

"Tan-ee-aa?" the Bad Phlebotomist calls out.

"Yes, I'm here, but I forgot something in my car, so go ahead and take the next patient."

"You always forget something in your car. I wait for you," she says.

"That's OK, you can help someone else and I'll wait for the next phlebotomist."

"No other phlebotomist on staff today, just me."

I'm tucked into the beige grade-school desk. As I extend my arm for the Bad Phlebotomist, I try to find the love and peace in this situation. The reality is that the Bad Phlebotomist is a petite four-foot-seven Filipina with a delightful laugh and a kind look in her eyes. I focus on those features as I extend my arm. I even make a little

joke, "Make sure to get a good one." She smiles her
delightful little smile and plunges the needle into my skin.
Everything seems to be going fine; I'm not even sure why I
was so afraid of this phlebotomist in the first place.
I'm feeling a little discomfort. Now I'm feeling a lot of discomfort. OH, MY GOD.
"What's going on?" I ask as I feel the needle lancing everything that is soft and sensitive but not a vein.
"Oh, we have trouble finding a vein. We keep looking."
We ain't doing nothing, lady. I want off the *We* ride. Now
she's moving the needle around with such abandon that it
feels like she's on an archaeological dig. I can't help but
visualize what's going on inside my arm, and before I can
get a clear picture, the sweat that has been beading up on
my upper lip gives way to shaking, and soon...
I wake up to the smell of rubbing alcohol near my nose.
"You pass out," she says and laughs her demonic little
laugh. "Are you OK?"
"I'm fine."
"Good. Then you get up and follow me to the room."
"The room?" What now? Is she going to practice her
lobotomy skills on me?
I get up to follow her to the room. About halfway down the
hallway I start to feel faint. Voices that sounded crisp now
sound distant. I see a blur of white and as I begin to collapse,
the four-foot-seven Bad Phlebotomist screams for reinforcement, because in comparison to her, at five-foot-four, I'm a
gargantuan creature who could crush her if I fell on her.
Reinforcement comes in the form of the Good Phlebotomist.
The Good Phlebotomist takes two seconds to find a vein,
get three vials of blood, and send me on my way.

y-me?
(right breast—1992)

When the social worker at the hospital told me that Y-Me was the name of a support group, I thought she was joking. Y-Me? It sounds like a pity party where everyone's invited, women in their forties and fifties hanging out, whining about their conditions.

"Why me?" I ask Mom.

"Shh!" she barks.

We're in the middle of a Y-Me meeting. Mom blackmailed me to come, told me she would give me a surprise if I came. SURPRISE: She gave me nothing. She felt like a support group would be good for both of us. Me, I'm not so sure.

"Let's thank Dr. Springer for coming tonight and talking about hormone replacement therapy," the woman conducting the meeting says as she claps, encouraging us all to clap.

All of the women in the crowded hotel banquet room applaud. The woman continues, "Dr. Springer will now be taking questions from all of you. If you have a question, just stand up, say your name, and tell us why you're here."

Immediately a middle-aged woman, who looks to have two rather large organic-looking breasts, stands up.

"Hi, my name is Cindy. I'm thirty-four years old, and I was diagnosed with breast cancer two years ago." There's an audible gasp from the audience. "Is it my imagination, or are women getting breast cancer younger and younger?" Dr. Springer adjusts his small wire-rimmed glasses to focus on Cindy. "Unfortunately, that seems to be the case. I've even known of a woman as young as twenty-six being diagnosed with breast cancer."

This announcement produces a more audible and concerned gasp from the audience, followed by loud whispering. I can see my mother get excited, full of sensationalism and pride, like she's got her very own *People* magazine story sitting right next to her. "Mom, don't even think about—" She's up.

"Well my daughter is twenty-one years old and she has breast cancer. She had a mastectomy and everything," she says, full of pride.

The women are gasping, frenetically whispering to one another, falling all over themselves just to catch a glimpse of the freak, a.k.a. me. The mob of middle-aged women manages to push me to my feet so I'll say something, offer them some insight into the mind of twenty-one-year-old breast cancer survivor. I'm up.

"Hello, my name is Tania Katan, and like my mother told you moments ago, I have breast cancer. Had it? Have it? Actually I'm not sure, but I'm missing a boob, so I am qualified to be here."

The women go nuts, raising their hands, eager to ask questions. I am the president of the United States holding a press conference.

"Yes, you, in the back." I motion to a woman jumping out of her seat.

"I can't believe that a twenty-one-year-old woman has breast cancer! Where did you grow up?"

"In a microwave. Next question."

"Does your family have a history?"

"A long one, thank you for asking. Next question."

"How did you know?"

"Well, once the lump exceeded the size of a golf ball, I thought, *Maybe something's wrong.*"

The woman in charge of ceremonies saves me from the lions.

"We're going to take a fifteen-minute break. We have cookies and coffee in the lobby, so..." She ushers the ladies to leave the room, to leave me alone.

In the middle of a clean getaway I'm cornered by a handful of women.

"Are you going to get reconstruction?" one of the ladies asks.

"Well, I don't know, but probably n—" I start to respond.

"You're really too young not to. I have a great plastic surgeon. I'll give you his number," offers another woman.

"I didn't say I was—"

"I'd get silicon. They look more real," says another woman.

"And they feel real too," yet another woman adds. "Go ahead, feel 'em!" she says while lifting up her shirt, grabbing my hand, and placing it on her hard oval mound. With my stiff hand grazing this random woman's breast, I turn to my mother and ask her if we can please get the hell out of here. She sees my discomfort and agrees to leave, but the damage is done. I'm never going to go to a support group again. I'm never going to get fake boobs. I'm never going to feel a random woman's breast again. Well...

"Hey, Alexander. It's me." I'm standing outside my movement class leaning against the pay phone.

"What's happening, Chemolicious?" I hear him exhale a long drag of cigarette smoke.

"Um, do you have a second?"

"A million for you, darling. What's wrong? You sound queer, and by that I mean peculiar."

"I sort of, well, I kind of… OK, it started the other night with these crazy breast cancer ladies at the support group my mom took me to. They were all excited and freaked out about my age and the fact that I'm not going to get reconstructive surgery, and when I left I was totally riled up, feeling really angry and uncomfortable about my body, about my age. So, when I went to school yesterday I didn't wear a bra. No bra, no prosthetic, and a tight shirt. I thought, *Fuck those support group ladies. I'm fine just the way I am.*"

"Right on, sister!"

"I was gonna show them, show everyone, that I'm comfortable having only one breast. I'm fine. I'm more than fine. I'm spec-fucking-tacular!"

"Swing out, sister!"

"So, you know what I did?"

"Don't leave a brother hanging, sister!"

"I walked into my movement class, past all of my unsuspecting classmates, who said, as usual, 'Hello, Tania.' But today I knew better than to accept their salutations at face value. That's right. Today I knew what they were thinking, what they *really* meant by 'Hello, Tania.' They were clearly saying, *What's up with your chest? Do you only have one breast? Why are you lopsided, Tania?* So I did what anyone would have done when a group of people is staring at them—I confronted one of them: Emma, this sweet skinny eighteen-year-old girl in my program. I said, 'Emma, what are you looking at, huh? You want to share with the rest of the class why you're staring at me? At my chest? Stop looking at my chest!' And when she turned away from me I said, 'Oh, I disgust you so much you can't even look at me? So I only have one breast—big deal.' That's when Emma burst into tears and ran out of the dance studio. I'm losing it, Alex. It's like every time I feel fine, all of a sudden there's this huge wave of fear and anxiety that reminds me I'm not fine, I might never be fine."

"Whoa. This is big, Ms. T. At least it happened in a drama class, kind of apropos."

"Before class I walked around campus wanting people to look at me so I could say, 'What the fuck are you looking at?' Or to not look at me so I could say, 'What, I'm too much of a freak for you to look at me?' I looked at them as if somehow *they* gave me cancer, because I don't have anyone to blame, because cancer just happens, because I don't know what to do, because—"

"You know what you need?" Alexander pipes in. "You need to shake your groove thing with a hot homo like myself. I mean, what happened to fun little Tania? Where's that sassy dyke who'd ditch school at a moment's notice so we could drink mochas and cruise queers all day, huh? Where's the girl everyone wants to make out with at Trash Disco?"

"She's on sabbatical. Wait, who wants to make out with me?"

"Everyone, even some of the guys. They think you're a dude, especially from the right side, with no boob and all."

"Alexander—"

"What about the three Ds: drinking, dancing, and diving for muff? Trash Disco is this Thursday—it's exactly what you need to get back to the fabulous Miss Katanalicious. Are you with me?"

"I'll think about it," I say with no intentions of really going.

I love Alexander Billingford III, but I've got other things to worry about than the three Ds. I've got to finish writing my play and finish chemotherapy. The three Ds don't sound so hot to me anymore. Even though my vocabulary still includes "awesome" and "totally cool," I feel older than twenty-one. But then again, I am twenty-one and this is how I feel, so I guess I feel like a twenty-one-year-old who is me. I'm in what Fran calls the grieving stage of dealing with loss. I didn't know you could grieve the loss of a body part; I thought grief was reserved for death, for losing a mother or father or sister. Although I'm not exactly sure how one grieves the loss of a booby, I'm working on it. I'm also grieving the loss of control over my body, and the big scar across my chest, and the fact that chemotherapy has depleted most of my energy. And I'm grieving my relationship with Dawn, because no matter how toxic it was, it was a relationship I chose. Doesn't Alexander realize that I don't have time for cocktails, that I'm too busy grieving?

I am jamming on my play. I even came up with a title for it: *STAGES*. I've been reading Susan Sontag's *Illness as Metaphor*, and all she talks about are the stages of grieving and the stages of cancer and the stages of deterioration. *STAGES* feels right. At least it's better than the title my

brother came up with: *Why Tania Can't Go Swimming.* My
blood-cell count is as low as it can get and still be safe for
me. That's what happens when you approach the end of
six months of chemotherapy. I'm feeling good, though,
even a little peppy. Maybe it's because I have a date with
Fran; that's right, a real date tonight with Fran.
Unfortunately a first date requires a new outfit, which
requires a trip to the mall, which means braving the chaos
and confusion of determined shoppers. I don't like going
to malls, but I am in Arizona where the unofficial state
motto is: "We don't have a cultural center, but we do have
malls."

One hundred degrees will force Arizonans to leave the
comfort of their recliners and head for the free air condi-
tioning that only Scottsdale Fashion Square can provide.
There are thousands of people milling about the mall
today. And many of them are wearing these silly-looking
pink ribbons. What are those ribbons about? I know the
red ribbons are for AIDS, the yellow ones are for our
troops, the purple are pro-choice, but pink?
"Excuse me. What does the pink ribbon stand for?" I ask a
woman wearing a pink ribbon on her lapel.
"Oh, breast cancer awareness. They're having free screen-
ings and information in the mall today," she says, smiling
and continuing with her shopping.
Two women sit behind a banner that reads BREAST CANCER
AWARENESS: BE AWARE. On the card table bearing the banner sits a stack of glossy pink brochures. I tentatively
approach the table.
"Go ahead, take as much information as you'd like," one

of the women says to me.

"Thanks," I tell her. This smells a bit like Y-Me.

"Would you like to make a donation?" the other woman asks.

I look at her, then at my chest, then at her again and say, "I already gave, thanks."

"Do you know someone who's had breast cancer?" the first woman asks.

"Your mother?" the second woman asks.

"An aunt?" says the first.

"A teacher?" says the second.

"A friend of the family?" says the first.

"ME," I finally have an opportunity to say.

"Oh, my God," says the second.

"You're so young," says the first.

"Too young," says the second.

"How old are you?" asks the first.

TWELVE! is what I want to say, but instead I say twenty-one and you're right, I am young, here's a check for ten bucks, thanks for the ribbon. I run out of the mall with no new outfit. I'm too young to have breast cancer? I didn't wake up one morning and say, "I'm twenty-one, active, my social life is booming, but give me some cancer, yeah, I'd love some breast cancer." They have no idea what it's like to be me. They don't know what it's like to have a big Frankenstein scar where your breast used to be. I wanted to tell those ladies what it's like to have hair so thin that people can see your scalp. One breast, no hair, it's a real blast. And having a headache or pain in my stomach and thinking that it's the cancer spreading, or feeling lumps that aren't there, and checking and rechecking and checking again until my breast is sore. I'm going through stuff I shouldn't even know about. And whenever I feel like I'm getting over it, I get knocked back down by ladies wearing pink ribbons. I want one day without breast cancer awareness.

surfing my web
(left breast—2002)

It's 10 P.M. Time to pop my first Zofran. Round two of chemotherapy is complete and I can't wait to go to Arizona to visit Angela. My chemo fog is a little thicker this time, so Mom and I decide to relax by watching *Moulin Rouge*. The phone rings just as we find out that Nicole Kidman's character is afflicted with consumption. It's got to be Angela. "Hey!"

"I'm downstairs. I need to talk to you now." It's not Angela. It's Sal. Maybe she's finally developed my photos. I put on my fluffy blue slippers, combat my feeling of nausea, and head down the stairs.

"Are you dating Angela?" Sal is seething.

"First of all, WHAT? And second of all, HUH?" How could she know that I was dating Angela? Oh man, I know how: When I was dating Sal, in a moment of love and trust, I blurted out what I thought was a funny e-mail password: DYKEDRAMA. It was just a password, not a request. Who knew that she would memorize it and then go surfing my Web?!

"I read your e-mails," she confesses.

Maybe it's the chemo, or the fact that this doesn't seem out of character for Sal, but I'm surprisingly calm. "Wow, Sal, you have invaded my privacy in such an overt and nasty

manner that you have only succeeded in pushing me further away from you."

"Well, if you called to let me know how you were doing, I
wouldn't have to hack into your e-mail to find out."

Asperger's or Asshole, it doesn't matter what disease Sal's
got—I've heard enough from her.

"I want you to leave now. I want you to go home and
think about all of the juicy, sexy, loving, *articulate* e-mails
Angela has sent me. Hey, why don't you print them out
and wallpaper your place with them? I'm really sorry you
felt the need to read my e-mails. I want you to mail me
the photographs of my breast immediately, and I want you
to please leave me alone."

"I'm sorry. I'll drop the pictures in the mail tomorrow,"
she says, looking as sad as she is.

When I tell my mom what just happened she says, "We
need to change your password to *NOSAL*."

surviving reality
(left breast—2002)

In preparation for my date with Angela, I am conducting
an independent sociological study on the effects of
chemotherapy on one's libido. I began my study last night,
at approximately 11:30 P.M. After a rousing conversation
with Angela in which she told me how she wanted to be
my naughty chemotherapy nurse, I was facedown on my
bed with a blanket tucked between my legs—yes, I am a
blanket humper—and moving vigorously. What usually
takes about three minutes took an hour. And when it
appeared as if I had come, I searched the blanket for some
dampness, some sign of life between my legs, but there was

nothing. My vagina has dried up, leaving my libido far behind. I am putting myself on a strict diet of vanilla porn and lively masturbation until I go to Arizona.

In addition to losing my libido, I've misplaced my passion for movement. Sitting in front of the TV set is my new favorite sport. The sound of tribal drums beating pulls me closer to the screen. A camera pans around a seemingly calm oceanside paradise. Wild animals and foliage in all their brilliant colors and expressions are onlookers to a group of very thin people. A voice-over is heard, "Welcome to *SURVIVOR*." The announcer goes on to say that this is a reality show. I've never seen a reality show. This is great. *Survivor.* This is the show for me! I wonder what they're surviving? That one on the left looks like he's got a touch of the cancer, and the one on the far right looks like she had a double mastectomy. This is amazing! I guess I haven't watched television in a very long time.

I watch as the tribe known as Soup-Chai is forced to compete against their rivals, Chewy-Is-Gone, in a game of…SURVIVAL. Equipped with my Zofran and a voyeuristic gleam in my eye, I wait for the challenge at hand.

"Today's challenge involves skill, dexterity, and strength." I can so relate to that. I turn up the volume as the khaki-clad man continues to speak, "You will have ten minutes to move those wooden dowels from here…to there!"

I don't get it? What kind of lame-o challenge is that? Wait a second. These people aren't sick. What the hell kind of "Survival" are they doing? They're engaged in Contrived Surviving. This isn't "Reality."

For the duration of *Survivor*, the members of Soup-Kitchen

and Chew-My-Leg-Off prance around in very small swim-suits flirting with each other, rowing canoes, figuring out puzzles, and sunbathing. I'd give my left breast to be on a tropical island with twelve totally hot half-naked people—oops, too late. How are they surviving? By seeing who can guess what's under coconut number one the fastest? Why don't they kick it up a notch and inject those young healthy survivors with a dash of cancer, a pinch of multiple sclerosis, and a touch of HIV? Some challenges might include Puzzle of Paralysis; Ring Around the Lesions; and Ductal, Ductal, Carcinoma. The new *Survivor* could be like the island of misfit toys: breaking broken people's spirits, all set to a funky tropical soundtrack on the coast of Thailand. What do you think, MTV? Television sucks. I think I'll go masturbate.

I fear that I am becoming a curmudgeonly old man, and here's the reason why: constipation. There is nothing worse for one's personal morale than being stopped up. Due to all of the chemicals coursing through my body, I haven't been able to have a *movement* for the past five days, but right now, nudging, peeking, poking, pushing out of my bottom is the beginning of a doodie. I am elated. Halfway through my first real push I realize I need some reinforcement, some backup for my backup, so I grab the *Times*. I'm reading and squeezing, and that's when I read, "Lynda Carter is the face of Irritable Bowel Syndrome." And right there in *The New York Times* is Wonder Woman, and I'm guessing she has a difficult time getting it out too. But as I continue to push and read the article, I find out that Wonder Woman doesn't even have IBS. She is one of the many celebrities who get paid assloads of money to represent pharmaceutical companies. That's not very honest of a woman who's known for tying people up and making them tell the truth, is it? This act of betrayal by my childhood superhero provides me with the *oomph* I need to give birth to my toxic five-day-old mass. My ass feels as if a gospel church congregation decided to hold services in it. I wipe myself and see blood. The prospect of getting off the toilet seems just as bleak as staying on it. I'm in so much pain that I have no idea how I might get off this toilet. I wish Wonder Woman could get me out of this bind.

Tomorrow I go to Arizona, and today I hate Sal. This is going to come as a surprise, I know, but the photos never arrived in the mail. Sal is holding my breast for ransom. She is using my booby for emotional leverage. My first attempt to collect my debt included an incredibly beautiful and well-crafted piece of writing, the closest I could come to writing a Hallmark card. I wanted to speak to her in a language she could understand; Hallmark was perfect for this occasion. The typestyle I chose was Snell Roundhand. The sentiment was flowery, mildly dramatic, and suggested urgency under the guise of calmness. I expressed how that film was the only photo archive of my breast's untimely departure; how the pictorial documentation of a booby's life lived was only important to me. The e-mail was perfect. I even got a bit weepy reading it. I hit *send* and waited for what was bound to be a genuine and caring response. Sal's e-mail was genuine, all right—genuinely fucked up:

Tania: First of all, those pictures were taken with MY camera, so technically they are MY pictures. Second, I don't

*need you to threaten me. When I'm ready I'll CONSIDER
giving them to you. You have no idea what I'm going
through. I'm dealing with my newly diagnosed depression.
I'm fighting for my life too. —S*

Today she must pay. I dial the number that has almost
been withdrawn from my memory bank.
"Hello, Sal?"
"Yes."
"It's Tania. How are you?"
"I'm great. Actually I've been really great ever since you
and I stopped talking to each other. As a matter of fact,
I'm not even suffering from depression anymore. My ther-
apist can't figure it out. I've even started to play the drums
again. It's amazing how much time and energy I have since
you're out of my life."
"That's great," I tell her. "Listen, I wanted to see if you
would send me my pictures, please."
"Well…I was actually thinking of sending them to you
just yesterday, and I think that I might be ready to do that.
Yeah, I'll send them to you."
"Great, I really appreciate it."
"But I have to tell you, Tania, I think you're an egocentric
bitch, and you fucking left me when I needed you the
most, when I was diagnosed with depression, and I'm still
pissed at you."
"I'm sorry. So you can send the pictures to my dad's. The
address is fifteen…"
"I know the address. I told you I'd send them. I've been
really angry with you. You know?"
I exert diplomacy in order to maintain my dignity and get

my freaking pictures already. "Well, I really hope you're taking care of yourself and…"

"What the fuck does that mean? Are you implying that something's wrong with me?"

"No, I just meant that I hope you're being kind to yourself, that's all."

"Fine. Whatever. I'll send you the pictures."

"Thank you. Take care."

Mission accomplished. The photos will soon be MINE. The phone rings.

"Hello?"

"Yeah, it's Sal."

"Hey, what's up?"

"I decided not to give you the pictures. If you want me to tell you why, I will, but I'm not going to give them to you."

"No, I don't want to know why." I slam the phone down hard.

Right now I want Sal to die. Is that wrong? Or is that the most right, visceral response I could have in this situation? I feel like I'm a character in one of those *Choose Your Own Adventure* books we used to read in junior high. You know, those books where the main character, a white, middle-class new girl in school, navigates her way toward popularity by choosing the right answers to high-stakes morality questions like, "Do you decide to go to the prom with John or Ron?"

Sal, your most psychotic ex, offers to give you back the pictures of the breast you just had removed due to cancer, but then quickly reneges. This makes you very upset. After talking to your parents about it, and writing furiously in your journal, you decide to take action. If you go over to her house and try to get your pictures back guerrilla-style, turn to page 33. If you decide to teach Sal a lesson she'll never forget, turn to page 56. If you decide to meditate and employ Thich Nhat Hahn's teachings, turn to page 89.

Page 33: You're in your car parked outside of Sal's nasty little brown adult tree house. It is approximately 7 P.M. Monday night. You know she is home because her SUV is in the drive-way. You take a large steel hook, and with all the anger that you possess regarding someone using your illness as a hook, you decide to make the metaphor literal and stab the hook into each one of her tires. As the air hisses out of Sal's tires you smile with a sense of accomplishment. You're feeling so empowered that you casually approach Sal's front door and knock. A stunned Sal hesitantly lets you in. You cut to the chase and ask for the photos. She feels out of control. She knows that if she gives you these photos, she gives up all the control she thinks those photos give her. She is not ready to do that. You ask her again, nicely. She insists that you leave her home. You see a golf club within reach. A five-iron. You grab it and knock Sal unconscious. You get your photos and leave. This is the end of your story.

Page 56: You arrive at Sal's workplace, where she is not out to her coworkers—except for the fact that she looks like a man. Sal is standing by the copier when you approach her. You calmly ask for your photographs. Sal asks you, rather angrily, to leave her place of employment. You see some toner within reach. You grab the toner, shake, and rip it open in Sal's direction. Sal is covered in ink. She seems very upset. You try to explain to her how toner, although toxic in nature, is not being injected into her veins, thus killing both her white and red blood cells, "So pipe down, missy!" Before leaving Sal's office you find an intercom system and broadcast the following: "Sal, in Technical Support, is the biggest dyke on earth! OH, and Sal thinks that [name all the coworkers she's been bitching about for the duration of your relationship] are FUCKING COCKSUCKERS. Have a nice day!"

You dash out of the building with a smile on your face. En route to your car you see an extremely attractive woman who says, "I loved what you did in there. I've always thought Sal was a jerk. Would you like to go out to dinner sometime?" If you opt to go to dinner with the hot chick who hates Sal, turn to page 109. If you get into your car and leave, this is the end of your story.

Page 89: You light some aromatherapy candles, draw a bath, and grab a copy of Peace Is Every Step. *Instinctively you open the book to the section titled "Relationships." Your breathing is fluid and deep. As you read you begin to understand that everyone is on a journey. You recognize the beauty in understanding and loving and helping. You mentally embrace the image of Sal. You give her a hug because you know she is in pain and coming from a place of fear and anxiety. You feel Zenlike. You feel as though you've feng shui-ed your worries away. While getting out of the tub you slip and black out. When you awaken you find yourself outside of Sal's house knocking on her door. She answers. You tell her that Thich Nhat Hanh has sent you. She is taken aback. You tell her you love her and wish her well and that what you are about to do is Buddha's will, sort of. You see a camera within reach. You grab it. You beat Sal unconscious with the camera. When you are finished, you take pictures of her in various incriminating poses. You will use them for blackmail at a later date. You look through a few drawers and find your pictures. You are happy. Before you leave you write Sal a loving note, "Thanks. See, it does feel good to give." This is the beginning of your story.*

i love fozzie
(right breast—1992)

Fran kissed me! It started with the play. We went to see a play, and when the lights went down, she took my hand in hers and held it, even caressed it, and from that point on, with all my theatrical training, I had no idea if the play we saw was a comedy, tragedy, or melodrama. I didn't care what we were watching because I was busy falling in love with Fran. After the show, Fran invited me back to *her place.* We walked on the Saltillo tiles lining her front porch to get to the screen door, which was locked. She opened the screen, then the main door, and as soon as we set foot inside her home she closed the door and said, "If I don't kiss you now, I'm going to die." Then she plants one juicy, fantastic kiss on my mouth and runs off to the bathroom. She's got good lips, she's cute, she's smart, she's not psychotic. True, she's eleven years older than me, but I'm pretty mature. So I'm thinking, yeah, this is gonna happen, and then I think, I hope she doesn't want to have sex with me, not that I wouldn't have sex with her, but she's older than me and, statistically speaking, has probably had more sexual experiences than I've had, which would be any number above two. When she comes back from the bathroom she says it's late and asks me to spend the night. And

I blurt out, "Do you want to have sex with me?" She says she does, at some point, but not tonight. I agree to spend the night. She gives me a pair of pink boxers with little pigs on them and a soft white T-shirt to wear to bed. Once in bed we kiss and cuddle until we can no longer keep our eyes open.

After Alexander Billingford III invited me to go to Trash Disco and I said I'd think about it and never went, we sort of drifted apart. No declarations like "I'm never talking to you again!" but more of a shift in interests. I ran into Alex eight months later at a fancy salon where he was cutting hair. Fran had given me a FREE HAIRCUT coupon for when my hair had grown in and was long enough to be cut. Alexander Billingford III cut my hair as we relived what seemed like old times, even though they had only happened a year ago. After my haircut, which looked fabulous, we decided to get a drink at Fosters and see what the place looked like during the day.

Lackluster is the only word to accurately describe a bar during the day, with natural light exposing all the tears in the shabby carpet and the chipped wood on the edges of the pool table. We ordered two vodka collins, and before I even had time to twirl the red plastic stirrer, blending the vodka and fruit juices together, Alex said, "Tania, I have to tell you something." He took a moment to stare into his drink as if the words to explain what he needed to say would be swimming around in his cocktail, forming sentences that could be easily skimmed off the top. "I have HIV."

He would go on to tell me that he was moving to New York

in a month to pursue his dream of being a hairstylist to Broadway's elite. I would tell him that after *STAGES* was produced in Arizona it went on to Connecticut, where *The New York Times* caught wind of it and interviewed me for their prestigious pages. He was busy collecting tips from the salon for a plane ticket, and I was busy being in love with Fran and getting my hair cut. We talked for a little bit about the similarities between HIV and cancer; there were many. Alex had to get back to the salon, and I had to show Fran my new hairdo. We hugged goodbye in the parking lot of Fosters. He told me he would call when he got set up in New York. Maybe Alex did call, but I never got the message, and soon we would lose contact altogether. Periodically I think about Alexander Billingford III shaking his groove thing at a New York hot spot and giving Patti LuPone a trim before she saunters onstage.

I'm in the Breast Clinic waiting to get a mammogram. It's my first one since chemo ended a year ago. The receptionist seems to think I'm in the wrong place. "Are you here for a mammogram?" she asks.
"Yes," I say.
"You're so young," she says.
"Yep."
I've learned not to get upset when people say, "You're so young." I mean, it's better than having them say "You're so old," right?
"Tania, why don't you come back with me?" a nurse says, bringing me to a room with a mammography unit. She asks me to take off my shirt and stand with my left breast parallel to the unit.

"Hold still. This is going to be a little uncomfortable," she says.

She has no idea how right she is. This has all been a little uncomfortable. Losing hair has been a little uncomfortable, waiting for blood work with tumor markers is a little uncomfortable, finding out that Alex has HIV has been a little uncomfortable. What *should* be comfortable is the fact that my doctors say I'm cancer-free, but whenever I get a bill from my oncologist or have to go in for a mammogram I feel like I have cancer all over again. I'm cancer-free until my mother has taped a special on the subject, until it's National Breast Cancer Awareness Month, or until I turn on the news. I try to check for lumps only once a day now, and I wait. For five years. A cure. Another lump. The next stage.

my first bald date
(no breasts)

I made Mom and Dad drop me off a block away from Angela's house. I'm so nervous. I'm bald and nervous. On the long drive to Arizona, while my parents argued in the front seat, I listened to my Walkman while visualizing swimming naked with Angela.

Angela opens the door. She is more beautiful than I remembered. We stand in the doorway for a long time. Words that have come so easily for both of us in writing and on the phone are long gone. We are left staring at each other.

"Wow," I say.

"I know," she says.

When the majority of a relationship is spent on a computer

or phone or postcard, being in front of the real deal is overwhelming.

"You look beautiful, Tania. Your head is so round and perfect."

"I know. I lucked out, huh?"

And the ice is broken and there's no turning back and it's easy to be present with someone you adore.

Even though we each have a history of taking off our clothes on the first date, we're both a little shy. We manage to get over our shyness, get out of our clothes, and get into the pool before the other has a chance to look. The water is a perfect temperature, and when Angela suggests that I lie on my back so I can feel the water on my head, I do. She slowly moves my body around the pool, allowing me to feel the water swirling around my head.

"When we kiss, who do you think will make the first move?" Angela asks, reminding me that even though I have had a lot of fantasies about Angela, and a lot of them have been sexual in nature, we haven't even kissed yet. This is so exciting.

"I will," I say and lean in for a kiss.

It's a sweet kiss—mouths closed, lips full, energy exploding.

We continue to float, face-to-face, around the pool, our bodies wrapped around each other's, our vocabulary restored. We talk in complete sentences, whole paragraphs, entire stories.

Once we're out of the pool and dried off, Angela presents me with a gift: two of the kookiest wigs ever constructed. One looks like it was procured from the head

of Laurie Anderson and the other looks like it belonged
to Pamela Anderson.
"They're for the photo shoot later this evening," Angela
says, laughing.
I love our first date.
We've showered and are in our pajamas. Angela wears a
vintage black slip, and I'm in my men's red-striped Brooks
Brothers pajamas. We jump into Angela's bed. When she
gets up to go to the bathroom I quickly check the tag on
the sheet to find that her thread count is off the charts.
Angela grabs a box of photos to show me what she looked
like when she was bald. We're sitting on her bed, close; her
bare legs are brushing against mine. We look at slides of
her work; we read a short play of mine together, both of us
changing our voices to become various characters; we kiss
in between all of the parts that make our connection a
whole. I love this woman.
"I want to give you a foot massage," Angela announces at
2 A.M. as she squeezes a tube of eucalyptus/mint lotion. Is
she for real? I fall asleep to her massaging my feet.

A good morning indeed! This morning, after Angela
served me fresh-squeezed orange juice in bed, after our
photo shoot where we put on the wigs, filled up wine
glasses with cherry juice, and pretended to be at a cocktail
party, after we found out that both of us use only one yolk
and two egg whites in our omelets, after Angela asked if I
ate the rind on cheese and I said, "Duh, I'm French," and
she was pleased, after all the good stuff, we end up here, in
bed again, with Angela underneath me, her black vintage
slip slipping up to expose the fact that she's not wearing

panties. We are kissing so furiously that I'm going to have to break my mental rule of not making love with her on the first date. She stops.

"Tania, I'm not going to make love with you today. I want to, but I want to wait. Because when we finally do make love it's going to be spectacular."

It's a nice sentiment, and I do agree with her, but she is so sexy and her slip keeps working its way up and my libido is back! We're kissing again and this time it doesn't look like either of us is going to stop. But looks can be deceiving. Angela stops. "I've got an idea. We can each touch each other anywhere we want for five seconds."

"That sounds fair. Why don't you go first?" I say.

Her fingers work their way down my chest, across my belly. "Don't start my time yet," she says and continues to work her way to my pussy. "OK, you can start now."

I count slowly, "One...one thousand, two...one thousand..."

It's my turn. I place my hands on either side of her ass. I dip my head down, toward her crotch. She gasps, "I didn't know we could use our mouths!"

"You said we could touch anywhere we wanted. You didn't say we had to use our hands."

My mom and dad arrive at the designated time, on the designated street, one block away from Angela's house, to pick me up. I'm smiling the kind of mischievous smile that appears when it's early Sunday morning and you can't find your car because you're not familiar with the neighborhood, because you don't live there. Your panties—if you were wearing any—are in your back pocket. You've got fucked-up rock star hair, you reek of pomade and pussy, and when you finally find your car you get inside and somehow your fingers brush against your nose as you inhale the images that made up last night, and a smile comes across your face. That's the kind of smile I'm talking about.

whose gene is it anyway?
(no breasts)

I call my oncologist with two important questions, but I get the nurse instead.

"So, could you tell Dr. Moore that it's going to be my thirty-first birthday in a couple of days and I'll be celebrating with my friends in San Francisco, so…do you think it would be OK if I have a cocktail? And my second question is: Are the results from my genetic test in yet?"

The nurse notes my questions and says she'll have the doctor get back to me.

Three minutes pass. The phone rings. I'm impressed.

"Hello?" I say.

"Hello, may I speak with Tania Katan?"

"Dr. Moore?"

"Yes, hi, Tania. How are you doing?"

"OK," I say, anxious for the answers to my questions.

"Great! So you have a couple of questions?"

"Yes. Can I have a drink, and has my genetic test come back?"

"Right. First of all, who told you you couldn't drink?"

"I just thought that because of the chemo—"

"You can have a drink. Hell, you can have two drinks. You can safely have two drinks every day for the duration of your chemotherapy if you want to."

"Whoa, I'm not asking for a prescription to be an alcoholic. I just want a cosmo."

"Now, about the genetic testing. Yes, your results are in, and yes, you *do* have the BRCA-1 gene."

Wait, wait, wait! It's my birthday. I'm gonna be thirty-one years old. I'm not supposed to be issued a genetic death sentence by a cheerful doctor. I called for good news. This is the wrong extension. I'll try back later.

"I'm sorry, but I have the gene? Did you say I have the gene?"

"Yes. Did you think you weren't going to have the gene? I told you I was hedging my bets on your having it."

While my doctor is pleased with being right, I'm feeling wronged in a monumental way.

"Now, with the BRCA-1, you have about a forty-percent risk of developing ovarian cancer, as we discussed in our first meeting. To give you an idea of what that means, women who do not possess the gene have a one-percent chance of developing ovarian cancer in their lifetime. Ovarian cancer *can* be treated. However, we don't have a way of detecting it. Unless, of course, you become symptomatic, but by that time it's too late. Are you going to have children?"

"I kind of… I was planning on… I really want to…"

"Because my recommendation is to get your ovaries out as soon as possible. The more you menstruate, the greater your chances are for developing ovarian cancer."

What happened to my buddy Dr. Moore? The guy who stood up for me?

"Your aunt who had breast cancer, did she die of it?" Dr. Moore asks.

"No. She died of ovarian cancer."

"Mmmm. Well, at least you can drink, right? Have a couple of glasses of red wine and enjoy your birthday!"

As soon as I get off the phone with Dr. Moore I feel defeated. I tell Mom and Dad about the gene, then peacefully go to my room with the phone to call Angela and cry. Angela's not home, so I leave a message. I already know that I'm going to get ovarian cancer and die—why would the gene spare me that? My aunt had breast cancer, then ovarian cancer, and then death; that's my cancer role model. I try to stop the images from playing out in my brain, but they're coming too fast and developing into tears and now moans.

I hear Mom and Dad fighting in the other room. It's reminiscent of being four years old in New York. The discovery of a gene that causes death brings a lot of blame with it. From what I can hear, Mom is blaming Dad and his Ashkenazi family, and Dad is screaming for Mom to shut the fuck up, and I'm really sorry that I have this gene for everyone. I'm sorry.

In between my gulping for air and sobbing, the phone rings. Needing to talk with Angela, I pick up.

"Hello, Tania?" Oh, my God, Sal? Not now.

"It's Stephanie—"

With that heavy tone on the other end of the phone I thought it was Sal. But it's Stephanie, my old buddy and Angela's most recent ex-girlfriend.

Here's the deal with getting cancer, with having a terminal gene, with feeling unattractive and having the looks to match; I'm going to let you in on a little known fact about illness: Just because you get sick doesn't mean the world stops. That's right, banks still want their money back, tele-marketers still call late at night, and ex-girlfriends still have bones to pick. Just because you've received the worst news of your life doesn't mean people stop being jealous, stop ripping you a new asshole because they're still pining away for your current girlfriend, stop talking long enough to hear that you're crying. I'm just telling you the facts about illness, the facts that nobody lists in their brochures. Just because you're bald doesn't mean you can change the date of your license-renewal photo. Just because you feel intense guilt for having a genetic mutation doesn't mean your parents, in the next room, feel any better knowing they've given you this gene. People keep calling, photos continue to be taken, and the world keeps spinning.

"I have to get off the phone now, Stephanie. I'm sorry you feel this way. I'm really sorry."

the labyrinth
(no breasts)

I'm in San Francisco for my thirty-first birthday. Angela couldn't make it, but I traded in my Cell Phones Are For Losers status for a cell phone, so I can talk with my girl-friend for 600 minutes during the week and unlimited weekend minutes.

For the past three years, on my birthday, I have engaged in my own self-imposed adult-type ritual: walking the labyrinth at Grace Cathedral. Today I really need to walk the labyrinth.

The sun is shining through the saturated colors of stained glass that line the cathedral, illuminating all of the people here, hunched over, taking off sneakers in preparation to walk the labyrinth. There is a sign at the beginning of the labyrinth that gives a brief history of what it signifies and why one might walk the path. It says, "The labyrinth is used as a meditation and prayer tool. It is a metaphor for life's journey. It takes us out of our ego. It is a journey to the center of our deepest self."

At first I'm always a little self-conscious, especially when there are a lot of people walking the labyrinth, like today. Focusing more on *looking* Zen rather than *being* Zen. Should I speed up and pass someone, or walk slower and let them pass me? If I choose to pass someone, is that a metaphor? Breathe, Katan. OK, I'm allowing my brain to let go of being self-conscious, to let go of ego. My breathing is falling into a rhythm, and my feet are following suit. No longer are there other people on my path. It's just me, here, breathing, walking, and clearing my mind. I curve around the soft clovers, down the narrow straightaways, into the center.

I'm sitting in the middle of the labyrinth, closing my eyes and breathing. I feel like I have arrived somewhere, not sure where, but it feels good. Even through my closed eyes I can see the brilliant colors of the stained glass. Wow, I'm thirty-one years old! This has been a long journey. And I have a feeling that I've only completed the first leg of it. The twenty-one-to-thirty-one leg. The growing years? The cancer years? The falling-in-love years? The toxic-girlfriend years? Assuming that I've completed one leg, what's next? I'm almost finished with chemotherapy, I'm in love with Angela, my genetic code is uncertain: Now what? It's like I'm entering a second adolescence: thinking about moving out of my parents' place, getting a job… Maybe I'll write a memoir about this leg of my journey. Can a person under the age of ninety write a memoir?

I think that before I start on my next journey I need to get rid of some crap. Here goes: It's a visualization that my friend Julia taught me. It's a little woo-woo, but I think it's perfect for the occasion. I'm picturing a pink bubble, a big pink bubble, a huge pink bubble. It's soft, like chewing gum, like millions of pieces of pink chewing gum, blown out of the mouth of God to form an enormous bubble. I am delicately placing Sal in this enormous pink bubble. I am placing the photographs of my breast in the bubble. Dawn, Stephanie, and icky doctors. I am placing hard feelings and anger in the bubble. And the final guest I will be placing in the bubble is cancer. I see all of these people and ideas that don't work for me anymore, and I gently blow, watching as the bubble floats away until I can no longer see it.

mapping the human genome
(no breasts)

Dr. Quiet takes the stage, and as her name might suggest, a hush falls over the congregation. Dr. Quiet looks like Joanne from HR, or Sue from accounting, or basically any woman you've ever seen by a cooler, corner, or counter. The light from her sleek Japanese laptop illuminates her plain but knowledgeable face.

"Mapping is the construction of a series of chromosome descriptions that depict the position and spacing of unique, identifiable biochemical landmarks," Dr. Quiet claims without looking up from her computer screen.

It's the day before my 10K and I'm in Arizona, sitting in a synagogue surrounded by my people. There are at least twenty-five breast cancer survivors; four, no, definitely five lesbians; and presumably a whole temple full of Jews. I should feel calm, comforted, but instead my grungy red suede Reebok sneakers are twitching, bouncing up and down, dancing around the floor. They are nervous. I'm fine. Angela sits next to me. We are two cancer survivors in a pod. How lucky am I to have found a girlfriend who has also had cancer, albeit lymphoma, but cancer just the same? We're here to listen to Dr. Quiet speak about the breast cancer gene and how it affects Eastern European Jews.

Dr. Quiet's lecture begins with basic breast cancer facts: lumps, mammograms, treatments. Although I appreciate the fact that there are other people here, some dealing with breast cancer for the first time, as an unofficial expert on breast cancer, I would like detailed information on my gene, the BRCA-1, now, please.

"Now, as far as the BRCA-1 and BRCA-2…" Dr. Quiet says, picking up on my telepathic signals, "if you're of Eastern European Jewish decent with a family history of breast or ovarian cancer, you might want to consider being tested for BRCA-1 and BRCA-2."

OK, been there, done that, got the gene, now what?

"Now I'll answer your questions," she says, pecking at her computer in hopes of turning it off.

That's all? That's it? No more time spent following the "identifiable biochemical landmarks"? I look around this temple, this sanctuary, to discover that I'm the youngest one in here by at least ten years. When I was twenty-one and dealing with my first round of breast cancer, I was young. But now, at thirty-one, with three surgeries, five scars, and ten rounds of chemotherapy under my belt, I am weathered and worthy of fitting in. Where is my sanctuary? I raise my right hand as high as it will go. The doctor skims the crowd for a worthy question. Using my left hand I hold the side of my chair and push, lifting my body and thus my arm higher, trying to increase my chances of being seen. The doctor looks in my direction and then…and then…passes over me. If it were Passover, I would be revered. They would call upon me to ask the four questions: *Am I the only one in this room with the gene? How many times will I get cancer in my lifetime? What else will I need to have removed from my body? Why is tonight different from all other nights?*

Dr. Quiet calls upon the person whose arms are flailing in the most flamboyant manner.

"Is stem cell replacement an acceptable form of treatment for advanced breast cancer?" asks an older woman in the twelfth row.

As the doctor begins to answer the question, another question is launched into the air, like a grenade, by the older woman in the second row: "Are mammograms really the best method of detection?" Again the doctor attempts to answer the question, but now there's an all-out air raid of inquiries. The last question to be catapulted is, "What about sleeping with circumcised men? Does that cause ovarian cancer?" This is asked by a ninety-year-old woman in my row.

Dr. Quiet, holding back a smile, addresses the woman, "Actually, that's cervical cancer, and there are no conclusive studies to suggest that's true."

I wonder if this ninety-year-old woman is having sex with men who are circumcised, or uncircumcised for that matter? The ninety-year-old has a follow-up question: "You just mentioned something about cesareans. Did you say that having a cesarean increases your risk for getting breast cancer?"

Dr. Quiet is obviously processing this information, as she hasn't said anything about cesareans. "Oh, no, I was talking about stem cell replacement."

The half-deaf ninety-year-old woman, who is clearly sexually active and undoubtedly fertile, says, "Oh."

A man on a mission is next to ask a question. He begins with a three-minute presentation of *everything* he knows about hormone replacement therapy, or as he says, "HRT." His speech ends with a question that can't be answered.

My hand is still in the air; I have a question that can be answered. I even have a few questions for this man: Why are you here, sir? Why do you need to assert your knowledge of a disease that is primarily linked to a gender other than your own? Is this about your wife? Sister? Mother? Does one of them have breast cancer? Is she still alive? What do you really want to ask the doctor? Are you going to be all right?

I'm certain all religions and cultures have their own unique way of getting their needs met. The Jews are no exception. As an American Jew, I've noticed that one need my tribe has is the need for reassurance. We need to be reassured that sometimes a shower is just a shower; that we are, in fact, funnier than people of other faiths; and, most important, that a headache is not necessarily a brain tumor. The Jewish body is a sensitive one. There is the Jewish

Stomach, for example, which is an undocumented medical phenomenon characterized by a pain in the stomach, which seems to be caused by anything from eating to breathing. Then there's the Jewish Lower Back, which is characterized by a pain in the lower back caused by everything from lifting a cup of coffee to lifting a bran muffin. And Jews don't even need to be symptomatic in order to feel like they need reassurance. Simply knowing someone in our family has a disease is enough for us to believe that we too have that disease. In our pursuit to understand our bodies, we *love* the doctor, the medical professional whose only job is to indulge us in our symptoms, real or imagined, and offer us advice.

Shooting up my arm is a startling and constant pain that suggests I should put it down. But I can't. If my question goes unanswered I will experience a pain deeper than that of my arm. Questions and answers shift to free advice as the congregation seeks to be collectively reassured. A disembodied female voice wants to know if she made the right decision to take estrogen for the last eight years. Another woman wonders aloud why she suffers from vaginal dryness. A man explores the implications of a lump he found in his testicle.

Dr. Quiet attempts to regain control of this emotional free-for-all by addressing the next arm she sees waving in the air; it is not mine. The arm is that of a forty-something unnaturally blond woman with breasts up to her neck that are not planning on moving down anytime soon. "Dr. Quee-ette, our family is riddled with breast cancer. My sister was diagnosed with breast cancer three years ago, and my aunt Rose had it—"

Aunt Rose interjects with the authority of a neurosurgeon, "That's right, doctor, I had it just twelve years ago."

The blond continues, "And I had breast cancer three years ago and—"

Her mother interrupts, "And we also have a cousin who died of a brain tumor, and then there's Vivienne, who had precancerous cells in her uterus. OH, and I have a melanoma."

The blond continues, "So Dr. Quee-ette, do you think I should get tested for the gene?"

My arm sways, suspended in the air; it's been hanging there for ten minutes now. I want to ask a question about my map, about how my chromosomes are constructed, about any possible roadblocks I might encounter. I've been forming this question ever since I found out about my genetic mutation. This question is not only for my benefit but for the benefit of anyone in this sanctuary who has the gene. Dr. Quiet continues to indulge this family in a private therapy session for public consumption. The family is now talking at whim. Long gone is the etiquette of hand-raising, waiting to be acknowledged, and then speaking. It feels more like a kooky game show than an informative lecture. If Richard Dawson were here, he'd know how to facilitate this *Family Feud*.

"YOU say, every female member of your family has had breast cancer. SURVEY SAYS...Aunt Marilyn, Cousin Jody, and Grandmother Rebecca had OVARIAN Cancer. I'm sorry, but the Cohens are in the lead."

Family therapy hour seems to be winding down. I crawl up on my chair, stretching my now-tired arm higher.

Finally, I catch Dr. Quiet's eye.

"Yes…?" she says.

"Are you aware of how many women who…" My voice starts to trail off, less fierce and direct than the question sounded in my head. As I listen to myself speak, I sound weak and start to shake. The shaking travels from my feet up to my legs, into my stomach, and then my throat, constricting my speech, forcing me to reach into the depths of my soul for an ounce of momentum. "Umm, uh, how many women who have the BRCA-1 gene and have developed breast cancer…" My whole being is shaking. I am far away. In slow motion. I can't even see Angela anymore. I feel like I'm in one of those dreams where I'm about to fall off a bridge or someone's gonna kill me or I'm on a plane that's going down and the only way I can escape the grip of death is to scream. I open my mouth and…nothing. I scream air.

"…Uh, and develop breast cancer, go on to develop ovarian cancer?" I ask.

"BRCA-1 carriers have an eighty-five–percent chance of developing breast cancer and a forty-percent chance of developing ovarian cancer," she succinctly answers.

But I knew that, I know that, what I really want to know is, of the eighty-five percent who have had breast cancer, what percentage *also* get ovarian cancer? How many of the forty percent end up dying of ovarian cancer? What about the sixty percent and the fifteen percent? Do they ever have feelings of guilt? Will I get ovarian cancer? Am I in the forty percent or the sixty percent? Why am I always such a rarity? Who here knows that I'm a genetic time bomb that might go off at any second? Can I scream my way out of my DNA? Am I the only woman who goes for a jog and when my body feels like giving up, mentally motivates herself by saying, *Tania, if you run one more mile, you won't get ovarian cancer*? "Thanks, Dr. Quiet," I say, fighting back tears.

The talk is over. Angela says something to me; it could be anything—I can't hear her. Tears temporarily distort my vision, my hearing. I race out of the sanctuary with Angela running to keep up. We drive home in silence.

At home, in bed, while trying to understand the statistics and ramifications of being with me, Angela says, "I want to be with you whether you're in the forty percent or the sixty percent; I just want to be with you." I feel her wet face pressing into my cheek as she wraps her arms around me and pulls me into her. In the privacy of the dark I allow myself to sob.

What does 6.2 miles look like, feel like, sound like? When you're driving from Long Beach to Phoenix to join your girlfriend to run that 10K you committed to doing when you were under the influence of morphine and new love, 6.2 miles is a long way. Right after Blythe, when there's no real semblance of a town, click your odometer to clear all the miles that have come before. While you blow through tumbleweeds and wilting cacti, in hundred-degree heat, you will see how slowly 0.1 becomes 0.2 becomes 0.3. And you're not even at one mile when you realize that if you were stranded in this unseasonably hot desert and had to walk or, God forbid, run 6.2 miles to the nearest sign of life, you'd be a mess.

My 10K training was kind of like a boxing-film montage: sweats, steps, and slow motion. Only instead of me running up steps, for my last chemotherapy treatment I could barely walk up the eight or so steps without breaking into a sweat. Instead of wearing sweats I was drenched in sweat. And the slow-motion part of my less-than-triumphant montage consisted of me attempting to run on the treadmill at the gym. Feeling strong now? As I only had a few more days before Angela and I would run the Phoenix *New Times* 10K to raise money for heart disease, I celebrated my final day of chemo—along with my lowest cell count to date—with a training run at the Long Beach Jewish Community Center.

Hopefully this would be the last time my mom accompanied me to the gym. I was ready to be a grownup again. With a stack of magazines almost tipping over the Lucite rack resting on the digital display of her stationary bicycle, my mother looked like an average middle-aged woman as she pedaled and previewed all the magazines that would soon be resting on her coffee table at home. Nearby, with two strands of aspiring blond hair poking out of my head, I tried to run five miles on the treadmill. When I say try, I mean that one mile into this fun run I frantically, repeatedly pressed the arrow that pointed down on the treadmill display, reducing my speed from slow to slower. There's something about watching your chubby fifty-year-old mother, who has never played sports at any point in her life because, as she puts it, "I have no sense of balance," deftly and energetically pedal a bicycle faster than you can even think. Which makes me think, *How am I going to run 6.2 miles?*

Weeks earlier Angela had said to me, with great tenderness, "Tania, if I need to run a little bit faster, you know, go ahead, would that be all right with you?"

"Of course," I told her, wanting her to achieve her goal as much as I wanted to achieve mine. Angela had been training to run a 10K long before I was bald and in her life. She had been training for about a year now. Her body was strong—and sexy—and her mind was focused and connected to her body. She was ready to run. Her goal was to run the entire 10K in as close to an hour as possible. My goal, a bit different, was to run without stopping, dropping, or dying.

I look like I'm racing for the wrong cure: Bald, tired, and yellow, I'm clearly not a poster child for heart disease. Angela is the embodiment of health as she bounces up and down, wearing her shiny, tight black running pants with two continuous white stripes on either side, her pink long-sleeve lightweight running shirt, and a matching mesh baseball cap, with her cute dark locks purposefully placed behind her ears and slightly sticking out from under the cap to contrast with her smooth skin. She's doing all the cool runner stretches too: foot on sidewalk, leaning weight down to stretch the calves, left leg over right leg, crossed at the ankle, bending at the waist all the way down, hugging face against shins. Meanwhile I'm stretching my nerves, shifting my weight between being nervous and having the nerve to run in a race I haven't properly trained for. With my soft black running pants, mesh blue hooded running jacket, and running shoes, I kind of look like a runner. From the outside no one notices that I'm an imposter, that underneath my stylish orange baseball cap is a bald head covered in three layers of SPF 50. For all intents and purposes I can run ten kilometers. I am one of them.

The map for the race is a unique arrangement of rock bands, landmarks, and roadblocks, creating a feeling of weaving in and out of Arizona's history. Seeing what's ahead should be calming, but instead it's stifling to see how much ground we will cover.

As I review the course over and over again, Angela grabs my hand. "We're really doing this, Tania!" she says, smiling. Her excitement infiltrates my body and I'm excited too, not thinking about the roadblock on Central and Thomas but thinking about the fact that I'm free. I'm free of chemotherapy, free to be with Angela in Arizona, free to drive myself to the gym or anywhere else I choose. I'm free!

Arizona has a way of getting hot while other states are still sleeping. By the time the announcer says, "10K runners, take your marks..." it's ninety degrees and steadily getting hotter. Angela and I inch toward the starting line, holding hands and smiling.

"Are you ready, 10K-ers?" The crowd screams. "Go!" And we're off! Well, actually it's not as fast or fluid as I imagined. I thought it would be more like when you see Olympian sprinters and the gun is fired and they bolt as fast as they can down the long stretch of compact dirt—just them against the yards. This is different; this is human bodies bottlenecking. We're jam-packed, barely able to move, let alone run. If this pace persists, I'll be fine. The first few minutes we're basically jogging in place while optimistically leaning forward. Soon the crowd thins and begins its separation process. There are three distinct groups that emerge: professional runners, people in shape,

and people with something to prove. Naturally I filter into
the third category, along with people who just gave up
smoking, recent divorcées, and prosthetic-limb wearers.
Angela looks amazing. Her strides are steady and confident. I know she will leave my side soon. "Tania, I love
you. Is it OK if I go ahead?" she says, building up momentum, looking ahead.

"Kick some ass, honey!" I tell her, giving her a firm pat on
the back. And she's off.

It's now ninety-five degrees, and I've passed at least three
Arizona bands that will never be heard from outside the
local scene. My body continues to lurch forward like a car
with a crappy transmission. With the sun taking jabs at
my head and people walking faster than I'm running, I
need a mantra: *If I make it the whole way without stopping,
I won't get ovarian cancer.* OK, that's a fucked-up mantra.
(I think the DSM calls it "magical thinking.") It's time for
a new mantra: *If I make it the whole way, I will get to snuggle with Angela for the rest of my life.* Good one. (Yeah, I
know, it's still magical thinking, but it's very happy magical
thinking.) Passing the three-mile marker, reciting my magical mantra, and picturing Angela waiting for me at the
finish line propels me to the four-mile marker. En route to
the five-mile marker I grab cups of water without stopping, toss the water into my dry mouth, crumple up the
cups, and throw them to the ground like I'm King Kong.
A cup won't slow me down. Fog created by sweat and heat
overtakes the lenses in my glasses, reducing my visibility to
about one foot. In trying to use the sleeve of my fancy
moisture-extracting shirt to wipe the condensation from
my glasses, I only succeed in smearing and adding to the

damp concoction.

Somehow I'm able to see the finish line, and in seeing the finish line I'm able to see Angela, and in seeing Angela I'm able to see myself finishing. I sprint toward the finish line—as fast as someone with no cells can sprint. The long banner that reads FINISH LINE practically hugs me as I lean into it. In slow motion sweat drips off my accomplished brow and onto the tarmac. Like Chris Cahill in *Personal Best*, I am a winner. My arms throw themselves into the air, celebrating what the rest of my body is too tired to comprehend: I made it! I wait for Angela to run up to me, throw her arms around me, and give me a victory kiss. But I don't see her; maybe she was a hallucination. Where is she? Did she make it all right? I wait. I wait some more. Then I head over to the designated if-we-get-separated-from-each-other-here's-where-we'll-meet place. As I pass all the booths with smiling people peddling PowerBars and juice I want to tell everyone that I did it. I take off my baseball cap to feel the heat, to be in the moment.

Angela is not at the designated safe place. After an hour and fifteen minutes of waiting for her, when the last Powerbar stand has packed up for the afternoon, I decide to go to the car; maybe she's waiting there for me, maybe we had a miscommunication regarding where to meet. Yeah, that's it, she's at the car. Angela is not at the car, and now it's getting really late and I'm worried about her and simultaneously sad that we couldn't share in each other's accomplishments. All of a sudden a weary and confused figure approaches the car. It's Angela. She's crying.

"Oh, my God, Tania, I'm so glad you're OK. Oh, God." She hugs me hard and sniffles through her words. "I thought you didn't make it. When I finished the race I ran to a booth to grab some water and then went back to the finish line to wait for you. I waited ten minutes, fifteen, then thirty-five…When the stragglers started coming in and there was still no sign of you, I panicked. I ran back down the course, following the map to a T, but there was no one around except for a security guard talking on a CB about a woman who had passed out at the three-mile marker. I thought you were the one who passed out, Tania." Angela's crying has softened. "I didn't know where you were. I thought you'd gotten sick and passed out."

"Honey, I did it! I made it! I ran the whole way!" I tell her.

"Oh, I'm so happy for you!"

"Yeah, and you'll never guess what my time was."

"What?" she asks.

"One hour and eleven minutes."

"That's impossible—you were so far behind me. My time was an hour and six minutes."

"We missed each other in the five minutes it took for you to get water."

topless 10K

It's Sunday morning, 6 A.M., and really cold outside. If I had nipples, they'd be hard right now. I'm thirty-three years old and at the City of Hope's 10K to raise money for breast cancer. Angela and I have been living together in Los Angeles for almost two years. Today Angela and our friend Mary Kay are acting as cheerleaders for this event, holding signs that read, RUN, TANIA, RUN! and NO BOOBIES, NO PROBLEM! TANIA KICKS ASS! This 10K is now my third. Two months after the 10K for heart disease (Angela:

1:06:12, me: 1:11:03), Angela and I ran in the 10K for diabetes (Angela: 1:04:32, me: 1:05:00), and now it's time to run for my peeps. I have two goals for this 10K: to run the entire 6.2 miles in less than an hour, and to do it without my shirt on.

I don't know if you're aware of this, but at every breast cancer conference, fund-raiser, or 10K, women are given copious amounts of cosmetic products. I could never make sense of this: Are women who are dealing with cancer supposed to feel healthier if their eye shadow matches their baseball cap? Because when I think of looking and feeling healthy, I think of a body in motion, a body moving so calmly and quickly that it inspires other bodies to move. In deciding to bare it all, or at least half, I want to present a healthy body in a different form. That's all. Last night, however, I was freaking out about this action. I mean, could I get arrested for indecent exposure? What if people see my scars and get scared? What if they see my scars and don't say anything? So, at two in the morning I got on the computer and looked up California state laws on indecent exposure. It turns out that because I no longer have areolas and I'm not going to derive any sexual pleasure from the act of running ten kilometers (well, maybe a little), I'm safe from the law.

When I was imagining the City of Hope's 10K I never imagined *thousands* of people at this event. Nope, not once. But, alas, this pink wonderland is filled with my people. Frenzied people, running from booth to booth, loading up on free Luna bars, pink hats, and T-shirts. I'm no exception. Fortunately Angela and Mary Kay hold all the pink stuff, in pink plastic bags, that I will probably never use but right now seem necessary, almost urgent. Every time I make eye contact with someone I excitedly say, "Hey, have a good run!" and "Good luck!" and "You can do it!" Sometimes the women smile back, but mostly they're confused by my enthusiasm, like I'm blissfully unaware of why we're all gathered here, like I'm too young to possibly understand breast cancer and its serious nature. I remain undaunted in sharing my excitement with every person who crosses my path. Yeah!

There is definitely a heaviness at this event that didn't exist at the other two 10Ks. Women wearing T-shirts with lists of names printed under headings like WE MISS YOU and WE'RE RUNNING FOR YOU. Women walking slower, holding the hands of their daughters tighter, taking note of the women around them and asking silent questions of comparison: *I wonder if her cancer metastasized? Is she going to actually run? Will she make it? Will I make it?*

As the announcer calls for all the 10K runners to head to the starting line, Angela, Mary Kay, and I work out a strategy for my taking off my jacket.

"OK, I'm going to be right here on the sidelines next to you," Angela says, firmly planting herself in front of the thousands of onlookers. "Then, like thirty seconds before the announcer says 'Go,' unzip your jacket and hand it to me."

"Meanwhile," Mary Kay adds, "I'll be at the finish line taking pictures of your beautiful bare chest, OK?"

"OK," I say, gulping as more and more people surround me. Within moments there's a sheet of people in sneakers extending at least a quarter of a mile back and seventy feet

across. *How am I going to take off my jacket? Why am I going to take off my jacket? Help! Oh, great, the Cub Scouts of America are the official helpers of this event. So now I'll have to run half-naked through a human starting line made up of awkward preteens stuffed into khaki uniforms. Shit.*
Angela looks at her watch, then at me.

"Tania," she says in a loud whisper, "it's time."

Just as I'm about to disrobe I realize I'm standing only inches away from a kind-looking woman on the sidelines and that perhaps I should fill her in on my little action before I freak her out.

"Excuse me," I say nervously.

"Yes?" she says calmly.

"Um, in like a second, I'm going to take off my jacket, exposing my mastectomy scars, and I just wanted to tell you so you won't freak out."

The woman pauses for a moment and says, "Can I hug you?"

We embrace. I unzip my jacket, toss it to Angela, who smiles upon receiving it, and wait for the announcer.

"10K runners, take your marks and...GO!"

My shoulders are relaxed, legs are moving fast, breathing is efficient and easy. I almost forget that I'm half-naked until I reach the first water station, where several stunned cub scouts are barely able to hand me a cup of water. Somehow the fifty-five degrees feels warm to me. I am booking, running so fast that I have to remind myself, *Tania, pace yourself.*

When I spot the three-mile marker just ahead I wonder what happened to miles one and two, but by that time I'm nearing the finish line and it's time to sprint.

"HEY, Tania!" Mary Kay shouts from the finish line, snapping photos as fast as she can. "You look amazing!"

A larger-than-life digital display hangs over the finish line. One of the cub scout leaders, an older guy with a whistle around his neck, yells to me, "You did it! Good job!" I look up at the digital display to see 57:03. Angela is in front of me taking pictures and simultaneously hugging me. My body doesn't want to stop running; I keep moving forward until I land in a crowd of cub scouts, who adorn my neck with a pink ribbon with a heavy gold medallion hanging down and sticking to my sweaty chest.

Angela and Mary Kay hug me and tell me how proud they are of me as we stroll around the woodsy grounds of the City of Hope, and even though everyone is wearing a winter coat, I am naked, sweaty, and glowing. Slowly people begin to notice me, my chest, sneaking peeks, tenderly avoiding eye contact. I see a woman tap another on the arm and gesture in my direction. I see a group of teenage boys, who under any other circumstance would be considered tough, look at my scars and soften.

Children are the only ones who look directly at me, no shyness, just curiosity.

In the car on the way home, Angela, Mary Kay, and I can't stop talking about what we just experienced.

"You know what I was thinking," Angela says, "is how many people will go home tonight and, while lying next to someone they love, bring up your image and talk about it."

"Yeah," Mary Kay adds. "How many conversations over the next week, month, or year will people have about what they saw. I love this idea that art creates dialogue and connection that wouldn't otherwise happen."

"You made art," Angela says. She pauses and starts to cry. "Do you understand how big this is, Tania?"

the end

Angela and I have made a home together in Los Angeles. During the day she sends out applications and slides for artist residencies and makes beautiful drawings in nontraditional ways, which usually involve pedaling, running, or throwing. And I wear tangerine sneakers with Tiffany-blue stripes while writing for hours by a window that overlooks the little beige grade school and the colorful crossing guard, Dee.

We both hyperventilate when we think about having to get health insurance or day jobs, but those moments are small compared to all the time we spend snuggling in our pajamas, talking about art and creating it.

Periodically Sal e-mails me to say she's going to send me my photographs. And right after she sends those e-mails, she follows up with e-mails that say she's not going to send me my photographs. I don't respond to any of them. I've let go of those photographs to make room for new ones.

Cancer has a funny way of leaving as quietly as it arrived. We move on with our lives, forget about genetic mutations, and things appear to be the same as they were before the cancer. Except for the differences. Now my family hugs each other all the time and I'm in love with a healthy woman. And now when my father squeezes my hand he's hard-pressed to let go. And at thirty-three years old, when I go out of town I call my mother to let her know I've arrived safely at my destination. When I hear that a friend of a friend has been diagnosed with breast cancer, I offer to listen. I guess what I've figured out is that life is precious and temporary, so there's no need to pretend to be someone other than who you are, even if you don't always fit in.